BEST PRACTICES IN GIFTED EDUCATION

BEST PRACTICES IN GIFTED EDUCATION

AN EVIDENCE-BASED GUIDE

ANN ROBINSON, PH.D.

BRUCE M. SHORE, PH.D.

DONNA L. ENERSEN, PH.D.

PRUFROCK PRESS INC.
WACO, TEXAS

a service publication of

Library of Congress Cataloging-in-Publication Data

Robinson, Ann, 1949–
  Best practices in gifted education : an evidence-based guide / Ann Robinson, Bruce M. Shore,
Donna L. Enersen.
     p. cm.
  ISBN-13: 978-1-59363-210-6 (pbk.)
  ISBN-10: 1-59363-210-X (pbk.)
  1. Gifted children—Education—Handbooks, manuals, etc. I. Shore, Bruce M., 1945– II. Enersen,
Donna L., 1942– III. Title.
  LC3993.R614 2007
  371.95'6—dc22
                                        2006024716

Edited by Jennifer Robins
Cover and Layout Design by Marjorie Parker

ISBN-13: 978-1-59363-210-6
ISBN-10: 1-59363-210-X

This study was partially supported by a contract from the Javits Gifted and Talented Students program of the United States Education Department. Any opinions, findings, conclusions, or recommendations expressed in this publication are those of the authors and do not necessarily reflect the
views of the Department of Education.

Printed in the United States of America.

At the time of this book's publication, all facts and figures cited are the most current available. All
telephone numbers, addresses, and Web site URLs are accurate and active. All publications, organizations, Web sites, and other resources exist as described in the book, and all have been verified.
The authors and Prufrock Press Inc. make no warranty or guarantee concerning the information
and materials given out by organizations or content found at Web sites, and we are not responsible
for any changes that occur after this book's publication. If you find an error, please contact Prufrock
Press Inc.

Prufrock Press Inc.
P.O. Box 8813
Waco, TX 76714-8813
Phone: (800) 998-2208
Fax: (800) 240-0333
http://www.prufrock.com

CONTENTS

PART I: HOME

PART II: CLASSROOM

PART III: SCHOOL

FOREWORD

What is the evidence to support a given practice? Is the evidence grounded in solid research? These are the questions we need to ask ourselves as we consider the best ways to educate and support gifted and talented students.

Too often in education we are persuaded to choose programs, materials, or practices without enough consideration of the evidence that support them. As a result, there are disagreements about what should be done, because without the evidence one person's opinion is as good as the next.

Fortunately, we now have a publication that helps us consider many of the common practices used with gifted and talented students. The authors, with the aid of a steering group of experts in gifted and talented education, have taken on the considerable task of identifying many of the practices that are typically used with these students and have analyzed the research that informs these practices. This is difficult enough. But, they also have managed to summarize the research in a way that is accessible to a general audience, so that the findings can be used by everyone to help make decisions on how to best support gifted and talented students.

Ask yourself—is the evidence on a particular practice convincing? Do we know enough about this practice to use it with our children? Is the research that is offered strong and compelling? What do we need to know more about? This publication is a useful starting point for these discussions and should help us all shape better and more effective programs for gifted and talented students.

—Pat O'Connell Ross
U.S. Department of Education

ACKNOWLEDGEMENTS

We have been fortunate in the assistance we have received on this project. We must begin with the monetary support from the Javits Gifted and Talented Students program of the United States Department of Education. Under the leadership of Pat O'Connell Ross, the need for a book on evidence-based practices for the development of talents was viewed as an important undertaking. We thank Pat for honoring us with the foreword to this book.

We owe a great debt to the steering group members, who convened in Washington, DC, for the project. They worked intensely and face-to-face at the beginning of the project to shape it and to suggest which practices should be considered for further examination. This was an extremely challenging task—one that they discharged with spirit! We were aided by Phyllis Aldrich, Saratoga Warren Board of Cooperative Educational Services (BOCES); Joan Becker, University of Massachusetts, Boston; Laurence J. Coleman, University of Tennessee; Peggy Dettmer, Kansas State University; Bessie Duncan, Detroit Public Schools, Emeritus; Evie Hiatt, Texas Department of Education; Scott Hunsaker, Utah State University; James Kulik, University of Michigan; Rosa Perez, City Schools, San Diego, CA; Joyce VanTassel-Baska, College of William and Mary; and Herbert J. Walberg, University of Illinois, Chicago Circle, who had undertaken such a project for general education in the 1980s. Members of the steering group also served as reviewers of text. We thank them and several anonymous reviewers for their invaluable insights.

We enjoyed the assistance of several colleagues and students in the preliminary drafting or editing of several of the chapters in this volume. Special thanks and credit are therefore offered to Andrea Newman, Rebecca Leib, and F. Gillian Rejskind (Chapter 4); Katie Boisvert (Chapter 10); Andrea Newman (Chapter 12); Rola Helou (Chapter 15); Jeff Powell and Lisa Linders (Chapter 20); Jan Ellsworth (Chapters 22 and 27); Rebecca Leib (Chapter 23); and Yuan Jin-Hong (Chapter 26). Their suggestions and contributions to this book were invaluable.

We must also collectively thank our universities that provided additional support through graduate assistantships and clerical assistance. These contributions were invaluable and kept the project moving forward when it might have foundered.

At the University of Arkansas at Little Rock, students and staff at the Center for Gifted Education found themselves called upon repeatedly to find some reference, react to drafts, or to do some needed service. We especially thank Gwen Millen and Benjamin Hardy for their bibliographic searches, Lorna Bryant for her thoughtful reaction to text, and Tommie Anthony and Alicia Cotabish for the loan of key materials. To Paulette Edison and Cynthia Jackson, we owe capable support at crucial times in the past year. From colleagues Jan Ellsworth, Corliss McCallister, and Betty Wood, we appreciated their insights about particular areas of research.

At McGill University, a number of students contributed to the project. They include Katie Boisvert, Rola Helou, Yuan Jin-Hong, Rebecca Leib, Lisa Linders, Andrea Newman, and Jeff Powell. We were also fortunate to enjoy the collaboration of colleague F. Gillian Rejskind on this project, as well as the original *Recommended Practices in Gifted Education: A Critical Analysis*. Zalman Usiskin was most helpful with regard to the evidence-based practice on mathematics.

At Purdue University, we enjoyed the interest and support of gifted education colleagues at the Gifted Education Resource Institute and the Shared Information Services office. Mary Lou Mattes stepped in to assist in the transfer of key readings to our Purdue author. Indeed, authors Enersen and Robinson are alumnae of the graduate program in gifted education begun by John Feldhusen and carried forward by Sidney Moon. Connections forged there last a professional lifetime. We must especially thank John Feldhusen for mentoring two of us and for being an enthusiastic supporter and friend to all three of us.

Finally, this book simply would not appear without the capable and energetic manuscript management of Linda Fiddler, formerly of the Pulaski County School District and the Center for Gifted Education at the University of Arkansas at Little Rock. As the former secondary language arts coordinator in her district, she is able to spot a comma splice from a very great distance.

Her fearless mastery of the eccentricities of the computer in manuscript preparation was a mainstay over the years of textual preparation.

We acknowledge that any errors must be ours, but hope that we have captured the "story" that evidence-based practices tell us.

INTRODUCTION

Parents want the best for their children; educators want their students to do well. Both parents and educators have questions about what works at home and at school to foster the talents of children and adolescents. The collection of practices based on research provides homes and schools with practical information upon which parents and educators can act.

The 29 practices in this volume are the result of an extensive, but by no means comprehensive, examination of educational research on what works with talented youth. The practices selected for review are supported by systematic inquiry and research evidence. They are offered not as a complete picture of how to develop talents in high-ability youth, but as recommendations for specific actions parents and teachers can take in the upbringing and schooling of their talented children.

The practices are organized into three sections: the home, the classroom, and the school. To a certain extent, the sections are not mutually exclusive. Many of the practices are shared by home and school. However, the research often focuses on one arena more than the others, so the practice is placed in the section where the actions are most likely to take place. A list of the practices is found in Table 1.

TABLE 1

Evidence-Based Practices That Work With Talented Youth

Home	Classroom	School
Parent Involvement	Encouraging Creativity	Mathematics Curriculum
Social-Emotional Adjustment and Peer Relations	Multiple Intelligences	Arts in the Curriculum
Students Who Are Twice-Exceptional	Higher Level Thinking	Learning Multiple Languages
Gender Differences	Inquiry-Based Learning and Teaching	Career Education
Developing Specific Talents	Compacting the Curriculum	School Programs
Early Literacy Experiences for Precocious and Emerging Readers	Flexible Grouping	Acceleration
Mentors and Mentorships	Instructional Technology	Multiple Criteria for Identification
University-Based Programs	Using Primary Sources in History	Developing Talents in Culturally Diverse Learners
	Language Arts Instruction	Promising Learners From Low-Income Backgrounds
	Reading Instruction	Professional Development for Teachers
	Science in the Classroom	

The reviews of each practice are organized in four sections. First, a summary statement sets the stage for the review. Second, the research literature is presented in a section titled "What We Know." Third, recommendations or actions derived from the research are bulleted in a section titled "What We Can Do." Finally, a list of references is included at the end of each discussion. The reviews of the practices are not interlocking: The reader of this text may browse the practices like the reader of a collection of short stories.

The need for this information was considered sufficiently pressing that the Javits Gifted and Talented Students program of the United States Department of Education convened a steering group of practitioners and academics to identify which practices are of greatest interest to practitioners and which of these have research support. The group represented higher education, state departments of education, regional educational service districts, and local school districts. Three editors or former editors of journals in gifted child education also participated. The steering group included individuals representing 2 countries, 11 states, and 1 province, and included university, state department, and school district personnel.

The overall framework for the project reported here is guided by the importance of connecting empirical evidence with practitioner, parent, and policymaker concerns. The connection between research and practice is often loosely coupled with the marked frustration of researchers, practitioners, and policymakers alike. This text seeks to bridge the gap.

Because this text is written for the general reader, the convening scholars were asked to generate a list of questions about talent development, giftedness, and high-ability youth they believed to be of interest to the general reader. In Phase One of the project, they were also encouraged to suggest questions that interested them as experts in the development of talent. They asked three general questions. "What questions do we need to be able to answer about educational and home practices effective with high-ability youth?" "How do we frame these questions to be maximally useful to practitioners?" And, "What existing research informs these practical questions?" Initially, the scholars generated 150 questions. Small groups of scholars elaborated, combined, and selected the most important questions and suggested research that might inform them.

In Phase Two, Javits program staff and the three authors met to translate the questions into electronically searchable terms. The 150 questions were translated into 61 terms and searched electronically using both ERIC and PSYCHINFO. When searched, 31 of the 61 terms produced sufficient empirical research to remain in the pool of practices to be reviewed. During the writing phase, two practices were incorporated into other reviews because of overlapping or related research evidence, and the final count of practices stands at 29. For example, *emotional adjustment* and *peer relations* were searched separately but reviewed together, because they complimented one another. In later revisions, *advanced placement* was integrated into *acceleration*. The authors also sought out studies and followed up leads in addition to the electronic searches. The reviews focus on research studies that have explicitly investigated high-ability youth, and on studies that have investigated the kinds of educational outcomes considered important to the development of talents. These are outcomes that emphasize higher level thinking and challenging curriculum opportunities.

In Phase Three, the research was reviewed, and practices were drafted and circulated among the writing team members. The resulting text is a set of 29 individual evidence-based practices grounded in empirical research and offering specific guidance to educators, parents, and policymakers on what works with talented youth.

The practices in the collection are diverse and reflect several of the preoccupations of the field. The importance of parents, the interest in culturally diverse and low-income learners, the means to identify talents, and the need for curriculum that appropriately challenges high-ability youth constitute many of the 29 practices. The reviews of the individual practices also reflect the variability of perspectives in the field. Nowhere is this variety more evident than in the use of terminology to describe the population of interest—gifted, talented, high-ability, promising learners—we found them all, and we have used them interchangeably. We acknowledge the work of theoreticians who grapple with the issues of terminology; these efforts advance the field. But, we are school people in need of the best practical advice we can find, and we took the literature as we found it and looked for the "story" it could tell us. This volume will not answer every question a parent or a teacher asks about what works with talented youth, but it is a start.

PART I
HOME

CHAPTER 1

PARENT INVOLVEMENT

More than 80 years of research and experience demonstrates that the education of any child is made more effective by sustaining and increasing the role of parents at home and in partnership with the schools. Because high-ability children require academic interventions, parents and teachers must work together each year of the child's school life.

WHAT WE KNOW

Parents of gifted children are notoriously accurate in identifying their children's abilities, especially if they have some ideas about how children normally develop. Louis and Lewis (1992), Jackson (1992), Robinson and Robinson (1992), and Robinson, Dale, and Landesman (1990) report that parents dependably describe their children in terms of characteristics and behaviors that are indicative of advanced reasoning and skill. Even when they do not completely understand the extent of these abilities, they are aware of their children's differences from other children (Munger, 1990; Silverman, 1997). Because research has long supported the early identification and development of talents, educators must welcome and rely on parents for vital information about children's special abilities. This becomes the first kind of involvement schools should pursue and parents should offer.

Generally speaking, homes that are strong in support, stimulation, and exploration, and that function effectively, develop and nurture a gifted child's native abilities. It is not so much the economic wealth that matters, although special classes and other opportunities can be costly. VanTassel-Baska's (1989) study of disadvantaged gifted adolescents served to validate the powerful influence of parents over material comforts or even levels of parental education. It is much more advantageous for children to live in a child-centered home where parents spend time with them, engaging in conversation, reading, playing, and doing daily activities together (Robinson et al., 1990). This concept crosses all cultural and economic lines. An in-depth case study of eight minority students from low-income homes (Tomlinson, Callahan, & Lelli, 1997) yielded compelling information about the importance of this kind of involvement. These students had at least one parent who unconditionally believed in them and wanted to have an active role in their lives. The parents were determined to help with their children's education, and sought ways to learn how to do it well. It is conversely true that children whose parents are disengaged have the poorest developmental and school patterns. The resultant lack of self-esteem and competence multiplies over the school years (Steinberg, 1996).

A 1998 qualitative study of 34 gifted children and their families (Corbin & Denicolo) is representative of research to determine the impact of parental involvement on school success. Their findings revealed that students who thrived had parents who sought to know the educational system, were supportive of the school, valued education, set high expectations for their children and themselves, worked to establish rapport with teachers, and were not distracted from active parenting by marital crisis. There was additional evidence of Clark's (1983) findings that highlighted the ways parents' behaviors impact children's lives: in providing emotional support, especially when the children experience failure; teaching that practice and work are important; monitoring children's time and activities (such as TV watching and friendships); discussing school events; and taking responsibility for learning in their homes (Finn, 1998). These findings echo research from the wider fields of child development and education in studies such as Martini's (1995), which point out that stimulating home preparation is essential for school success. Martini found that there are certain specific parenting practices that override factors such as socioeconomic status and parent IQ and education. These practices include parents involving themselves extensively in structuring their children's lives, modeling life strategies that have been successful for them, and having frequent contact with teachers. Moss and Strayer (1990) found similar favorable parenting practices even with mothers and their preschoolers. A study by Crane (1996) corroborated Walberg's (1991, as cited in Crane) earlier findings that pointed to the role parents play in their children's learning success by providing a home environment—which means affection, expectations, opportunities, and guidance—that is conducive to the development of cognitive skills. Entwisle and Alexander (1990) looked at this same environment in terms of the large and significant effect it has on children's mathematics achievement, and Dai and Schader (2000) extended the impact of such efforts to music training. Coleman and Cross (2005) continue to confirm the unmatched effects of parents' involvement on academic and school success.

In all cases, children benefit from having their parents involved in their education by being interested in their homework, investigating topics of interest together, communicating regularly with teachers and administrators, and championing their children in scholastic arenas. It is also interesting to note that teachers who actively involve parents receive higher ratings from administrators for their overall teaching ability and interpersonal skills. A school with good marks in this area receives positive publicity and honors (Epstein, 1985).

Although it is abundantly clear that parents' involvement positively impacts their children's lives and schooling, the actual events are not always smooth. School policies may convey the message that all children are the same, and that there are not differences that need instructional modification. Some teachers find well-informed, bright parents "pushy" and make them feel unwelcome in the classroom (Cole & Della Vecchia, 1992); others feel threatened and defensive about their teaching practices (Enersen, 1993). There are some children who are highly gifted, and the school's resources are unable to meet their needs (Gross, 2004). In a detailed study of 15 highly gifted children (from a larger study of 40 such children), Gross traced family and school experiences that show how much of the burden is placed on parents and how difficult they find it to work with teachers and administrators.

There has long been controversy around the notion of early entrance to school (as with all aspects of acceleration). Parents approach the school with reports of their children reading well at age 3 or 4, speaking in vast detail about dinosaurs or space or some topic, understanding place value and being able to do mathematical computations, or perhaps showing talent in art or music. In some cases, the preschool teacher has alerted the parents to the ways in which their children are precocious. Because of these encouragements and the day-to-day evidence seen at home, the parents feel their children are ready for school. Research on the success of children who enter school early is mixed and often reported with cautions about adjustment and long-term benefits (Gagné & Gagnier, 2004; Rogers, 1991; Sankar-DeLeeuw, 2002; Schiever & Maker, 2003). Many school districts are reluctant or have policies against early entrance. In most cases, parents must vigorously work to gain early entrance or other accommodations for their children. Thus begins a years-long process that often leads to poor home-school relationships (Enersen, 1993).

Parents can choose to stand in the gap for their children, providing instruction for them at home in those early years, later in the afterschool hours, and even homeschooling them, or they can forcefully try to bring changes at school. However they work to solve the problem, they have two great needs: the support of others who are experiencing the same kind of challenges and information about gifted children and the resources that are available to them (Enersen, 1993). Knowing this, schools can seize the opportunity to equip parents and teachers to build a partnership through educational interventions. The most workable and successful plans are those that center on building communication skills, sharing information about the nature and needs of gifted children, and experiencing the viewpoints of others. There are several dependable formats for such interventions, all of which create an atmosphere conducive to open discussion and questioning and develop community among parents (i.e., Supporting Emotional Needs of the Gifted [SENG]; Webb & DeVries, 1993). Experts are often invited to present information about topics such as identification methods, career counseling, and emotional needs of gifted children. The sessions can be held during the day, in the evenings, or while the children are taking part in enrichment classes. It is interesting that even a short course is evaluated by the participants as extremely helpful, and that the most important part is finding other parents who share their experiences and concerns (Enersen). After such a course, the parents feel they are more prepared to approach the schools with appropriate advocacy and understanding.

WHAT WE CAN DO

To use the strong evidence that parents' involvement is good for the child and the school, there must be positive and team-like communication between educators and parents. Parents can be helped to develop effective parenting skills and teachers can develop effective ways of involving parents in their children's education.

At School

≥ Include in preservice teachers' training rationale and methods for working productively with parents of gifted children. This should be part of a larger effort to infuse undergraduate teacher preparation classes with awareness and techniques for teaching gifted students.

≥ Equip practicing teachers with strategies for working with parents of gifted children. Hold workshops that focus on effective communication and collaboration. Include specific strategies for teachers to employ to engage parents of culturally diverse families (see Ford & Grantham, 2003, among other authors who address the need to develop better relationships with parents of Black, Hispanic, and Native American students).

≥ Hold parenting classes when services are initiated for gifted children. Include the following:

- information about identification measures,
- nature and needs of gifted children,
- resources and options locally available,
- communication skills such as effective dialoguing and active listening,
- authoritative, child-centered parenting skills,
- specific training in how to promote learning at home, and
- plans for parents' assistance through classroom involvement.

ઽ Train teachers to put parent volunteers to good use. Working together will build a relationship from which to draw when the situation becomes stressed.

ઽ Encourage administrators (especially principals) to attend the teacher and parent training and reinforce the concept of partnership through their leadership.

ઽ Assume that parents, teachers, and administrators all want what is good for the children. Do not assume that everyone has all the information needed to make the best decisions. Provide a way for parents to get resource materials and access to professionals and other parents: open a small library and meeting room at school; offer workshops, speakers, Web site, or other clearinghouses for information and communication.

ઽ Keep at it. As children move through the grades and leave the school, others with their own needs enter; as new teachers join a school's faculty, the education and advocacy process must be renewed (Robinson & Moon, 2003).

Parents need to be actively involved in all facets of their children's lives, and most certainly in their children's education. Parent and teacher collaboration can make such involvement extremely beneficial to the children.

REFERENCES

Cole, L. C., & Della Vecchia, R. (1992, March). *From the voices of parents: Understanding the challenges for families of gifted children.* Paper presented at the Eastern Educational Research Association, Hilton Head, SC.

Coleman, L. J., & Cross, T. L. (2005). *Being gifted in school: An introduction to development, guidance, and teaching* (2nd ed.). Waco, TX: Prufrock Press.

Corbin, H. L., & Denicolo, P. (1998). Portraits of the able child: Highlights of case study research. *High Ability Studies, 9,* 207–218.

Clark, R. M. (1983). *Family life and school achievement.* Chicago: University of Chicago Press.

Crane, J. (1996). Effects of home environment, SES, and maternal test scores on mathematics achievement. *Journal of Educational Research, 89,* 305–314.

Dai, D. Y., & Schader, R. (2000). Parents' reasons and motivations for supporting their child's music training. *Roeper Review, 24,* 23–26.

Enersen, D. L. (1993). *Positive partnerships: Improving interactions among parents and educators of gifted children.* Unpublished doctoral dissertation, Purdue University, IN.

Epstein, J. L. (1985). A question of merit: Principals' and parents' evaluation of teachers. *Educational Researcher, 14*(7), 3–10.

Entwisle, D. R., & Alexander, K. L. (1990). Beginning school math competence: Minority and majority comparisons. *Child Development, 61*, 454–471.

Finn, J. (1998). Parental engagement that makes a difference. *Educational Leadership, 55*(8), 20–24.

Ford, D. Y., & Grantham, T. C. (2003). Providing access for culturally diverse gifted students: From deficit to dynamic thinking. *Theory Into Practice, 42*, 217–225.

Gagné, F., & Gagnier, N. (2004). The socio-affective and academic impact of early entrance to school. *Roeper Review, 26*, 128–138.

Gross, M. U. M. (2004). *Exceptionally gifted children* (2nd ed.) New York: Routledge-Falmer.

Jackson, N. E. (1992). Precocious reading of English: Origin, structure, and predictive significance. In P. S. Klein & A. J. Tannenbaum (Eds.), *To be young and gifted* (pp. 173–203). Norwood, NJ: Ablex

Louis, B., & Lewis, M. (1992). Parental beliefs about giftedness in young children and their relation to actual ability. *Gifted Child Quarterly, 36*, 27–31.

Martini, M. (1995). Features of home environments associated with children's school success. *Early Child Development and Care, 111*, 49–68.

Moss, E., & Strayer, F. F. (1990). Interactive problem-solving of gifted and non-gifted preschoolers with their mothers. *International Journal of Behavioral Development, 13*, 177–197.

Munger, A. (1990). The parent's role in counseling the gifted: The balance between home and school. In J. VanTassel-Baska (Ed.), *A practical guide to counseling the gifted in a school setting* (2nd ed., pp. 57–65). Reston, VA: Council for Exceptional Children.

Robinson, A., & Moon, S. M. (2003). The national study of state and local advocacy in gifted education. *Gifted Child Quarterly, 47*, 8–25.

Robinson, N. M., Dale, P. S., & Landesman, S. (1990). Validity of Stanford-Binet IV with linguistically precocious toddlers. *Intelligence, 14*, 173–186.

Robinson, N. M., & Robinson, H. B. (1992). The use of standardized tests with young gifted children. In P. S. Klein & A. Tannenbaum (Eds.), *To be young and gifted* (pp. 141–170). Norwood, NJ: Ablex.

Rogers, K. L. (1991). A best-evidence synthesis of the research on types of accelerative programs for gifted students (Vols. 1 & 2). *Dissertation Abstracts International, 52*, 796A. (UMI No. 9122206)

Sankar-DeLeeuw, N. (2002). Gifted preschoolers: Parent and teacher views on identification, early admission, and programming. *Roeper Review, 2*, 172–177.

Schiever, S. W., & Maker, C. J. (2003). New directions in enrichment and acceleration. In N. Colangelo & G. A. Davis (Eds.), *Handbook of gifted education* (3rd ed., pp. 163–173). Boston: Allyn & Bacon.

Silverman, L. K. (1997). Family counseling with the gifted. In N. Colangelo & G. A. Davis (Eds.), *Handbook of gifted education* (2nd ed., pp. 382–397). Boston: Allyn & Bacon.

Steinberg, I. (1996). *Beyond the classroom*. New York: Simon & Schuster.

Tomlinson, C. A., Callahan, C. M., & Lelli, K. M. (1997). Challenging expectations: Case studies of high-potential, culturally diverse young children. *Gifted Child Quarterly, 41*, 5–17.

VanTassel-Baska, J. (1989). The role of family in the success of disadvantaged gifted learners. *Journal for the Education of the Gifted, 13,* 22–36.

Webb, J. T., & DeVries, A. R. (1993). *Training manual for facilitators of SENG model guided discussion groups.* Dayton, OH: Ohio Psychology Press.

CHAPTER 2

SOCIAL-EMOTIONAL ADJUSTMENT AND PEER RELATIONS

lthough the stereotype of the gifted child as a physical, emotional, and social misfit has been dispelled by many studies, it must be understood that there are unique stresses and dynamic issues associated with a person's giftedness. It is important to consider all of the dimensions of a gifted child's life: academic, self-concept, social skills and well-being, emotional health, and talent maturation.

WHAT WE KNOW

As long ago as Terman (1925) and Hollingworth (1926), we have known that the picture of the "egghead," scrawny, bespectacled genius child is a myth, and that gifted children are more likely to be healthy, attractive, active youngsters with above-average emotional stability, personalities, and social competence (Colangelo, 1991; Gallagher & Crowder, 1957; Grace & Booth, 1958; Ludwig & Cullinan, 1984; Oram,

Cornell, & Rutemiller, 1995; Pollin, 1983; Robinson & Noble, 1991). However, we also know that continuing to expect excellence from these children without taking into account the emotional and social dimensions of their lives exacts a cost in the development of healthy self-concept and in family and peer relationships (Buescher, 1987; Gross, 2004).

The Family and Self-Concept

The family is the first place where gifted children build their understanding of who they are. The sense of belonging to the family, yet having one's own unique identity, leads to the gifted child's social and emotional adjustment (Sowa & May, 1997). Families that function well are those that accept their children, are not permissive, do not speak negatively about school, foster independence and exploration, and hold realistic expectations for all members (Landau, 1990; Silverman, 1993). These families pave the way for their children's stable social and emotional adjustment.

Silverman (1993) and Tolan (1992) stressed the need for parents to feel strong in their ability to raise bright children and to acknowledge the likelihood of their own giftedness. Parents may have personally encountered experiences similar to their children's and can identify with them and help them cope—if they are healthy themselves. For example, in some dysfunctional families, parents may allow the gifted child to dominate, leading to anger and depression within the family and extinguishing the ability and the desire in the child to adapt to relationships (Hollingsworth, 1990; Rimm, 1990). Many parents search for help from teachers and other professionals; the greatest needs that parents of gifted children report are the support of other parents raising gifted children and the attention of educational professionals so they can gain dependable information about rearing and educating gifted children (Enersen, 1993a).

Peer Relations and Self-Concept

Self-concept is also built through relationships with others, in fact, with all whom the child comes in contact. The child develops knowledge about him- or herself by comparison with others, particularly similar peers, and then makes assertions about his or her personal identity (Plucker & Stocking, 2001; Sowa & May, 1997). Cross, Coleman, and Stewart (1993) used an attitude questionnaire in a large-scale study to understand the stigma of feeling different and the coping behaviors students employ to maintain normal relationships with peers and teachers. For many bright students, finding true peers is a daunting and disappointing task.

Csikszentmihalyi (Csikszentmihalyi, Rathunde, & Whalen, 1993) found that gifted children tend to be introverted and like to have time alone. Even though gifted adolescents like times of solitude during which they can read, paint, and do other activities that are important for the development of their talent, they also yearn for peer contacts. It is difficult for them to find others who understand these seemingly contradictory desires and who will give them space and time to be alone, yet be available at other times. Winner (2000) suggested that advanced classes help these students find and get to know others who share their need for both friendship and solitude. Feldhusen, Sayler, Nielsen, and Kolloff (1990), Olszewski-Kubilius (1997), and Enersen (1993b) are among many researchers who observed enhanced self-concept and the discovery of true peers in children who take part in special programs for those with similar abilities and interests.

Many of the problems gifted children experience in relationships stem from their uneven development (Columbus Group, 1991; Silverman, 1993). It is important to help them see that relationships with different peer groups for different activities can meet their various physical, intellectual, and social levels; having one peer group at chess club and another for skateboarding is healthy.

Kerr (1991) reported a number of findings dealing with self-concept and peer relations. Her studies showed that there are interactions of gender: Gifted girls appear to be better adjusted than gifted boys or average girls and boys, although there is evidence that gifted girls have less confidence in their academic abilities and also tend to be particularly sensitive to the social impact of giftedness during their adolescence. Kerr also reported that young gifted children have some difficulties finding age-mates with whom they have common interests. They may feel frustration that the other children cannot read, do not like chess, or do not understand their vocabulary. Children who excel in different talent areas may experience unique problems, such as mathematically gifted students whose interests are so unusual that other children do not understand them, or those who are not being sufficiently challenged may eventually reject their own interests. Those who have high levels of talent in music, dance, or art can feel consumed with the discipline necessary to succeed, and may get out of touch with peers who have no such driving interest.

Research over the last decade (Gross, 2004; Kerr, 1991; Robinson & Noble, 1991; Silverman, 1993) agrees with earlier findings (Hollingworth, 1942; Terman, 1925) that exceptionally gifted children are aware that they are quite different from others their age and that they have greater difficulties with social adjustment than those who are moderately gifted. A key finding is that these children are friendly and outgoing when they are with others who are like themselves (Rogers, 1991; Silverman, 1993).

Bickley's (2002) case studies of 12 gifted children ages 5–16 found common difficulties resulting from their perceptions of others' expectations of them, and their high sensitivity, social ineptitude, and emotional vulnerability. She named coping strategies these children used to survive in academic settings including making difficult choices, using withdrawal, creating their own challenge and stimulation, and interacting with different groups of peers.

School and Self-Concept

There are persistent and significant relationships between self-concept and success in school. It is common for a gifted child to relate his or her individual worth as a person to school success and to derive personal identity from teachers' perceptions (Delisle, 1992). The belief that perfection is attainable and expected becomes the point at which self-esteem suffers when the child cannot be satisfied with lesser achievements. Because school is such an integral and important part of a child's daily life, understanding the complex interplay of effort, challenge, specific and deserved praise, and the comfort of a supportive environment is essential to the student's sense of worth (Katz, 1994; Tomlinson, 1994).

Plucker and Stocking's (2001) study of talent search students showed the disparity that can exist between high ability and high self-concept. They used the internal/external frame of reference model (I/E model) proposed by Marsh (1986) to explain how students base their self-concept on a personal (internal) appraisal of their ability simultaneously with an evaluation of their peers' (external) ability. The comparison can make them feel less positive about their own abilities.

Coleman and Cross (2005) contend that while there may be a lower incidence of severe emotional problems among gifted children than the general population, there are particular and unique problems that they encounter due to their developing abilities. They name the source of conflict gifted children face, especially at school, as "not something inherent in the traits of gifted children, but rather in the interplay between the individual and his or her surroundings" (p. 165). Gross (2004) would agree, as she found in her study of 15 highly gifted children that when the surroundings—the schools in particular—were a good match for them, they thrived; when they were not a good match, the children were bitter, frustrated, and very unhappy. Kerr (1991) listed five common adjustment disorders associated with school that gifted students may experience:

- stress from loneliness, academic expectations placed on them by others and those they place on themselves, and overcommitment to school activities (particularly by students who have multipotentiality) and the stress of being asked to make decisions beyond their capacity or maturity to make;
- depression that can come from many of the same situations as stress and from an existential struggle about the meaning of life and the depth of feelings for situations they cannot control (Hollingworth, 1926; Webb, Meckstroth, & Tolan, 1982);
- perfectionism that is not a positive push for excellence, but a compulsion to reach unrealistic goals;
- unsatisfactory peer relationships; and
- in rare cases, suicide.

In nearly all situations, counselors who are adept with and enjoy gifted children can help guide the students in managing their differentness, finding friends, dealing with perfectionism, and setting goals (Buescher, 1991; Coleman & Cross, 2005; Shore, Cornell, Robinson, & Ward, 1991).

Programming Considerations

There are wide differences within the population of gifted students; therefore, it is a fallacy to think that one kind of program or provision will meet the educational and affective needs of all gifted students. Among the factors that must be considered are:

- the degree of giftedness, especially for the highly gifted student;
- the racial, cultural, and socioeconomic differences, which may alter the definition of talent;
- the gender of the student, because males and females encounter and deal with giftedness differently;
- the talent area, such as the performing artist, the creative or divergent thinker, or the athlete whose expressions of giftedness may not fit the school environment;
- the emotional factors of the student's home life, such as abuse, parental strife, and illness or death in the home, or less catastrophic incidents, such as the death of a pet or the family's relocation; and
- other variables, such as learning disabilities, physical challenges, or emotional illness within the child (Coleman & Cross, 2005; Fiedler, 1999; Gross, 2004; Kerr, 1991; Morrison, 2001; Silverman, 1993; Stormont, Stebbins, & Holliday, 2001).

Any one of these factors could radically impact decisions made about the best way to nurture and educate a child, yet many children have more than one of these stressors in their lives. General school guidance programs that promote acceptance for the differences in how children move through developmental stages and cope with daily issues are helpful. All school personnel must team with families and the children themselves to create an environment that is supportive and conducive to building healthy self-concepts. More acute-care counseling interventions may be needed to address more serious issues, and a mental health care professional who has had training to understand and treat gifted children is needed. Moon (2002) makes a powerful point in highlighting two problems with depending on counselors who are not trained to work with gifted children:

First, very few mental health professionals know how to adapt their counseling strategies to better meet the needs of individuals with high abilities, and second, untrained counselors may pathologize normal characteristics of gifted individuals, such as adaptive perfectionism and overexcitabilities. (p. 218)

Families and educators are responsible for building the environment in which gifted children live and develop their abilities and personalities. The child's social-emotional health depends on the supports provided for healthy interactions of the child and the environment.

WHAT WE CAN DO

It is interesting that much of what we know to be helpful to gifted children as they grow and develop strong self-concepts was first designed by Leta Hollingworth in 1939. Her "emotional education" curriculum integrated particular affective and cognitive aspects that her students (in their 70s at the time of interview) reported as having had a lifelong impact on their success and self-actualization (Harris, 1992; White, 1990). Today's gifted children have many similar needs. The following may bring about those same, desired results:

At Home

ھ Nurture the child's talent. Active exploration of the environment, interactions with people, "crystallizing" events (Gardner, 1983), and even chance occurrences (Tannenbaum, 1983) are significant factors in the identification and unfolding of talent.

In the Classroom

ھ Help the child understand his or her giftedness and set reasonable goals based on ability, interests, and personality (VanTassel-Baska, 1998). Using techniques such as surveys, journals, one-on-one conferences, talent development growth plans (Feldhusen, 1992), and carefully selected small-group projects can legitimize the process of self-reflection and progressive improvement. Be alert for mixed messages about the value of the child as a person and the talent he or she may possess.

At School

ھ Understand that a child's social and emotional development is an integral part of his or her educational setting and program. Much of the growth in healthy self-concept is tied in with appropriate challenge of a curriculum that is a good fit in pace, depth, and concept, and with a group of mental peers (like-minded peers) with whom the child can work (Gross, 2004; Hollingworth, 1939; VanTassel-Baska, 1998).

❧ Build a positive partnership between parents and educators for the mutual sharing of information from the varying perspectives of home and school (Coleman & Cross, 2005; Enersen, 1993a).

❧ Help parents and teachers model for and instruct children on basic social skills that can ease their way in the school and neighborhood. Learning how to understand situations from another's perspective, how to defuse anger, how to make needs known in a positive manner, and other similar social considerations can promote smoother relationships (Hollingworth, 1939; Kerr, 1991; Silverman, 1993).

❧ Assist parents and teachers in ways to model and instruct children to manage stress, and provide resources if they need more help. Often, children learn the finer points of perfectionism and overcommitment from adults in their lives. Learning together how to set priorities and realistic goals, to relax, and to communicate effectively, as well as to deal with mistakes and failures, will benefit the child and the home and classroom (Colangelo, 1991; Cross, 2004; Hollingworth, 1939; Kerr, 1991).

❧ Provide individual, group, and family counseling on a preventative basis, as well as counseling for crises (Kerr, 1991; Silverman, 1993).

Gifted children sometimes talk and have interests like adults. They also may behave like an adult one moment and be very childlike the next. It can be easy to forget that they are children who have the right to be instructed in the ways of living in our society and that they need time to experience life. Because they are gifted, they have particular characteristics and needs, and parents and educators must work together to maximize the development of every aspect of the children's lives. Schneider's (1987) acknowledgment remains true: "As is the case for any minority, the social acceptance of the gifted depends in part on the readiness in society to accept, even appreciate, their unique attributes" (p. 13). Our responsibility begins with honoring the child as a person and continues with providing the best in academic, social, and emotional growth, and talent development.

REFERENCES

Bickley, N. Z. (2002). *The social and emotional adjustment of gifted children who experience asynchronous development and unique educational needs*. Unpublished doctoral dissertation, University of Connecticut.

Buescher, T. M. (Ed.). (1987). *Understanding gifted and talented adolescents: A resource guide for counselors, educators, and parents*. Evanston, IL: Northwestern University.

Buescher, T. M. (1991). Gifted adolescents. In N. Colangelo & G. A. Davis (Eds.), *Handbook of gifted education* (pp. 382–401). Needham Heights, MA: Allyn & Bacon.

Colangelo, N. (1991). Counseling gifted students. In N. Colangelo & G. A. Davis (Eds.), *Handbook of gifted education* (pp. 273–284). Needham Heights, MA: Allyn & Bacon.

Coleman, L. J., & Cross, T. L. (2005). *Being gifted in school: An introduction to development, guidance, and teaching* (2nd ed.). Waco, TX: Prufrock Press.

Columbus Group. (1991, July). *Manuscript of the meeting of the Columbus Group.* Unpublished manuscript.

Cross, T. L. (2004). *On the social and emotional lives of gifted children: Issues and factors in their psychological development* (2nd ed.). Waco, TX: Prufrock Press.

Cross, T. L., Coleman, L. J., & Stewart, R. A. (1993). The social cognition of gifted adolescents: An exploration of the stigma of giftedness paradigm. *Roeper Review, 16,* 37–40.

Csikszentmihalyi, M., Rathunde, K., & Whalen, S. (1993). *Talented teenagers: The roots of success and failure.* New York: Cambridge University Press.

Delisle, J. R. (1992). *Guiding the social and emotional development of gifted youth: A practical guide for educators and counselors.* New York: Longman.

Enersen, D. L. (1993a). *Positive partnerships: Improving interactions among parents of gifted children and educators.* Unpublished doctoral dissertation, Purdue University, IN.

Enersen, D. L. (1993b). Summer residential programs: Academics and beyond. *Gifted Child Quarterly, 37,* 169–176.

Fiedler, E. D. (1999). Gifted children: The promise of potential/the problems of potential. In V. L. Schwean & D. H. Saklofske (Eds.), *Handbook of psychosocial characteristics of exceptional children* (pp. 401–441). New York: Kluwer Academic/Plenum.

Feldhusen, J. F. (1992). *Talent identification and development in education (TIDE).* Sarasota, FL: Center for Creative Learning.

Feldhusen, J. F., Sayler, M. F., Nielsen, M. E., & Kolloff, M. B. (1990). Self-concepts of gifted children in enrichment programs. *Journal for the Education of the Gifted, 13,* 380–384.

Gallagher, J. J., & Crowder, T. (1957). The adjustment of gifted children in the regular classroom. *Exceptional Children, 23,* 306–312, 317–319.

Gardner, H. (1983). *Frames of mind: The theory of multiple intelligences.* New York: BasicBooks.

Grace, H., & Booth, N. (1958). Is the gifted child a social isolate? *Peabody Journal of Education, 35,* 195–196.

Gross, M. U. M. (2004). *Exceptionally gifted children* (2nd ed.). New York: Routledge.

Harris, C. R. (1992). The fruits of early intervention: The Hollingworth group today. *Advanced Development, 4,* 91–104.

Hollingworth, L. S. (1926). *Gifted children: Their nature and nurture.* New York: Macmillan.

Hollingworth, L. S. (1939). What we know about the early selection and training of leaders. *Teachers College Record, 40,* 575–592.

Hollingworth, L. S. (1942). *Children above 180 IQ Stanford-Binet: Origin and development.* Yonkers-on-Hudson, NY: World Book.

Hollingsworth, P. L. (1990, May/June). Making it through parenting. *Gifted Child Today, 13*(3), 2–7.

Katz, E. (1994). *Affective education: Self-concept and the gifted student.* Boulder, CO: Open Space Communications.

Kerr, B. (1991). *A handbook for counseling the gifted and talented.* Alexandria, VA: American Association for Counseling and Development.

Landau, E. (1990). *The courage to be gifted.* Unionville, NY: Trillium Press.

Ludwig, G., & Cullinan, D. (1984). Behavior problems of gifted and nongifted elementary school girls and boys. *Gifted Child Quarterly, 28,* 37–39.

Marsh, H. W. (1986). Verbal and math self-concepts: An internal/external frame of reference model. *American Educational Research Journal, 23,* 129–149.

Moon, S. M. (2002). Counseling needs and strategies. In M. Neihart, S. M. Reis, N. M. Robinson, & S. M. Moon (Eds.), *The social and emotional development of gifted children: What do we know?* (pp. 213–222). Waco, TX: Prufrock Press.

Morrison, W. F. (2001). Emotional/behavioral disabilities and gifted and talented behaviors: Paradoxical or semantic differences in characteristics? *Psychology in the Schools, 38,* 425–431.

Olszewski-Kubilius, P. (1997). Special summer and Saturday programs for gifted students. In N. Colangelo & G. A. Davis (Eds.), *Handbook of gifted education* (2nd ed., pp. 180–188). Needham Heights, MA: Allyn & Bacon.

Oram, G. D., Cornell, D. G., & Rutemiller, L. A. (1995). Relations between academic aptitude and psychological adjustment in gifted program students. *Gifted Child Quarterly, 39,* 236–244.

Plucker, J. A., & Stocking, V. B. (2001). Looking outside and inside: Self-concept development of gifted adolescents. *Exceptional Children, 67,* 535–548

Pollin, L. (1983). The effects of acceleration on the social and emotional development of gifted students. In C. Benbow & J. Stanley (Eds.), *Academic precocity: Aspects of its development* (pp. 160–179). Baltimore: Johns Hopkins University Press.

Rimm, S. B. (1990, May/June). Parenting and teaching gifted children: A model of relativity. *Gifted Child Today,* 33–36.

Robinson, N. M., & Noble, K. D. (1991). Social-emotional development and adjustment of gifted children. In M. C. Wang, M. C. Reynolds, & H. J. Walberg (Eds.), *Handbook of special education. Research and practice: Vol. 4. Emerging programs* (pp. 57–76). New York: Pergamon Press.

Rogers, K. B. (1991). *The relationship of grouping practices to the education of the gifted and talented learner.* Storrs: National Research Center on the Gifted and Talented, University of Connecticut.

Schneider, B. H. (1987). *The gifted child in peer group perspective.* New York: Springer-Verlag.

Shore, B. M., Cornell, D. G., Robinson, A., & Ward, V. S. (1991). *Recommended practices in gifted education: A critical analysis.* New York: Teachers College Press.

Silverman, L. K. (1993). *Counseling the gifted and talented.* Denver, CO: Love.

Sowa, C. J., & May, K. M. (1997). Expanding Lazarus and Folkman's paradigm to the social and emotional adjustment of gifted children and adolescents (SEAM). *Gifted Child Quarterly, 41,* 36–43.

Stormont, M., Stebbins, M. S., & Holliday, G. (2001). Characteristics and educational support needs of underrepresented gifted adolescents. *Psychology in the Schools, 38,* 413–423.

Tannenbaum, A. J. (1983). *Gifted children: Psychological and educational perspectives.* New York: Macmillan.

Terman, L. M. (1925). *Genetic studies of genius: Vol. 1. Mental and physical traits of a thousand gifted children.* Stanford, CA: Stanford University Press.

Tolan, S. S. (1992). Only a parent: Three true stories. *Understanding Our Gifted, 4*(3), 1, 8–10.

Tomlinson, C. A. (1994). The easy lie and the role of gifted education in school excellence. *Roeper Review, 16,* 258–259.

VanTassel-Baska, J. (1998). *Excellence in educating gifted and talented learners.* Denver, CO: Love.

Webb, J. T., Meckstroth, E. A., & Tolan, S. S. (1982). *Guiding the gifted child: A practical source for parents and teachers.* Columbus, OH: Ohio Psychology Press.

White, W. L. (1990). Interviews with Child I, Child J, and Child L. *Roeper Review, 12,* 222–227.

Winner, E. (2000). The origins and ends of giftedness. *American Psychologist, 55,* 159–169.

CHAPTER 3

STUDENTS WHO ARE TWICE-EXCEPTIONAL

hildren and adolescents with talents may also have specific disabilities; these children are twice-exceptional. Retrospective case studies of talented adults indicate that individuals with physical, sensory, or learning disabilities can achieve at high levels over the course of their lives. Children and adolescents also achieve, often in a context outside the school setting. Twice-exceptional children are characterized by intense motivation and the tendency to use intellectual abilities to ameliorate the effects of the disability. For example, even without expressive speech, early and fluent reading occurs among some learners with disabilities. Family and supportive teachers, counselors, and mentors play an important role in talent development by recognizing a twice-exceptional child's strengths, rather than exclusively focusing on the child's disability. Opportunities at home and school that focus on talents, provide assistance in bypassing the disability, or offer instruction in compensating for the disability foster giftedness in the twice-exceptional child.

WHAT WE KNOW

Talent and Disability

Because giftedness and talent are often identified by academic achievements and school success, children and adolescents with disabilities may be overlooked. They may have sensory or communication disabilities that make the expression of their talents invisible to others in the mainstreamed school context. If they are educated in specialized settings like residential schools for the blind or deaf, the disability orientation of the school program may overwhelm concerns about identifying and serving talented learners. Yet, history and popular literature offer numerous stories of the disabilities of eminent adults. Although the stories may be largely apocryphal, Thomas Edison's hearing loss or Albert Einstein's learning problems, for example, are offered as evidence that talent and disability are not mutually exclusive (Goertzel & Goertzel, 1962). More systematic evidence is available from case studies of adults who exhibit one or more disabilities, but who achieve despite them (Reis, Neu, & McGuire, 1995, 1997; Whitmore & Maker, 1985). Other case studies of children and adolescents with a range of talents and disabilities also shed light on the patterns of strengths and weaknesses and the home and school environments that maximize the development of the twice-exceptional child (Bailey & Sinclair, 1992; Hua, 2002; Kershner, 1995; Moon & Dillon, 1995; Willard-Holt, 1994, 1998).

Definition of Twice-Exceptional

The term *twice-exceptional* has been used to describe children "with special intellectual-processing problems [i.e., those with learning, communication, and/or behavioral disabilities], that nevertheless, maintain an extraordinarily high general intellectual potential" (Gallagher, 1988, p. 110). More broadly, these children may also have physical or sensory disabilities or a combination of multiple conditions identified through the Individuals with Disabilities Act (IDEA; 1990). For example, children affected by cerebral palsy, orthopedic impairments, deafness or hearing impairment, blindness, visual impairment or low vision, and a variety of specific learning disabilities may also be gifted (Cline & Schwartz, 1999; Johnsen & Corn, 1989). In terms of prevalence, the greatest numbers of twice-exceptional learners are likely to be those with a specific learning disability (Hokanson & Jospe, 1976). Nielsen (2002) notes, however, large-scale incidence figures "are virtually nonexistent" (p. 94).

Patterns of Talent Development and Disability

Information about the development of talents in children and youth with disabilities is found in case studies (Bailey & Sinclair, 1992; Ingraham, Daugherty, & Gorrafa, 1995; LaSasso, 1992; Moon & Dillon, 1995; Moon, Zentall, Grskovic, Hall, & Stormont, 2001; Reis et al., 1997; Willard-Holt, 1994, 1998); intervention studies (Baum, 1988; Coleman, 1992; Karnes, Shwedel, & Lewis, 1983a, 1983b; Nielsen, Higgins, & Hammond, 1993); and one longitudinal study (Vernon & LaFalce-Landers, 1993).

Although the patterns of talent development reported in the case studies differ widely, there are some commonalities among twice-exceptional individuals. First, motivation plays an important role in the development of talent among individuals with disabilities. For example, in the case study of Myron, a highly successful doctor and researcher, Whitmore and Maker (1985) noted that his intense desire to learn and early reading ability masked his hearing loss until he was 6 or 7 years of age. As an older student, he resisted the messages he was given about choosing another profession or an easier career path because of his deafness. Myron described his motivation as "perverse" and indicated that he often set challenging goals in order to "show them" he could succeed. As an adult, he directed a medical research center—an impressive career achievement for any physician. A second case reported by Whitmore and Maker displayed the same pattern of persistence in the face of obstruction; Abe, a congenitally blind mathematician with some light perception, was repeatedly denied employment in his field. Rather than give up his love for mathematics, Abe was encouraged by his family to attend graduate school in mathematics. Ultimately, he devised and was assisted in publishing the Nemeth Code, a means of transcribing mathematics for the blind that is in wide use today. Reis and her colleagues (1995) noted the same motivation and tendency toward persistence in 12 university students and graduates with learning disabilities. She reports that the majority of the students in this qualitative study "believed their capacity for hard work was their greatest asset" (p. 74). This pattern was also discernible in younger twice-exceptional students. Baum and Owen (1988) noted that gifted/learning-disabled students were persistent even though they were more likely to have lower academic self-efficacy when compared with learning-disabled students not identified as gifted. Willard-Holt (1994) reported that Jan, age 6, and Brad, age 14, repeatedly tried challenging tasks for hours at a time, sometimes without success. Both youngsters have cerebral palsy, are unable to speak, and have severely restricted movement. However, parents, teachers, classmates, and observers commented repeatedly that each boy is intensely motivated. For example, Willard-Holt (1994) reports in an interview with Brad's math teacher that "even when he feels sick, he wants to be here, like he's going to miss out on something. I think he shines at being motivated, way above and beyond the call of duty . . ." (p. 5).

Second, twice-exceptional learners develop coping strategies that compensate for their disabilities. In some cases, the strategies may have resulted in the masking or late identification of either the disability or the talent area. For example, as stated earlier, Myron was not identified as deaf until the age of 6. He was able to learn to lip-read without formal instruction and filled in the gaps in conversations he could not hear so successfully that he carried on telephone conversations without assistance (Whitmore & Maker, 1985). Of the gifted/learning-disabled students studied by Reis et al. (1995, 1997), the learning disability was not isolated until secondary school or beyond for 7 of the 12. Two others were not identified as having a disability until fifth or sixth grade. Only 2 of the 12 were identified as talented by the schools, and this was not until middle school; one was formally placed and the other was referred but not placed. These students report a variety of coping strategies to overcome their disability: computer use, books on tape, borrowing notes from classmates to fill in gaps, mnemonics, note taking, time management, and setting work priorities. Identification of specific learning disabilities in high-ability learners may require longitudinal monitoring during the first 3 to 5 years of schooling (McCoach, Kehle, Bray, & Siegle, 2001).

Third, twice-exceptional learners frequently report or are observed to have feelings of isolation from others, which they attribute to the disability or to others' responses to the disability. In some cases, the disabilities are the source of isolation. For example, Alec's severe allergies required homebound instruction and the social isolation from peers that accompanied it (Moon & Dillon, 1995). Ingraham et al. (1995) reported that isolation from peers was exacerbated for three deaf-blind students by the presence of interpreters in inclusive classrooms. According to the authors, students viewed the interpreters as supervisory adults rather than as support personnel. The college students interviewed by Reis and her colleagues (1995, 1997, 2000) generally reported peer difficulties and feelings of isolation in school; however, the two students identified at the earliest grade levels were the exceptions, as they reported positive peer relations. Peer and adjustment problems were reported for elementary boys with co-occurring Attention Deficit/Hyperactivity Disorder (ADHD) and giftedness (Moon et al., 2001; Zentall, Moon, Hall, & Grskovic, 2001).

Finally, reading ability is one of the frequently mentioned indicators of giftedness among children without disabilities. Even though a number of the disabilities manifested in twice-exceptional children involve impairments in receptive and expressive language abilities, fluent reading is also a pattern among many of the individuals reported in the case study literature. Both Jan and Brad were early readers: Jan by age 3 (Willard-Holt, 1994). Moon and Dillon (1995) detailed a child who was a verbally gifted, fluent reader, but who also was learning disabled and sufficiently health impaired to receive homebound instruction. Toscano, McKee, and Lepoutre (2002) and Whitmore and Maker (1985) also reported fluent reading in the case of deafness—a disability that affects receptive and expressive communication. The pattern of fluent and intense reading was reported in the case studies of learners with physical or sensory impairments; it was not typical of individuals with specific learning disabilities.

Importance of Talent Recognition Among Learners With Disabilities

Identifying talented learners with disabilities is made more difficult by the many variations and combinations of conditions that may affect students' abilities to learn or to demonstrate what they can do. For example, the educational needs of a student who is deaf and one who is deaf and blind differ. The needs of a student who is deaf from birth or one who loses hearing after language develops also differ. The needs of a student with a specific writing disability differ from one who presents a disability in mathematics learning. The nature and severity of a student's disability affects the means used to identify his or her talents. For example, assessments for students with sensory or physical impairments are adapted to provide alternative means for responses by the learner (Cline & Schwartz, 1999; Whitmore & Maker, 1985). The performances of twice-exceptional students should be compared with the performances of others with the same disabilities (Karnes & Johnson, 1991). Such comparisons help educators understand the nature of the talent occurring with the disability and to acknowledge it. In general, educators are not familiar with twice-exceptionality or how to identify it (Blough, Rittenhouse, & Dancer, 1999; Boodoo, Bradley, Frontera, Pitts, & Wright, 1989). For example, Minner (1990) noted that classroom teachers had difficulty identifying a student as gifted or as gifted and learning disabled from sample case studies. Thus, comparative information is important for educators charged with identifying twice-exceptional learners.

In two studies evaluating the effects of a program for young gifted children with mild to moderate disabilities, Karnes et al. (1983a, 1983b) noted that involving parents in the identification of and planning for their child assisted the family in viewing their youngster as having strengths rather than focusing solely on the disability. The importance of family recognition and support appears over the course of the twice-exceptional learner's development. In the reports of gifted/learning-disabled college students, Reis and her colleagues (1995) found that all 12 commented on the strength of maternal support in helping them to achieve their goals. Although the researchers noted that parents differed in the ways they offered support, all parents stepped forward to work with schools when problems arose. Patterns of familial support appear in reports of other gifted/learning-disabled college students, as well (Dole, 2001).

For parents and schools who wish to provide stimulation at home or plan educational services for twice-exceptional students, four factors are important in making decisions. In terms of students with sensory impairments, Ingraham and her colleagues (1995) suggested that the etiology of the disability should be considered. For example, with retinitis pigmentosa, the eye condition will worsen progressively. Second, the age of onset of the disability is important for educational planning. If the child is born with the disability (congenital), he may have no knowledge of a concept. If he acquired the disability later on (adventitious), there may be knowledge of a concept on which to build educational experiences. Third, the severity of the disability is a factor in educational planning. A child may be using remaining senses or other abilities to adapt well to the environment, and he or she may be capable of compensating significantly for the disability. Finally, the prior learning related to the disability will assist parents and educators in focusing on strengths. If the student can lip-read, use a communication board, read Braille, or take notes with a computer, key skills are already in place.

The overarching issue for parents with twice-exceptional children and the schools that serve them is to recognize the talent aggressively and plan individually to provide academic assistance and emotional support from the early years through the college experience.

WHAT WE CAN DO

At Home

❧ Resist the assumption that learners with physical or emotional disabilities, sensory impairments, lack of expressive speech, or specific learning disabilities cannot be academically talented. Evidence from case studies of children (Moon & Dillon, 1995; Willard-Holt, 1994, 1998) and adults (Dole, 2001; Whitmore & Maker, 1985) demonstrates that twice-exceptional individuals can be found early and do develop into successful and creative adults.

❧ Share with parents the importance of family support. Case studies of children, college students, and adults repeat the theme of parental support, especially by mothers (Reis et al., 1995; Whitmore & Maker, 1985; Willard-Holt, 1994).

In the Classroom

❧ Overtly teach compensating and coping strategies, particularly to talented students who also have a specific learning disability (Sah & Borland, 1989). Reis and her colleagues (1997, 2000) noted that assistance is welcomed and incorporated by students even when they have reached college age.

At School

❧ Modify identification procedures to include assessments that have been adapted for specific physical, hearing, or visual impairments. When using the assessments, compare the students' performance to the performance of others with similar or a combination of similar disabilities (Karnes & Johnson, 1991).

ॐ Adopt a talent development orientation to educational planning. If a student is in a setting that focuses exclusively on remediation, the talent area should be addressed. Educational planning teams should include professionals who concentrate on academic strengths, as well as those whose expertise is in assistive technology and adaptations to learning disabilities (Nielsen, 2002; Nielsen et al., 1993).

ॐ Explain to family and schools that the particular educational adaptations need to account for the age of the onset of the disability. For example, adaptations for deaf students differ depending upon whether the child has heard speech during the early formative years or has been without hearing since birth (Ingraham et al., 1995).

REFERENCES

Bailey, S., & Sinclair, R. (1992). Out of sight but not out of mind. *Gifted Education International, 8,* 114–116.

Baum, S. M. (1988). An enrichment program for gifted learning disabled students. *Gifted Child Quarterly, 32,* 226–230.

Baum, S. M., & Owen, S. (1988). High ability/learning disabled students: How are they different? *Gifted Child Quarterly, 32,* 321–326.

Blough, L. K., Rittenhouse, R. K., & Dancer, J. (1999). Identification of gifted deaf children: A complex but critical educational process. *Perceptual and Motor Skills, 89,* 219–221.

Boodoo, G. M., Bradley, C. I., Frontera, R. L., Pitts, J. R., & Wright, L. P. (1989). A survey of procedures used for identifying gifted learning disabled children. *Gifted Child Quarterly, 33,* 110–114.

Cline, S., & Schwartz, D. (1999). *Diverse populations of gifted children: Meeting their needs in the regular classroom and beyond.* Upper Saddle River, NJ: Prentice-Hall.

Coleman, M. R. (1992). A comparison of how gifted/LD and average/LD boys cope with school frustration. *Journal for the Education of the Gifted, 15,* 239–265

Dole, S. (2001). Reconciling contradictions: Identify formation in individuals with giftedness and learning disabilities. *Journal for the Education of the Gifted, 25,* 103–137.

Gallagher, J. J. (1988). National agenda for educating gifted students: Statement of priorities. *Exceptional Children, 55,* 107–114.

Goertzel, V., & Goertzel, M. G. (1962). *Cradles of eminence.* Boston: Little, Brown.

Hokanson, D. T., & Jospe, M. (1976). *The search for cognitive giftedness in exceptional children.* New Haven, CT: Project SEARCH, Educational Center for the Arts. (ERIC Document Reproduction Service No. ED140563)

Hua, C. B. (2002). Career self-efficacy of the student who is gifted/learning disabled: A case study. *Journal for the Education of the Gifted, 4,* 375–404.

Individuals with Disabilities Education Act, 20 U.S.C. §1401 et seq. (1990).

Ingraham, C., Daugherty, K. M., & Gorrafa, S. (1995). The success of three gifted deaf-blind students in inclusive educational programs. *Journal of Visual Impairment and Blindness, 89,* 257–261.

Johnsen, S. K., & Corn, A. L. (1989). The past, present and future of education for gifted children with sensory and/or physical disabilities. *Roeper Review, 12,* 13–23.

Karnes, M. B., & Johnson, L. J. (1991). Gifted handicapped. In N. Colangelo & G. A. Davis (Eds.), *Handbook of gifted education* (pp. 428–437). Boston: Allyn & Bacon.

Karnes, M. B., Shwedel, A. M., & Lewis, G. F. (1983a). Long-term effects of early programming for the young gifted handicapped child. *Exceptional Children, 50,* 103–109.

Karnes, M. B., Shwedel, A. M., & Lewis, G. F. (1983b). Short-term effects of early programming for the young gifted handicapped child. *Journal for the Education of the Gifted, 6,* 266–278.

Kershner, J. (1995). The career success of an adult with a learning disability: A psychosocial study of amnesic-semantic aphasia. *Journal of Learning Disabilities, 28,* 121–126.

LaSasso, C. J. (1992). Speaking of "learning disabilities," whatever happened to Erin? *Perspectives in Education and Deafness, 11*(2), 2–4.

McCoach, D. B., Kehle, T. J., Bray, M. A., & Siegle, D. (2001). Best practices in the identification of gifted students with learning disabilities. *Psychology in the Schools, 38,* 402–411.

Minner, S. (1990). Teacher evaluations of case descriptions of LD gifted children. *Gifted Child Quarterly, 34,* 37–39.

Moon, S. M., & Dillon, D. R. (1995). Multiple exceptionalities: A case study. *Journal for the Education of the Gifted, 18,* 111–130.

Moon, S. M., Zentall, S. S., Grskovic, J. A., Hall, A., & Stormont, M. (2001). Emotional and social characteristics of boys with AD/HD and giftedness: A comparative case study. *Journal for the Education of the Gifted, 24,* 207–247.

Nielsen, M. E. (2002). Gifted students with learning disabilities: Recommendations for identification and programming. *Exceptionality, 10,* 93–111.

Nielsen, M. E., Higgins, L. D., & Hammond, A. N. (1993). The twice-exceptional child project: Identifying and serving gifted/handicapped learners. In C. M. Callahan, C. A. Tomlinson, & P. M. Pizzat (Eds.), *Contexts for promise: Noteworthy practices and innovations in the identification of gifted students* (pp. 145–168). Storrs: National Research Center on the Gifted and Talented, University of Connecticut.

Reis, S. M., McGuire, J. M., & Neu, T. W. (2000). Compensation strategies used by high-ability students with learning disabilities who succeed in college. *Gifted Child Quarterly, 44,* 123–134.

Reis, S. M., Neu, T. W., & McGuire, J. M. (1995). *Talents in two places: Case studies of high ability students with learning disabilities who achieved.* Storrs: National Center on the Gifted and Talented, University of Connecticut.

Reis, S. M., Neu, T. W., & McGuire, J. M. (1997) Case studies of high ability students with learning disabilities who have achieved. *Exceptional Children, 63,* 463–479.

Sah, A., & Borland, J. H. (1989). The effects of a structured home plan on the home and school behaviors of gifted learning-disabled students with deficits in organizational skills. *Roeper Review, 12,* 54–57.

Toscano, R. M., McKee, B., & Lepoutre, D. (2002). Success with academic English: Reflections of deaf college students. *American Annals of the Deaf, 147,* 5–23.

Vernon, M., & LaFalce-Landers, E. (1993). A longitudinal study of intellectually gifted deaf and hard of hearing people: Educational, psychological, and career outcomes. *American Annals of the Deaf, 138,* 427–434.

Whitmore, J. R., & Maker C. J. (1985). *Intellectual giftedness in disabled persons.* Rockville, MD: Aspen.

Willard-Holt, C. (1994). *Recognizing talent: Cross-case study of two high potential students with cerebral palsy.* Storrs: National Research Center on the Gifted and Talented, University of Connecticut.

Willard-Holt, C. (1998). Academic and personality characteristics of gifted students with cerebral palsy: A multiple case study. *Exceptional Children, 65,* 37–50.

Zentall, S. M., Moon, S. M., Hall, A. M., & Grskovic, J. A. (2001). Learning and motivational characteristics of boys with AD/HD and/or giftedness. *Exceptional Children, 67,* 499–519.

CHAPTER 4

GENDER DIFFERENCES

The literature on gender differences in gifted education is mostly about gifted girls, and heavily focused on performance in mathematics and science. The general literature on gender differences rarely addresses high ability. The number of important research-based generalizations about gender differences and the education of highly able children is therefore small. While there are interesting differences in how female and male children or adults think or feel in some circumstances, the differences are typically contextual, and the final or potential performance differences are minor or nonexistent. This does not argue for the educational status quo, because existing contextual differences are often large, changeable, and inequitable.

WHAT WE KNOW

A convincing case is yet to be made that, all other things being equal, there are gender differences that matter in education or gifted education in particular (Olszewski-Kubilius & Turner, 2002). But, "other things" are not equal, hence the difficulty of systematically testing this assertion. Given the inequalities in parenting, schooling, and other societal inputs, it may be helpful to look at what appear to be gender differences as a means to address these inequalities, not as compensation for deficiencies usually characterized as "girl problems," for example, underperformance in mathematics rather than biases in mathematics education (cf. Secada, Fennema, & Adajian, 1995), underrepresentation in certain occupations rather than sexism in the workplace, or personality shortcomings such as lack of competitiveness rather than the undervaluing in many societies of cooperative or collaborative personalities or processes. Following are some examples of where recent and contemporary research is guiding thinking and action on these issues.

Spatial Versus Verbal Abilities

One of the most widely assumed differences, based on outcomes from IQ testing, is that girls' abilities exceed those of boys in the verbal domain, and boys are higher in the spatial and mathematical domains (Lubinski & Benbow, 1992). IQ subtest data have certainly demonstrated such performance outcomes, but the conclusion that these reflect a potential or ability difference is, in fact, no longer clear. For example, there is no significant difference between elementary girls and boys on mathematical reasoning ability (Springler & Alsup, 2003).

Borkowski (1990) examined SAT-Mathematics gender differences and concluded that they were small and were accounted for by differences on just 2 of the 40 items. These differences still predict later mathematics performance, but they are inadequate in light of simultaneous social influences to explain all the differences that follow. Nevertheless, in litigation these scores have been confirmed to discriminate against girls (cf. Stone, 1992). Stumpf (1998) looked at the performance of 553 girls and 730 boys from grades 7 and 8 and found that the girls got lower scores because they took more time working on time-limited tests. There was no difference in test performance when the time constraint was removed (also observed by Gallagher & Johnson, 1991, and in creativity measures—cf. Rejskind, Rapagna, & Gold, 1991). In her thorough overview, *Sex Differences in Cognitive Abilities*, Halpern (1986) cited a related real-world U.S. Air Force study that compared male and female officer trainees on both paper-and-pencil tests and flight simulator performance (McCloy & Koonce, 1982). The usual differences occurred on the timed tests, but there were no differences in final performance on the flight simulator. The instruction was not modified, and only one other difference was found; the men reached criterion performance in slightly fewer trials. We add to this evidence the increasing numbers of women in occupations traditionally dominated by males and perhaps thought to be more in accord with male abilities.

In the literature comparing gifted learners' and expert performance on spatial and mathematical tasks, one of the interesting and consistent outcomes is that gifted children and experts are more likely to spend more time in a response-planning phase and to proceed more quickly in the execution of the final answer, and go more quickly over the whole problem when it is trivial (Shore & Lazar, 1996). It has also been shown that learners will use strategies more attuned to their intellectual strengths to achieve similar levels of final performance (Shore, Hymovitch, & Lajoie, 1982), or solve an apparently spatial problem by verbalizing (Shore & Carey, 1984) if that is their strength. What looks like a gender issue need not be so construed.

In a meta-analysis of 75 studies, Friedman (1995) found that the general cohort verbal scores are actually more highly correlated with mathematical performance than spatial. Furthermore, in college bound and high-ability samples, the spatial-mathematical correlations are stronger in female than male students. Our understanding of differences in spatial abilities needs to be carefully set in context.

Gender issues should be biologically driven. The spatial-verbal difference between men and women apparently cannot be accounted for by social variables. However, the gender impact is not simple and straightforward.

> At least among subjects with high reasoning ability, left handed males performed poorer [*sic*] than right handed males, but left handed males had the advantage over right handed males on verbal ability tests . . . Left handed females were better on the spatial ability tests than right handed females with an opposite pattern among females for the verbal ability tests. (Halpern, 1986, p. 150)

The existence of these biological differences is interesting, but it may be educationally irrelevant unless all students are faced with a single-tracked, time-pressured curriculum in which students' strengths are ignored, or in which systematic bias occurs. Stanic and Hart (1995) reported a classroom observational study that demonstrated that the total number of student-teacher interactions, and specifically those that were academic—that is, focused on the subject matter and learning—were associated with only small differences in classroom scores across gender and race. In contrast, small differences in the numbers of procedural interactions—those having to do with behavior—were related to large differences. African American girls and White boys fared more favorably than White girls and African American boys, in that order. The race-gender interaction is most closely associated not with ability, but with confidence. In terms of classroom achievement, student groups score in the same order as above, with little gap between the first two, but larger gaps between the others. The issue of confidence is explored in more detail in the chapter on mathematics learning.

Psychosocial Issues

There are many psychosocial variables whose influence may exaggerate the importance of gender differences (Halpern, 1986).

Although there is an assumption that females and males receive an equal education when they are in the same classrooms, with the same teachers using the same books (Benbow & Stanley, 1983), the assumption is false. . . . Classroom activities are chosen more often to appeal to boys than to girls (Fennema & Peterson, 1987; Stallings, 1985). Boys receive more praise, a greater number of disciplinary contacts, and more general teacher-initiated contacts. Teachers respond more often to boys' requests for help and criticize girls more frequently for the academic quality of their work. Even when overall sex differences are not found in patterns of interaction, a few male students often dominate teacher attention in mathematics classes (Eccles, 1989, p. 226).

In her benchmark work on gifted girls, Kerr (1995) cited several educational barriers. These barriers include boys being called upon three times as often as girls and receiving more informative replies, the continuing dominance of male characters in texts, and girls being allowed or even encouraged to choose less demanding courses. According to Kerr, gifted girls may be too well-adjusted for their own good. They adjust to unacceptable situations, and supposed gender differences bear remarkable resemblance to status inequalities. However, in the 20 years since the beginning of her longitudinal study, Kerr continued to note increased career goals and lower mathematics anxiety in bright women; equal aspirations to men in law, medicine, and business; and less fear of success and compliance to men's opinions. Callahan, Cunningham, and Plucker (1994) reported that problem-solving abilities and family support helped girls cope with these barriers.

In a study of 5,385 fourth- and eighth-grade gifted and talented students, Siegle and Reis (1998) found that teachers generally perceive girls as working harder and producing better quality work. Only in language arts did teachers perceive any ability difference—in favor of the girls. However, girls' self-perceptions of their own abilities remained negative and lower than the boys'. The girls continue to deny their giftedness (Walker, Reis, & Leonard, 1992). In a study of readiness for advanced mathematics, Ablard and Tissot (1998) found neither gender differences nor gender-by-age interactions in formal reasoning in 150 children finishing grades 2 and 6. It is possible that apparent gender differences in performance and measures of potential, commonly seen in the general literature, are disappearing among talented individuals, but social issues remain. Zohar and Sela (2003) found boys' matriculation physics test scores to be higher than girls', but girls' teacher-based scores were higher. They uncovered excessive competitiveness and inadequate focus on learner understanding as disadvantages for girls. Inzlicht and Ben-Zeev (2003) conducted a telling study demonstrating that high-achieving female students' performance is significantly lowered when they are merely tested in the presence of a majority of males. They also pointed out that girls slightly outperform boys in class, but suffer on timed or speeded tests.

Persistent gender-related differences continue to surface in self-efficacy, a quality reflected in measures of self-concept (Luscombe & Riley, 2001; Schober, Reimann, & Wagner, 2004; Swiatek, 2005; Yun Dai, 2001), locus of control (Reis & Park, 2001), and course-choosing behavior: "when adolescent girls are also identified as gifted, the problems of conformity, peer acceptance, and low self-esteem often become exacerbated" (Frey, 1998, p. 437). In Cramer and Oshima's (1992) review, girls continued to ascribe difficulties in mathematics to lack of ability, in contrast to boys' attributions to effort. In contrast, Li and Adamson (1995) found that gifted girls attributed both success and failure in mathematics, science, and English more to effort and strategy than did boys. Nevertheless, they also cited Dweck's (1986) observation of a repeated maladaptive pattern of "a tendency toward unduly low expectancies, challenge avoidance, ability attribution for failure, and debilitation under failure in bright girls" (p. 1043). Wright and Leroux (1997) found no gender differences or changes over a school year in global self-concept. On some subscales of the Harter Self-Perception Profile there were, however, significant gender-by-time interactions. The first was the growth of gifted girls' internal or ability attributions for school competence and the growing importance of close friendships. Their end-of-year interview produced an interesting result; some gifted boys saw their failures as the result of lack of ability, too. Similarly, on the Piers-Harris scales, school girls rate themselves more highly on behavior and school and intellectual status, but lower on anxiety. A single self-concept score is not meaningful (Lewis & Knight, 2000).

Several studies have found race-by-gender interactions that parallel the data for spatial and verbal ability, strengthening suspicions that environmental contexts are important. McLaughlin and Saccuzzo (1997) studied locus of control in 805 fifth to seventh graders with attention to giftedness, gender, ethnicity, and risk factors. The highest internal locus of control was for female Caucasian students with no risk factors. One interpretation of these findings is that, given the number of external barriers facing highly able women, taking personal responsibility may sometimes be maladaptive. When Plucker (1998) explored gender-by-ethnicity differences in 749 gifted adolescents' coping strategies, he found none uniquely related to gender. Heller and Ziegler (1996) reported two promising studies in Germany, one with preadolescent boys and girls and the other with university women only. Attribution retraining was associated with enhanced performance for both boys and girls, so there is some suspicion that attribution differences may not be an inherent gender difference.

Family influences have not been studied as thoroughly as they deserve. There is accumulated evidence that girls are more likely to choose science careers if their fathers are in science (F. G. Rejskind, personal communication). Dickens and Cornell (1993) reported that parents' own self-concept with regard to mathematics was related to their expectations for their high-ability daughters. It was the parents' expectations that directly related to their daughters' mathematical self-concept, although the relations were reciprocal: The daughters' self-concept and achievement could equally influence parental expectations. No evidence has been found of a parallel study focusing on sons.

Single-Sex Schooling

Silverman (1993) asserted that "one factor that clearly undermines gifted adolescent girls' self-esteem is their belief that high ability means achieving good grades effortlessly" (p. 304). This may explain why they do not attribute success to effort. Despite the dominance of boys in interactions with teachers in mixed-gender classes, Subotnik and Strauss (1995) found that single-sex classes did not increase girls' participation in an Advanced Placement calculus class. Feldhusen and Willard-Holt (1993) noted that bright boys ask more questions than bright girls do. Teachers do not stop girls from calling out the answers (only a small part of classroom discourse) and do not address the appropriateness of calling out answers by either boys or girls. The potential advantages of girls-only classes are not fully known.

In a history of Hunter College Campus Schools, Stone (1992) repeated the common experience of educators and students in girls-only schools; they hold many advantages for girls and gifted girls in particular. "At a single-sex school, the girls did not feel like second-class citizens, or fall silent in classroom discussions, or develop math anxiety, or settle for running for student government secretary" (p. 72). "The boys' presence dulled the sharper edges of the girls' competitiveness. . . . The boys' presence and the boys' performance deterred the girls" (p. 75). Ironically, the admission of boys to the Hunter College Schools in the 1970s doubled the size of the applicant pool and raised the secondary school entrance criterion from being 2 years ahead of classmates to 4. As a consequence, the presence of boys affected choices of which girls were not admitted, and thereby lost the opportunity to attend Hunter. Kerr (1995) reflected on the successes of women's colleges in producing eminent women. She noted that the result is not necessarily causal, but rather may be the result of selection factors. One must test a prediction, not merely evaluate an outcome. It is also not yet fully known if the benefits of single-sex schooling can be achieved in mixed classes and schools. The role of female role models for girls also remains of considerable interest (Hébert, Long, & Speirs Neumeister, 2001).

Conclusion

When examined carefully, gender differences between gifted boys and girls are equivocal. There may well be fewer gender differences than in the general population because highly able girls are increasingly nontraditional in their course-taking and career choices and because in education gifted boys are not discriminated against for less macho behavior and interests. On the other hand, sensitivity to gender-related outcomes in both general and gifted education is extremely important, especially as it directs our attention to ways to improve equity for all children, its relation to differences in social status and vulnerability, and the interaction with ethnicity. The possibility that gender differences themselves may be trivial and educationally unimportant is not justification for maintaining the educational status quo or failing to learn from differences in which gender is merely a correlate, not a cause. Some of these implications are outlined next.

WHAT WE CAN DO

At Home

ê Parents should consciously separate their own experiences with schooling, and mathematics in particular, from the expectations they communicate to their children, especially girls. Even though girls and boys may have different intellectual strengths or preferences, there is no evidence that any subject matter is thereby more difficult or less attainable.

ê Through the parent and teacher or home and school association, develop a dialogue and awareness about gender issues, parental expectations, differential treatment by teachers, and related topics.

In the Classroom

ê Teachers should consciously call upon girls and boys for responses and ensure that the levels of their questions addressed to both are equal. Girls or any children who do not volunteer readily should not be left out of the classroom discourse, but respectfully involved.

ê Criticism should be equitably provided. Do not assume that girls are having trouble with the content and boys are having trouble with paying attention.

ê Give value to planning and reflection before engaging in the demands of a task, rather than overemphasizing the rapid delivery of an answer. This is especially important in the case of novel or challenging tasks.

At School

ê Encourage the availability of female, as well as male, role models without their being cast into stereotypical careers.

᠊᠊᠊ Offer a balance of mixed-gender and single-sex learning opportunities, especially for young adolescent girls, while ensuring that equally high expectations are provided for both boys and girls.

᠊᠊᠊ Offer single-sex and mixed support groups that allow both boys and girls to openly discuss self-esteem and other issues.

᠊᠊᠊ Consider the optional or compulsory status of subjects such as mathematics and science. In most parts of the world, mathematics and science are not optional subjects at the secondary level, especially for college-bound students.

᠊᠊᠊ Try as much as possible to avoid program or educational decisions made exclusively on the basis of timed examinations; ensure that students' profiles also include assessments of criterion performance.

REFERENCES

Ablard, K. E., & Tissot, S. L. (1998). Young students' readiness for advanced mathematics: Precocious abstract reasoning. *Journal for the Education of the Gifted, 21,* 206–223.

Benbow, C. P., & Stanley, J. C. (1983). Sex differences in mathematical reasoning ability: More facts. *Science, 222,* 1029–1031.

Borkowski, J. (1990). "Small" gender differences on the SAT: A scenario about social origins. *Behavioral and Brain Sciences, 13,* 190–198.

Callahan, C. M., Cunningham, C. M., & Plucker, J. A. (1994). Foundations for the future: The socio-emotional development of gifted, adolescent women. *Roeper Review, 17,* 99–105.

Cramer, J., & Oshima, T. C. (1992). Do gifted females attribute their math performance differently than other students? *Journal for the Education of the Gifted, 16,* 18–35.

Dickens, M. N., & Cornell, D. C. (1993). Parent influences on mathematics self-concept of high ability adolescent girls. *Journal for the Education of the Gifted, 17,* 53–73.

Dweck, C. S. (1986). Motivational processes affecting learning. *American Psychologist, 41,* 1040–1048.

Eccles, J. (1989). Bringing young women to mathematics and science. In M. Crawford & M. Gentry (Eds.), *Gender and thought: Psychological perspectives* (pp. 36–58). New York: Springer.

Feldhusen, J. F., & Willard-Holt, C. (1993). Gender differences in classroom interactions and career aspirations of gifted students. *Contemporary Educational Psychology, 18,* 335–362.

Fennema, E., & Peterson, P. (1987). Effective teaching for girls and boys: The same or different? In D. Berliner & B. Rosenshine (Eds.), *Talks to teachers* (pp. 111–125). New York: Random House.

Frey, C. P. (1998). Struggling with identity: Working with seventh- and eighth-grade girls to air issues of concern. *Journal for the Education of the Gifted, 21,* 437–451.

Friedman, L. (1995). The space factor in mathematics: Gender differences. *Review of Educational Research, 65,* 22–50.

Gallagher, S. A., & Johnson, E. S. (1991). The effect of time limits on performance of mental rotations by gifted adolescents. *Gifted Child Quarterly, 36,* 19–22.

Halpern, D. F. (1986). *Sex differences in cognitive abilities.* Hillsdale, NJ: Erlbaum.

Hébert, T. P., Long, L. A., & Speirs Neumeister, K. L. (2001). Using biography to counsel gifted young women. *Journal of Secondary Gifted Education, 12,* 62–79.

Heller, K. A., & Ziegler, A. (1996). Gender differences in mathematics and the sciences: Can attribution retraining improve the performance of gifted females? *Gifted Child Quarterly, 40,* 200–210.

Inzlicht, M., & Ben-Zeev, T. (2003). Do high-achieving female students underperform in private? The implications of threatening environments on intellectual processing. *Journal of Educational Psychology, 95,* 796–805.

Kerr, B. A. (1995). *Smart girls: A new psychology of girls, women, and giftedness.* Scottsdale, AZ: Gifted Psychology Press.

Lewis, J. D., & Knight, H. V. (2000). Self-concept in gifted youth: An investigation employing the Piers-Harris Subscales. *Gifted Child Quarterly, 44,* 45–53.

Li, A. K. F., & Adamson, G. (1995). Motivational patterns related to gifted students' learning of mathematics, science and English: An examination of gender differences. *Journal for the Education of the Gifted, 18,* 284–297.

Lubinski, D., & Benbow, C. P. (1992). Gender differences in abilities and preferences among the gifted: Implications for the math-science pipeline. *Current Directions in Psychological Science, 1,* 61–66.

Luscombe, A., & Riley, T. L. (2001). An examination of self-concept in academically gifted adolescents: Do gender differences occur? *Roeper Review, 24,* 20–22.

McCloy, T. M., & Koonce, J. M. (1982). Sex as a moderator variable in the selection and training of persons for a skilled task. *Aviation, Space and Environmental Medicine, 53,* 1170–1172.

McLaughlin, S. C., & Saccuzzo, D. P. (1997). Ethnic and gender differences in locus of control. *Journal for the Education of the Gifted, 20,* 268–283.

Olszewski-Kubilius, P., & Turner, D. (2002). Gender differences among elementary school-aged gifted students in achievement, perceptions of ability, and subject preference. *Journal for the Education of the Gifted, 25,* 233–268.

Plucker, J. A. (1998). Gender, race, and grade differences in gifted adolescents' coping strategies. *Journal for the Education of the Gifted, 21,* 423–436.

Reis, S. M., & Park, S. (2001). Gender differences in high-achieving students in math and science. *Journal for the Education of the Gifted, 25,* 52–73.

Rejskind, F. G., Rapagna, S. O., & Gold, D. (1991). Gender differences in children's divergent thinking. *Creativity Research Journal, 5,* 165–174.

Schober, B., Reimann, F., & Wagner, P. (2004). Is research on gender-specific underachievement in gifted girls an obsolete topic? New findings on an often discussed issue. *High Ability Studies, 15,* 43–62.

Secada, W. G., Fennema, E., & Adajian, L. B. (Eds.). (1995). *New directions for equity in mathematics education.* Cambridge, UK: Cambridge University Press.

Shore, B. M., & Carey, S. M. (1984). Verbal ability and spatial tasks. *Perceptual and Motor Skills, 59,* 255–259.

Shore, B. M., Hymovitch, J., & Lajoie, S. P. (1982). Processing differences in the relation between ability and field-independence. *Psychological Reports, 50,* 391–395.

Shore, B. M., & Lazar, L. (1996). IQ-related differences in time allocation during problem solving. *Psychological Reports, 78,* 848–849.

Siegle, D., & Reis, S. M. (1998). Gender differences in teacher and student perceptions of gifted students' ability and effort. *Gifted Child Quarterly, 42,* 39–47.

Silverman, L. K. (1993). Social development leadership and gender issues. In L. K. Silverman (Ed.), *Counseling the gifted and talented* (pp. 291–327). Denver, CO: Love.

Springler, D. M., & Alsup, J. K. (2003). An analysis of gender and the mathematical reasoning ability sub-skill of analysis-synthesis. *Education, 123,* 763–369.

Stallings, J. (1985). School, classroom and home influences on women's decisions to enroll in advanced mathematics courses. In S. Chipman, L. Brush, & D. Wilson (Eds.), *Women and mathematics: Balancing the equation* (pp. 199–224). Hillsdale, NJ: Erlbaum.

Stanic, G. M., & Hart, L. E. (1995). Attitudes, persistence, and mathematics achievements. In W. G. Secada, E. Fennema, & L. B. Adajian (Eds.), *New directions for equity in mathematics education* (pp. 258–276). Cambridge, UK: Cambridge University Press.

Stone, E. (1992). *The Hunter College campus schools for the gifted: The challenge of equity and excellence.* New York: Teachers College Press.

Stumpf, H. (1998). Gender-related differences in academically talented students' scores and use of time on tests of spatial ability. *Gifted Child Quarterly, 42,* 157–171.

Subotnik, R. F., & Strauss, S. M. (1995). Gender differences in classroom participation and achievement: An experiment involving Advanced Placement calculus classes. *Journal of Secondary Gifted Education, 6,* 77–85.

Swiatek, M. A. (2005). Gifted students' self-perceptions of ability in specific subject domains: Factor structure and relationship with above-level test scores. *Roeper Review, 27,* 104–109.

Walker, B. A., Reis, S. M., & Leonard, J. S. (1992). A developmental investigation of the lives of gifted women. *Gifted Child Quarterly, 36,* 201–206.

Wright, P. B., & Leroux, J. A. (1997). The self-concept of gifted adolescents in a congregated program. *Gifted Child Quarterly, 41,* 83–94.

Yun Dai, D. (2001). A comparison of gender differences in academic self-concept and motivation between high-ability and average Chinese adolescents. *Journal of Secondary Gifted Education, 13,* 22–32.

Zohar, A., & Sela, D. (2003). Her physics, his physics: Gender issues in Israeli Advanced Placement physics classes. *International Journal of Science Education, 25,* 245–268.

CHAPTER 5

DEVELOPING SPECIFIC TALENTS

T alent development is a complex process involving the individual, the home, the school, and the community. Research on talented adults has been used to understand the process in specific domains. Talent development in children is influenced by parents' response to the talent and by the response of others in the family or community when the family environment is not optimal. In addition, talent development is fostered when the child or adolescent encounters the right teacher at the right time, has the opportunity to connect powerfully with the talent area, and has an outlet to express accomplishments.

WHAT WE KNOW

Much of what is known about the expression of talent in specific domains comes from studies of talented or eminent adults. These studies can take the form of retrospective investigations in particular talent domains (Bloom, 1985;

Roe, 1953; Walberg, 1969; Zuckerman, 1977), historical analyses of eminent figures (Gruber, 1976; VanTassel-Baska, 1995), or historiometry (Simonton, 1984, 1994). However, talent development has also been investigated among adolescents and children through both case studies and large sample studies (Coleman, 2005; Csikszentmihalyi, Rathunde, & Whalen, 1993; Feldman, 1991; Goldsmith, 2000; Golomb, 1992; Piirto, 1992).

For example, Bloom (1985) retrospectively investigated 35 highly successful individuals in adulthood. They excelled in areas as diverse as science, competitive sports, and music. He found patterns in the factors that influenced talent development among this sample. First, there was a nurturing and supportive family. If a child displayed an interest in a talent area, the family was quick to respond by providing the child with opportunities to learn about or gain experiences in exercising the talent. Second, the individual encountered important teachers along the way. During the early years, a teacher who felt the child was special, who encouraged and believed in the child was frequently reported as important. As the child grew and the talent began to mature, the child encountered a teacher who was a "taskmaster." This teacher focused on developing the habits of practice and dedication to the talent area. Finally, these highly talented adults encountered a master teacher, a person who was also an expert in the talent area. As the individual continued to mature, competitions were used to try out one's talent and develop a sense of the standards in the field.

Csikszentmihalyi and his colleagues (1993) focused on the motivational aspects of talent development in a study of 200 teenagers. Using a technique called the experience-sampling method, the researchers followed teenagers throughout the day and evening by giving them pagers. When the pager went off, the teens were to write down what they were doing at that moment and how they felt about the activity. Thus, the researchers were able to "see" the thinking and feeling of the youth, both in and out of school. They were able to contrast teenagers who developed their talents with those who did not. The researchers concluded that for talents to develop, it was necessary for the talent area to be considered useful in the culture, for the student to have the power of concentration, and for the student to be open to experience. Csikszentmihalyi and his colleagues also observed that students who "have learned habits conducive to cultivating talent" (p. 244) are more successful at developing their talents than those who do not. For example, students who shared challenging pursuits with friends, who had hobbies, and who spent time studying were more likely to develop their talents than students who spent time in nonspecific socializing. Talented teenagers were also able to vary the amount of concentration they put forth for various activities. They concentrated more in school, but were able to moderate the concentration during activities like socializing, doing household tasks, or watching television. Finally, they spent greater amounts of time in solitary pursuits, which gave them time to build skills and reflection in the talent area. In a later study of 526 high school students from 13 high schools, Shernoff, Csikszentmihalyi, Schneider, and Shernoff (2003) reported that students were more engaged when they encountered challenging tasks in school and perceived their skills to be up to the challenge. Although they did not analyze by ability level in this study, the researchers noted that students reported the greatest engagement in art and computer science. Sustained interest in particular talent areas occurs in school and outside of it. Olszewski-Kubilius and Lee (2004) found that for a highly able group of adolescents, the pattern of participation in out-of-school activities mirrored their specific academic choices in a summer program.

Case studies of child prodigies also reveal the pattern of perseverance, identification with the talent area, and supports that permit the unfolding of talents (Feldman, 1991). In a study of six prodigies, Feldman noted the extensive support network that developed around the talented child. Families were in the front line of involvement, but mentors, teachers, and peers also encouraged the development of the talent area. He observed that the course of talent development did not always run smoothly. Families and children would find a teacher or a school that met their needs for a period of time and then the arrangements would need to be revisited or abandoned for a new venue. In case studies of talented children living in poverty, VanTassel-Baska (1989) noted that for children who did not have an active parent, the grandmother often stepped in to perform the role of parental encouragement.

WHAT WE CAN DO

At Home

❧ Parents should be attuned to the interests of their children. It is not necessary to direct the child formally, but if the child expresses an interest in a talent area, further opportunities to be exposed to the domain should be a part of the family undertakings. For example, a child who inquires about the little pieces in a chess set may need the opportunity to learn to play with a family member or adult friend. Involvement with extracurricular and out-of-school activities are related to the development of specific talents.

❧ Understand that a child may identify profoundly with a talent area and be happy in it. It is not necessary to become alarmed about the intense interest or to worry about well-roundedness.

❧ To develop talents, youngsters need the luxury of reflection and the comfort of productive solitude. Winner (2000) suggested that "rich inner lives" (p. 163) sustain talented children. Families can make it possible for the child to have quiet time on a regular basis.

At School

↝ As talents develop, children and adolescents need outlets to try out or to display those talents through performance, exhibition, or publication. These may be available within the school context or outside of it.

↝ Accept that the development of talent takes time—the child's time and the adult's. There will be long hours of practice and apprenticeship. If the child or adolescent is happy and finds pleasure in the activity, the hours are well spent.

REFERENCES

Bloom, B. (Ed.). (1985). *Developing talent in young people*. New York: Ballantine.

Coleman, L. J. (2005). *Nurturing talent in high school: Life in the fast lane*. New York: Teachers College Press.

Csikszentmihalyi, M., Rathunde, K., & Whalen, S. (1993). *Talented teenagers: The roots of success and failure*. New York: Cambridge University Press.

Feldman, D. (1991). *Nature's gambit*. New York: Teachers College Press.

Goldsmith, L. T. (2000). Tracking trajectories of talent: Child prodigies growing up. In R. C. Friedman & B. M. Shore (Eds.), *Talents unfolding: Cognition and development*. Washington, DC: American Psychological Association.

Golomb, C. (1992). Eytan: The early development of a precociously gifted child artist. *Creativity Research Journal, 5*, 265–279.

Gruber, H. (1976). *Darwin on man*. London: Wildwood House.

Olszewski-Kubilius, P., & Lee, S-Y. (2004). The role of participation in in-school and out-of-school activities in the talent development of gifted students. *Journal of Secondary Gifted Education, 15*, 107–123.

Piirto, J. (1992). Does writing prodigy exist? In N. Colangelo, S. G. Assouline, & D. L. Ambroson (Eds.), *Talent development* (pp. 387–388). Unionville, NY: Trillium Press.

Roe, A. (1953). *Making of a scientist*. New York: Dodd, Mead.

Shernoff, D. J., Csikszentmihalyi, M., Schneider, B., & Shernoff, E. S. (2003). Student engagement in high school classrooms from the perspective of flow theory. *School Psychology Quarterly, 18*, 158–176.

Simonton, D. K. (1984). *Genius, creativity, and leadership: Historiometric inquiries*. Cambridge, MA: Harvard University Press.

Simonton, D. K. (1994). *Greatness: Who makes history and why*. New York: Guilford Press.

VanTassel-Baska, J. (1989). Case studies of disadvantaged gifted learners. *Journal for the Education of the Gifted, 13*, 22–36.

VanTassel-Baska, J. (1995). The talent development process in women writers: A study of Charlotte Bronte and Virginia Woolf. In R. Subotnik, K. Arnold, & K. Noble (Eds.), *Remarkable women*. New York: Hampton.

Walberg, H. J. (1969). A portrait of the artist and scientist as young men. *Exceptional Children, 36*, 5–11.

Winner, E. (2000). The origins and ends of giftedness. *American Psychologist, 55*, 159–170.

Zuckerman, H. (1977). *The scientific elite: Nobel laureates in the U. S.* New York: Free Press.

CHAPTER 6

EARLY LITERACY EXPERIENCES FOR PRECOCIOUS AND EMERGING READERS

Intelligent children are generally characterized as being verbally precocious with large vocabularies and advanced oral language. Not all talented children, however, are developmentally advanced in reading skills. Not all precocious talkers become precocious readers. Precocious readers, sometimes called early readers, show the ability to read before formal instruction begins. Other talented young children read "on schedule" when preschool or school lessons are begun. Although reading early may be a sign of intellectual giftedness, it is not always the case. Reading is the result of a long developmental process that begins in infancy and accelerates in childhood. It includes several developmental stages and many skill areas—reading, writing, speaking, listening, viewing, and representing. This development can be affected in many ways by the child's physical environment and social-emotional interactions. Parents and other caregivers contribute to children's literacy development by providing (a) an environment rich in print resources and (b) enjoyable interactions between the child, adults, and these resources. While parent activities are modestly associated with individual differences in children's reading and oral language development, parent efforts alone cannot "make" a precocious reader. Attitudes toward children who read early have changed over the years, and newer research on emerging literacy and the whole-language/ phonics debate have changed how educators view the instructional approaches for precocious readers.

WHAT WE KNOW

The current paradigm of emergent literacy posits that the foundation of a child's reading ability is the infant's experiences with the general patterns of oral language. According to Jackson and Roller (1993), literacy development can start as early as 2 or 3 years of age. The precocious reader can learn to identify letters, the sounds of letters, the nature of stories, and the function of print by listening to books read aloud, playing games, and talking to caregivers.

Identifying and Supporting the Early Reader

Case studies (Gross, 1992; Henderson, Jackson, & Mukamal, 1993; Stainthorp & Hughes, 2004a) and biographies (Bissex, 1980; Grost, 1970) of talented children who were early readers describe the challenges of parenting and teaching them. Conceptually, early readers are children who process information effectively in a specific domain and that processing, for some, is accomplished by decoding a specific closed symbol system (Jackson & Kearney, 1999). Jackson, Donaldson, and Cleland (1988) defined precocious readers as "children who have made substantial progress in reading comprehension before first grade" (p. 234). Stainthorp and Hughes (2004a) limited the definition further: "children who are able to read fluently and with understanding before attending school and without having received any direct instruction in reading." (p. 107). According to Jackson (1992), precocious readers are exceptional, but not rare; estimates vary on their incidence and prevalence (p. 173). Durkin's studies (1966, 1974–1975) have been cited by Jackson (1992) and Chall (2000) to illustrate the variability of these figures on geographical, historical, educational, and social factors. Studies have focused on development and achievement of readers from Black and bilingual families (Durkin, 1982; Jackson & Lu, 1992).

Researchers have been interested in the processes used by emerging readers. Mason (1980) studied 38 four-year-olds in preschool settings to determine if there was a hierarchy of skills and behaviors evidenced in emerging readers not receiving formal reading instruction. Although these were not children specifically identified as precocious readers, their reading experience began with the initial naming and printing of letters, then reading signs and labels to develop a sight word vocabulary of nouns and function words, and finally reading multisyllable words and abstract nouns. The last skill is considered advanced because it requires sound-letter knowledge usually developed through formal reading instruction.

In a review of the research on beginning reading achievement, Adams (1990) indicated that letter-name knowledge was the best predictor of success in reading, while the ability to discriminate sounds was also a good predictor. Precocious readers may develop sound-letter knowledge before formal reading instruction is given. Jackson et al. (1988) investigated 87 students between kindergarten and first grade, none of whom had formal reading instruction. Parents' reports about the precocious readers from this group indicated that the majority could recite the alphabet and identify capital letters before the age of 3. Sixty-eight percent recognized words on sight by age 3, 85% began reading preprimer books by age 4, and 92% were sounding out unknown words by the age of 5. These patterns may be considered an accelerated version of Mason's (1980) hierarchy of skills for emerging literacy. However, in contrast to Mason's study, Jackson and Cleland (1982) found that hierarchical skill development was less obvious among these precocious readers. Jackson and her colleagues (1988) documented diversity in reading styles and patterns of skill development. What is most critical to the success of precocious readers is "their ability to use relevant knowledge [strategies] appropriately, effectively, and flexibly" (p. 242). This ability leads to the development of skills that enable them to monitor comprehension, fill in the gaps, and apply "fix up" strategies in their reading to further improve comprehension.

Reading Storybooks to Children

In *What Works* (U.S. Department of Education, 1987), parents were told that the best way to help their children become better readers is to read to them, even when they are very young. That advice has been supported by numerous studies in the past two decades. More specifically, reading storybooks has been linked to oral language development (Anderson, Hiebert, Scott, & Wilkinson, 1984; Senechal, Le Fevre, Thomas, & Daley, 1998; Sulzby, 1985), a skill important for reading achievement. Senechal et al. studied an unselected group of predominantly middle-class children and found that storybook exposure contributed to oral language development, while parent teaching about words contributed to children's knowledge about written language. Sulzby studied the patterns of emergent readers and confirmed a progression of development related to storybook reading. She noted that children who were read to frequently tended to score higher on traditional measures of reading readiness and on independent reading. Sulzby also indicated that children who learn to read and write prior to formal instruction often teach themselves to read through storybook reading. They tend to have favorite books, which they ask to have read to them over and over again. They correct the reader if some of the story line is eliminated and often attempt to read the story themselves.

Like Mason (1980), Sulzby also reported predictable developmental behaviors of emergent readers leading to independent reading. The levels of progression identified in Sulzby's research suggest that children's storytelling is based on labeling the pictures in storybooks, commenting on the pictures initially rather than relying on print, treating the individual pages as discrete units with no story line, and eventually reading the book as a whole with almost verbatim recall of the story. Eventually the story line and interaction between the child who is "reading" and the person being read to is more dependent on print than on the pictures.

Parents and Motivation

Although empirical research is limited, results suggest that the emotional dimensions of shared storybook reading are contributors to the development of motivation for reading. A review by Baker, Scher, and Mackler (1997) stated that if early encounters with literacy are enjoyable for children, they are more likely to read frequently and broadly in subsequent years. Parents who create a positive socioemotional climate during reading are more likely to motivate children to read. Hildebrand (1998) suggested that parents share reading in a "relaxed, patient, and encouraging way" (p. 263). Research generally supports the associations between not only parent attitudes, but also parent activities, and children's individual differences in emerging literacy (Bus, van Ijzendoorn, & Pellegrini, 1995; Baker et al. 1997). Home activities, especially language-related activities with parents or caregivers, are associated broadly with reading success in the early school years. Current research shows correlation only—not causation. The effects of these activities are generally characterized as small when children's ability levels are controlled for. A meta-analysis by Bus et al. showed that parent-preschooler reading is related to language growth, emergent literacy, and reading achievement, but that this book reading accounted for only a small part of these outcomes, and that these effects tend to weaken as children begin school and become independent readers. Similar findings are reported by Stainthorp and Hughes (2000), who compared the family literacy practices for 15 precocious readers with 14 successful, but not precocious, readers. There were no systematic differences in the literacy activities of the two sets of parents. All parents tended to use the local library, purchase newspapers and magazines for the home, read across fiction and nonfiction genres, make copious lists, and expose their children to print at birth. There was a slight tendency for the parents of precocious readers and their children to play word games more frequently than successful, nonprecocious readers.

Interactions between all children and their parents can help develop vocabulary, basic reading skills such as top-down and left-right orientation, and higher level thinking skills. For young readers, parents may play the role of informal reading instructor by participating in an extended discussion of storybook reading. Parents can talk about pictures and name the objects illustrated, comment on the printed page, and discuss story elements.

Comparison studies of gifted accelerated readers and gifted nonreaders by Burns and Collins (1987) and Burns, Collins, and Paulsell (1991) found some differences in the activities of parents of high-IQ precocious readers and the activities of parents of high-IQ children who were not precocious readers. Parent reports indicated that mothers of accelerated readers provided more opportunities for interaction, discussion, and word identification than the mothers of the nonreaders. Burns et al. indicated, however, that these differences could have occurred *in response* to the children's abilities. This bidirectional nature of the exchange was also emphasized by Baker et al. (1997). Parents influence children, and children's behaviors influence those of their parents. The emerging interests of the children can prompt the parents' behaviors.

Teachers and Reading Instruction

Stanovich (1986) suggested another way in which children affect their own reading development. His review of the research literature reconceptualized the effects of individual differences on reading development. Stanovich stated that a student's aptitude can influence a student's reaction to "environmental quality," including reading instruction. He posited that a student's cognitive processing affects reading ability and that reading ability also affects cognitive processing. Good readers become better readers because they effectively process information on reading; students with strong cognitive processing abilities become better at processing information because they read widely and well. Because these differences do exist, Witty advocated "differentiated methods, materials, and means of evaluation" for early readers (Bonds & Bonds, 1983, p. 5). Since that time, several researchers and practitioners have echoed the need for identifying the early reader and providing appropriate reading instruction (Brown & Rogan, 1983; Feldhusen & Feldhusen, 1998). Sacks and Mergendoller (1997) suggest that different methods of instruction may produce different outcomes, depending on the student's stage of reading development. These authors also noted the importance of individual differences in classroom participation (e.g., discussion). Higher scoring students engaged in more verbal interactions, especially in whole-language classrooms. This aptitude-by-treatment interaction is an excellent rationale for both the early identification of precocious readers and the differentiation of instruction. Teachers may need to provide different kinds of support for children at different stages of development to maximize progress; higher scoring students need access to higher stage literacy tasks (Sacks & Mergendoller). Current practice, however, generally does not match this recommendation. Burns et al. (1991) found that when early readers are not challenged, their achievement scores regress; that is, without instruction on their level, their scores drop toward those of more average readers. Jackson (1992) noted that "precocious readers test the schools' ability to provide appropriately differentiated education for exceptionally able young children" because they have already mastered much of the curriculum (p. 172). Chall (2000) stated that in her previous studies she observed that teachers, when faced with widely varying ability levels, generally gave precocious readers enrichment material on grade level rather than more challenging material (p. 120). In a longitudinal study of precocious readers, Stainthorp and Hughes (2004b) found that students who begin school with high levels of reading maintain that advantage at age 11, but that their school experiences do not appear to have added any value to their progress. Precocious readers might have benefited from opportunities matched to their literacy needs, but did not receive them.

Both parents and teachers acknowledge the unusual challenges for early readers who prefer books on unusual topics, trade books rather than basal readers, reference books, and literature usually appropriate for older readers. They also face the physical challenges of turning pages. Harrison (1999) cites the story of Olivia who could read a book with flaps, but "her little fingers couldn't manage the flaps" (p. 28). These psychomotor challenges may also include frustration in writing activities that accompany reading in emergent literacy.

Fostering Literacy Development in the Talented Child Who Is Not a Precocious Reader

Not all children who talk early develop into precocious readers (Crain-Thoreson & Dale, 1992). Whether a child is talented in reading and begins to read "early" or is talented in another area, parents and teachers can support the emergence of literacy in a variety of ways. First, they can provide their children with enriching print resources. Second, they can read aloud to the child (Anderson et al., 1984). Third, they can verbally interact with the child to model and motivate the child to value literacy activities. Reading together with their parents motivates children to read, to value and appreciate reading, and to develop thinking strategies (Jackson & Roller, 1993). Positive and playful interactions are recommended rather than strained or highly controlled experiences, which can lead to negative attitudes toward school literacy (Leseman & de Jong, 1998). Interactions also are important because they serve as the raw material for concept development. For example, reading to young children establishes the concept that a reader can respond and interact with the literature. Parent comments encourage children to be active and to ask questions about what they read. Lastly, interactions may develop specific skills such as looking at illustrations for story clues.

Guidelines for Books

Halsted (2002), Jackson and Roller (1993), Feldhusen and VanTassel-Baska (1989), and Baskin and Harris (1980) have suggested guidelines for choosing books for young talented children. Reading choices should (a) tell a good story; (b) have strong characters with which children can identify; (c) be open-ended enough to require interpretation, evaluation, or problem solving; (d) include a variety of literature (folktales, fiction, fantasy, and poetry) and high-interest nonfiction (e.g. animals); and (e) feature language that is varied and rich—rhymes, repetition, and predictable language that allows participation. Additional information on choices for gifted readers is available from a variety of sources (e.g., Halsted, 2002, and Robinson & Schatz, 2002).

Although precocious readers maintain their performance through the first years of school, precocious reading achievement may be associated with rather modest long-term benefits for middle-class children (Burns et al., 1991; Coltheart, 1979; Jackson, 1992; Jackson & Kearney, 1999; Mills & Jackson, 1990; Stainthorp & Hughes, 2004b). Precocious reading generally is associated with good reading and language performance in later years, but intelligent children who are not early readers also may show similar achievements in these areas (Jackson & Kearney).

WHAT WE CAN DO

At Home

❧ Parents can support literacy development in all talented children whether or not they are precocious readers. This support includes providing home and preschool environments rich in both print materials and oral language experiences.

❧ Recommended practices at home include establishing a regular reading time, reading to children aloud and discussing what is read, and modeling by reading for both information and enjoyment. Reading experiences shared by parents and children should be warm, loving, and fun.

❧ Parents can help teachers to recognize and support precocious readers when they begin school. When the early reader enters preschool or kindergarten, let the teacher know he or she can read. If assessment data on the child's reading ability is available, share it with the teacher; if not, ask for an assessment of the child's instructional reading level.

In the Classroom

❧ Early childhood education experiences should include teachers and classrooms that allow meaningful and varied learning experiences at the child's developmental level. Teachers should be aware of the developmental stages of emergent literacy and provide developmentally appropriate activities to capitalize on children's readiness to learn. Reading should be integrated into all kinds of classroom activities.

❧ Elementary classroom teachers should identify early readers regardless of their other talent areas; assess their reading abilities, particularly in the areas of phonological awareness; and shape the curriculum and instruction to those ability levels and the child's interests. Parents should ask for a specific plan for appropriate reading activities that includes more than just enrichment.

❧ Parents and teachers should support literacy development in talented children who are emerging readers through environments and interactions that motivate, stimulate, and instruct at an appropriate level and pace.

At School

❧ Programs for young talented students must assess and provide for varying levels of language abilities, specifically for individual differences in reading abilities and interests. Instruction should be differentiated for precocious readers and those "ready to read."

❧ Schools should develop assessment policies and procedures for precocious readers on school entry. These assessments should include assessing the level of phonological awareness (the connections between sounds and words), decoding skills, spelling, and writing in order to plan a balanced and accelerated literacy program.

REFERENCES

Adams, M. J. (1990). *Beginning to read: Thinking and learning about print.* Cambridge, MA: MIT Press.

Anderson, R. C., Hiebert, E. H., Scott, J., & Wilkinson, I. (1984). *Becoming a nation of readers: The report of the Commission on Reading.* Washington, DC: National Institute of Education.

Baker, L., Scher, D., & Mackler, K. (1997). Home and family influences on motivations for reading. *Educational Psychologist, 32*(2), 69–82.

Baskin, B. H., & Harris, K. H. (1980). *Books for the gifted child.* New York: Bowker.

Bissex, G. L. (1980). *Gnys at wrk: A child learns to write and read.* Cambridge, MA: Harvard University Press.

Bonds, C. W., & Bonds, L. T. (1983). Teacher, is there a gifted reader in first grade? *Roeper Review, 5,* 4–6.

Brown, W., & Rogan, J. (1983). Reading and young gifted children. *Roeper Review, 5,* 6–9.

Burns, J. M., & Collins, M. D. (1987). Parents' perceptions of factors affecting the reading development of intellectually superior accelerated readers and intellectually superior nonreaders. *Reading Research and Instruction, 26,* 239–246.

Burns, J. M., Collins, M. D., & Paulsell, J. C. (1991). A comparison of intellectually superior preschool accelerated readers and nonreaders: Four years later. *Gifted Child Quarterly, 35,* 118–124.

Bus, A. G., van Ijzendoorn, M. H., & Pellegrini, A. D. (1995). Joint book reading makes for success in learning to read: A meta-analysis on intergenerational transmission of literacy. *Review of Educational Research, 65,* 1–21.

Chall, J. S. (2000). *The academic achievement challenge: What really works in the classroom.* New York: Guilford Press.

Coltheart, M. (1979). When can children learn to read—and when should they be taught? In T. G. Waller & G. E. MacKinnon (Eds.), *Reading research advances in theory and practice: Vol. 1* (pp. 1–30). San Diego, CA: Academic Press.

Crain-Thoreson, C., & Dale, P. S. (1992). Do early talkers become early readers? Linguistic precocity, preschool language, and emergent literacy. *Developmental Psychology, 28,* 421–429.

Durkin, D. (1966). *Children who read early: Two longitudinal studies.* New York: Teachers College Press.

Durkin, D. (1974–1975). A six year study of children who learned to read in school at the age of four. *Reading Research Quarterly, 1,* 9–61.

Durkin, D. (1982). *A study of poor Black children who are successful readers* (Reading Education Report No. 33). Champaign: University of Illinois, Center for the Study of Reading.

Feldhusen, J. F., & Feldhusen, H. J. (1998). Identification and nurturing of precocious children in early childhood. In J. Smutny (Ed.), *The young gifted child: Potential and promise, an anthology* (pp. 62–72). Cresskill, NJ: Hampton Press.

Feldhusen, J., & VanTassel-Baska, J. (1989). Social studies and language arts for the gifted. In J. Feldhusen, J. VanTassel-Baska, & K. Seeley (Eds.), *Excellence in educating the gifted* (pp. 213–217). Denver, CO: Love Publishing.

Gross, M. U. M. (1992). The early development of three profoundly gifted children of IQ 200. In P. S. Klein & A. J. Tannenbaum (Eds.), *To be young and gifted* (pp. 94–138). Norwood, NJ: Ablex.

Grost, A. (1970). *Genius in residence.* Englewood Cliffs, NJ: Prentice-Hall.

Halsted, J. W. (2002). *Some of my best friends are books: Guiding gifted readers from preschool through high school* (2nd ed.). Scottsdale, AZ: Great Potential Press.

Harrison, C. (1999). *Giftedness in early childhood.* Sydney, Australia: GERRIC, University of New South Wales.

Henderson, S. J., Jackson, N. E., & Mukamal, R. A. (1993). Early development of language and literacy skills of an extremely precocious reader. *Gifted Child Quarterly, 37,* 78–83.

Hildebrand, P. M. (1998). From the beginning: Parents as teachers and home as a reading resource. In J. Smutny (Ed.), *The young gifted child: Potential and promise, an anthology* (pp. 259–271). Cresskill, NJ: Hampton Press.

Jackson, N. E. (1992). Precocious reading of English: Origins, structure and predictive significance. In P. S. Klein & A. J. Tannenbaum (Eds.), *To be young and gifted* (pp. 171–203). Norwood, NJ: Ablex.

Jackson, N. E., & Cleland, L. N. (1982, March). *Skill patterns of precocious readers.* Paper presented at the annual convention of the American Educational Research Association, New York. (ERIC Document Reproduction Service No. ED214133)

Jackson, N. E., Donaldson, G. W., & Cleland, L. N. (1988). The structure of precocious reading ability. *Journal of Educational Psychology, 80*, 234–243.

Jackson, N. E., & Kearney, J. (1999). Achievement of precocious readers in middle childhood and young adulthood. In N. Colangelo & S. G. Assouline (Eds.), *Talent development III. Proceedings from the 1995 Henry B. and Jocelyn Wallace National Research Symposium on Talent Development* (pp. 203–217). Scottsdale, AZ: Gifted Psychology Press.

Jackson, N. E., & Lu, W-H. (1992). Bilingual precocious readers of English. *Roeper Review, 14*, 115–119.

Jackson, N. E., & Roller, C. M. (1993). *Reading with young children.* Storrs: National Research Center on the Gifted and Talented, University of Connecticut.

Leseman, P. M., & de Jong, P. F. (1998). Home literacy: Opportunity, instruction, cooperation and social-emotional quality predicting early reading achievement. *Reading Research Quarterly, 33*, 294–318.

Mason, J. M. (1980). When do children begin to read?: An exploration of four-year-old children's letter and word reading competencies. *Reading Research Quarterly, 15*, 203–227.

Mills, J. R., & Jackson, N. E. (1990). Predictive significance of early giftedness: The case of precocious reading. *Journal of Educational Psychology, 82*, 410–419.

Robinson, A., & Schatz, A. B. (2002). Biography for talented learners: Enriching the curriculum across the disciplines. *Gifted Education Communicator, 33*(3), 12–15, 38–39.

Sacks, C. H., & Mergendoller, J. R. (1997). The relationship between teachers' theoretical orientation toward reading and student outcomes in kindergarten children with different initial reading abilities. *American Educational Research Journal, 34*, 721–739.

Senechal, M., Le Fevre, J., Thomas, E. M., & Daley, K. E. (1998). Differential effects of home literacy experiences on the development of oral and written language. *Reading Research Quarterly, 33*, 96–116.

Stainthorp, R., & Hughes, D. (2000). Family literacy activities in the homes of successful young readers. *Journal of Research in Reading, 23*, 41–64.

Stainthorp, R., & Hughes, D. (2004a). An illustrative case study of precocious reading ability. *Gifted Child Quarterly, 48*, 107–120.

Stainthorp, R., & Hughes, D. (2004b). What happens to precocious readers' performance by the age of eleven? *Journal of Research in Reading, 27*, 357–372.

Stanovich, K. E. (1986). Matthew effects in reading: Some consequences of individual differences in the acquisition of literacy. *Reading Research Quarterly, 21*, 360–407.

Sulzby, E. (1985). Children's emergent reading of favorite storybooks: A developmental study. *Reading Research Quarterly, 20*, 458–481.

U.S. Department of Education. (1987). *What works: Research about teaching and learning* (2nd ed.). Washington, DC: Office of Educational Research and Improvement.

CHAPTER 7

MENTORS AND MENTORSHIPS

entoring is highly valued for both its psychosocial and vocational benefits by mentees or protégés. Role modeling is but one function of mentors. Mentorships may be short- or long-term, and arranged externally or informally discovered in reciprocal relationships. There may be optimal benefits from different kinds of mentorships at different periods of development. Evidence is emerging that long-term, self- or informally initiated mentorships are more potent than formal, short-term programs, and that talented students may especially value the psychosocial component. Despite the need for more research to clarify some of the contradictions in the present literature, mentoring is a useful component in the development of talents.

WHAT WE KNOW

Definitions of mentors and mentorships vary, but these definitions do show signs of convergence. The concept has its origins in classical Greek mythology. In Homer's *Odyssey*, Ulysses' close friend Mentor looked after his son during Ulysses' 10-year absence. Originally, then, a mentor's role is one of trust and more or less parental. In contemporary usage, Pleiss and Feldhusen (1995) defined mentors as "adults who introduce students to ideas, theories, tools, activities, or careers in their own fields of experience" (p. 159). This may be somewhat narrow because it does not explicitly include affective issues, but Pleiss and Feldhusen usefully differentiate the active role of a mentor—notably the direct and normally one-to-one interaction with the protégé (or mentee). This is in contrast to the role model, with whom the contact may be vicarious, and the hero who, like the role model, may also inspire action without direct contact. A mentor may or may not be a role model or a hero to the protégé. Boston (1976) noted that the mentor's goal is to engage the protégé in setting and moving toward his or her own goals in a domain of expertise in which they both share interest. Boston's definition, also somewhat cognitive, suggests a greater level of engagement or commitment by the protégé than Pleiss and Feldhusen's. Haensly and Parsons (1993) usefully suggested that mentorships comprise a range of helping relationships, from a short-term, externally arranged coaching of a less experienced person, to an informal arrangement "over a significant period" providing a "wise and reflective guide steering the individual's progress toward self-identification, particular accomplishments, and eventually to autonomous self-realization" (p. 204). They endorsed Yamamoto's (1988) criticism of the former as a "bastardization of the concept" (Haensly & Parsons, p. 204), especially when the coaching is linked to evaluation. The larger role takes us back to Ulysses and Mentor. The literature distinguishes clearly between mentorship programs that create opportunities for short- or fixed-term relationships, between career and psychosocial considerations, and the spontaneous growth of reciprocal relationships between generations versus planned matching.

The risk of dual roles presents an interesting challenge for education. Because teachers also have an evaluative responsibility, they may be constrained in their ability to form mentoring relationships with students in their classes. On the other hand, these risks may be overestimated. Burke, McKenna, and McKeen (1991) surveyed 94 managers about the relationships they considered to be of a mentor and protégé nature in contrast to regular supervisory relationships. From the point of view of the mentors, the results were not greatly different for the two groups. The mentor relationships were with employees more similar to themselves, were longer-lasting, involved less communication, and were at a greater distance. More psychosocial functions were provided, but career development input was regarded as equal by the mentors. This study did not examine opinions of outcomes by the mentored employees. However, Chao, Walz, and Gardner (1992) did so. They compared three groups on psychosocial and career outcomes: 212 protégés who benefited from informally developed mentorships, 53 who took part in formally organized mentorships, and 284 who were not associated with a mentor. Informal internship protégés received more career-related support (whereas the Burke et al. managers said there was no difference in the career support they gave) and higher salaries than those in organized or formal mentorships. They also replied more favorably in all dimensions than those who weren't mentored. The formally mentored group was superior to the group that wasn't mentored on only three psychosocial subscales. If these workplace studies offer hypotheses to educational practice, they would be that naturally developing mentorships are superior to organized formal ones, that psychosocial functions may, in general, be better served than career development, and that physical distance and personal distance are not a barrier and may even favor the growth of independence, confidence, and a sense of not being under constant surveillance. Teachers, like managers, may be able to serve as mentors, but perhaps not with students closely dependent upon them. Do any educational studies support these speculations?

Ambrose, Allen, and Huntley (1994) reported a case study of a very successful double mentorship that involved a gifted education teacher in a central role and a professor half a continent away. The student reported primarily psychosocial benefits, for example, enhanced awareness of his interests, greater valuing of his own thought processes, and focus in his life. He explicitly stated that while his career awareness was heightened, a career decision was not yet made. He especially valued that the guiding came without controlling, and this poses a potential conflict with a parallel role for a teacher-mentor. Fortunately, in this case, the teacher was a gifted education specialist in an extension program who may have been able to avoid some of the evaluation pressures of regular classroom teachers.

Several studies have reported that spontaneous mentoring relationships involving highly able youth last between 1 and 3 years on average, and sometimes up to 8 or 10 years (cf. Pleiss & Feldhusen, 1995). They noted that some end in conflict when the protégés supercede their mentor's accomplishments or otherwise find themselves in competition. Most, however, fade out uneventfully. This duration is considerably longer than the semester or school year experienced in typical program-based internships. There are other potentially important differences. Ambrose et al. (1994) briefly raised the question of benefits to the mentors, as well as to the protégé. Once more, the psychosocial domain was highlighted, primarily the opportunity and pleasure to help a young person find his or her way in a challenging world. Edlind and Haensly (1985) focused on the benefits to the mentor and noted "redefinition of a personal ethic, and renewed zest" (Haensly & Parsons, 1993, p. 206), as well as psychosocial development for both parties. Salary and career advancement were not mentioned. Perhaps a good teacher's first rewards lie elsewhere. Intentional, systematic mentoring interventions might, however, have the potential for lasting effects. It may take a number of years to evaluate the effectiveness of the direct impact of mentoring in regard to students' academic success, persistence, and aspirations (Moon & Callahan, 2001).

Casey (1997) explicitly examined the priority given by protégés to the contrast between vocational and psychosocial needs. She employed a sample of 39 upper elementary and junior high school students and a crossed design with two variables: having been mentored or not, and gifted or not based on having been in any kind of gifted, creative, or enrichment program in regular or summer school. Students not identified as gifted, even by this very loose criterion, expressed no preference for satisfying either vocational or psychosocial needs through mentoring. Gifted students more strongly endorsed components of mentorships addressing psychosocial needs. This may well be consistent with the data from Burke et al. (1991): The favored employees who were more like the managers and better paid (perhaps more able) were regarded by their managers as benefiting more from psychosocial than career mentoring. In relation to the Chao et al. (1992) study, however, the greater attention to career needs in informally arranged mentorships remains a puzzle. Perhaps our understanding of this research is constrained by a lack of knowledge of whether most of the mentorships to which employers and students refer are formal, informal, or somewhere between. There is also a more pervasive barrier to interpreting the literature, namely, that nearly all the studies are retrospective, so any participant who has had a mentor has more or less completed or sustained a mentoring relationship. The samples may be biased, therefore, to students and workers who have had longer and perhaps more successful mentorship experiences. Only the Chao and Casey studies included participants who were not mentored, but the Casey study had no data on the formality or other details of the mentorships that students acknowledged in their self-reports.

Gender

A specific literature has also developed on the special advantages of mentoring for women in general and gifted girls in particular (cf. Casey & Shore, 2000; Grau, 1985; Kerr, 1981, 1991; Shamanoff, 1985), although at the school level there may be some confusion between the need for mentors and role models. This literature, like the broader one, is also heavily weighted with discussions about career decision making. This may be appropriate, because Reilly and Welch (1994–1995) have shown that three times more young women than young men credit mentorship experiences for focusing career decisions, but they also mention self-confidence in career and personal domains. A related question is whether mentorships should be within gender. As well summarized by Pleiss and Feldhusen (1995), there are contradictions: Though same-sex pairings are generally recommended (e.g., Levinson, 1978), most women have had male mentors, and no relations have been empirically demonstrated between gender matching and outcomes. Indeed, Torrance (1984) reported that women expressed negative feelings about their mentors more commonly when they had been paired with women. Of course, if informal pairings were always possible, everyone would make the best personal match available.

Despite the limitations of the data, and the paucity of research studies explicitly on gifted children, the anecdotal and clinical literature is unanimous in supporting the benefits, however vaguely defined, of mentorships. Given the number of endorsements and their consistency, it is likely that mentorships are good for children and adults, including the gifted. The main difficulty is that once the nuances of the literature are explored, it is less clear exactly what comprise the qualities of an excellent or ideal mentorship, and there probably is no one best recipe. Before we can answer this question definitively with well-conceptualized alternatives, we need to know more about (a) the role of mentorships in cognitive development—a topic on which the literature appears to be silent; (b) what constitute the key variables on which mentors and protégés may regard themselves as similar or different, including gender, and if these matter; (c) the ages at which mentorships have particular effects or are most useful; (d) the role of informality or formality of organization; (e) how long a mentorship needs to last to have important long-term effects; (f) how to identify the protégé's "stake" in the relationship; (g) what differentiates successful from unsuccessful mentorships—a question that has not yet been posed to partners who might regard them as having failed; and (h) whether the subtle differences becoming apparent in gifted students' interests in mentorships require that they be specially designed, or whether the particular benefits of particular groups can be gleaned from more generic offerings. A conceptual shift is needed, from querying the advantages of mentorships, to a more detailed analysis of actual offerings and outcomes.

Conclusion

There are no published accounts of mentorships having a negative impact. Indeed, quite to the contrary, they are almost universally reported as important positive events, although perhaps few researchers have yet asked about the failures (as noted above, Torrance, 1984, did record some negative comments). Mentorships are useful additions to education in general (DuBois, Holloway, Valentine, & Cooper, 2002; Johnson & Ridley, 2004) and gifted education in particular (Bisland, 2001; Grantham, 2004; Hébert, 2002; Hébert & Olenchak, 2000; Hébert & Speirs Neumeister, 2000; Moon & Callahan, 2001).

WHAT WE CAN DO

At Home

Parents are children's fundamental mentors, and the idea of mentorships is essentially an extension of the parenting role into the community as an adolescent begins the process of creating independence from the parents. Perhaps the one thing that parents can do best is to ensure that their networks of friends and colleagues are exposed to their children and that they allow some time for their children to interact privately with this circle of friends and acquaintances. It may only require parents to remove themselves from the room for a few minutes to facilitate the initiation of an alliance between a child and an adult who can extend the parenting role in the manner foreseen for mentors.

The mentoring role is traditionally bestowed on godparents. The French word for godfather is "parrain," and the translation for sponsoring or mentoring is "parrainage"; although the connection is not so obvious in the English language, it is in French and other contexts. A specialized French-language dictionary of educational terminology (Legendre, 1993) furthermore located the word "mentorat" or mentorships under pedagogy for gifted pupils.

In the Classroom

Mentorships are not classroom pedagogy, therefore:

ᵊ❧ the teacher's primary contribution is in sponsoring students for mentorship opportunities; and

ᵊ❧ secondarily, and probably more rarely, if teachers are invited into a mentorship relationship with a protégé and wish to take part, they should feel free to do so. However, it is very important that this privileged relationship not translate into favoritism within the classroom, and the best way to avoid a conflict of interest is to acknowledge the relationship. As a result, the principal should know about any informal mentorship relationships within the school that involve school personnel.

Finally,

ᵊ❧ teachers can be on the watch for social isolation, stress, perfectionism (cf. Silverman, 1991), overchoice syndrome (related to multipotentiality—cf. Rysiew, Shore, & Leeb, 1999), and other barriers to the realization of potential by highly able pupils. These conditions might be eased by involvement in a mentoring relationship.

At School

School-based mentorships are almost always going to be of the arranged or formal type. These have been shown to have limitations, both in duration and in the balance between psychosocial and career thinking outcomes. Even if the contribution to lifespan development is limited in these ways, each component is still valuable. Mentorships usefully extend the curriculum in ways appropriate to high-ability children, including those in inclusive settings. They take into account areas of intellectual strength and interests, the ability to interact well with adults, and extended attention. They can, if done on school time and in school, enhance the security of mentoring relationships, give bright students personal attention they might not get in the regular classroom, and free up time for the teacher's attention to other students. The experiences must go beyond narrow school-like tasks and be preparation for life beyond school (Casey & Shore, 2000). As an additional benefit, mentorships for highly able students place excellent ambassadors in contact with the broader community and potentially pave the way for further interaction and collaboration. Pleiss and Feldhusen (1995) offered four specific suggestions about mentorships at the school level. Although they go somewhat beyond the evidence of empirical studies, they are generally defensible:

- start mentorships early and offer them across the years of schooling;

- start them for short periods of time, and let them become longer with maturity;

- structure them to address both the content of the mentor's expertise and the values and life experiences of the mentor as a person; and

- make explicit the recruitment, matching process, and supervision of school-sponsored mentorships.

We would add that:

- teachers should be welcomed into the formal mentor pool for students they do not directly teach or evaluate, and informally generated relationships within their teaching role should be accepted; and

- mentors engaged through the school need to be briefed on the goals of the program and on ethical conduct with adolescent children.

In conclusion, school-based or other arranged mentorship programs cannot provide all the elements of extended, informal, spontaneous relationships, and vice-versa. In addition, the latter are not available to all children, and the formal variety may be the best opportunity for some students to move on to a more personally constructed mentor relationship. Even though the research literature is incomplete, it points to support for mentorships in general and potential specific benefits for talented students.

REFERENCES

Ambrose, D., Allen, J., & Huntley, S. (1994). Mentorship of the highly creative. *Roeper Review, 17,* 131–134.

Bisland, A. (2001). Mentoring: An educational alternative for gifted students. *Gifted Child Today, 24*(4), 22–25, 64.

Boston, B. O. (1976). *The sorcerer's apprentice: A case study in the role of the mentor.* Reston, VA: Council for Exceptional Children.

Burke, R. J., McKenna, C. S., & McKeen, C. A. (1991). How do mentorships differ from typical supervisory relationships? *Psychological Reports, 68,* 459–466.

Casey, K. M. A. (1997). *Mentors' contributions to gifted adolescents' affective, social, and vocational development.* Unpublished master's thesis, McGill University, Montreal, Quebec, Canada.

Casey, K. M. A., & Shore, B. M. (2000). Mentors' contributions to gifted adolescents' affective, social, and vocational development. *Roeper Review, 22,* 227–230.

Chao, G. T., Walz, P. M., & Gardner, P. D. (1992). Formal and informal mentorships: A comparison on mentoring functions and contrast with nonmentored counterparts. *Personnel Management, 45,* 619–636.

DuBois, D. L., Holloway, B. E., Valentine, J. C., & Cooper, H. (2002). Effectiveness of mentoring programs for youth: A meta-analytic review. *American Journal of Community Psychology, 30,* 157–197.

Edlind, E. P., & Haensly, P. A. (1985). Gifts of mentorship. *Gifted Child Quarterly, 29,* 55–60.

Grantham, T. C. (2004). Multicultural mentoring to increase Black male representation in gifted programs. *Gifted Child Quarterly, 48,* 232–245.

Grau, P. N. (1985). Counseling the gifted girl. *Gifted Child Quarterly, 24,* 8–12.

Haensly, P. A., & Parsons, J. L. (1993). Creative, intellectual, and psychological development through mentorship: Relationships and stages. *Youth and Society, 25,* 202–221.

Hébert, T. P. (2002). Educating gifted children from low socioeconomic backgrounds: Creating visions of a hopeful future. *Exceptionality, 10,* 127–138.

Hébert, T. P., & Olenchak, F. R. (2000). Mentors for gifted underachieving males: Developing potential and realizing promise. *Gifted Child Quarterly, 4,* 196–207.

Hébert, T. P., & Speirs Neumeister, K. L. (2000). University mentors in the elementary classroom: Supporting the intellectual, motivational, and emotional needs of high-ability students. *Journal for the Education of the Gifted, 24,* 122–148.

Kerr, B. A. (1981). *Career education for the gifted and talented.* Columbus, OH: ERIC Clearinghouse on Adult, Vocational, and Career Education. (ERIC Document Reproduction Services No. ED205778)

Kerr, B. A. (1991). Educating gifted girls. In N. Colangelo & G. A. Davis (Eds.), *Handbook of gifted education* (pp. 402–415). Boston: Allyn & Bacon.

Johnson, W. B., & Ridley, C. R. (2004). *The elements of mentoring.* New York: Palgrave Macmillan.

Legendre, R. (1993). *Dictionnaire actuel de l'éducation* [Dictionary of current education] (2nd ed.). Montreal, Quebec, Canada: Guérin.

Levinson, D. J. (1978). *The seasons of a man's life.* New York: Knopf.

Moon, T. R., & Callahan, C. (2001). Curricular modifications, family outreach, and a mentoring program: Impacts on achievement and gifted identification in high-risk primary students. *Journal for the Education of the Gifted, 24,* 305–321.

Pleiss, M. K., & Feldhusen, J. F. (1995). Mentors, role models, and heroes in the lives of gifted children. *Educational Psychologist, 30,* 159–169.

Reilly, J. J., & Welch, D. B. (1994–1995). Mentoring gifted young women: A call to action. *Journal of Secondary Gifted Education, 6,* 120–128.

Rysiew, K. J., Shore, B. M., & Leeb, R. T. (1999). Multipotentiality, giftedness, and career choice: A review. *Journal of Counseling and Development, 77,* 432–430.

Shamanoff, G. A. (1985). The women mentor project. *Roeper Review, 7,* 162–164.

Silverman, L. K. (1991). Family counseling. In N. Colangelo & G. A. Davis (Eds.), *Handbook of gifted education* (pp. 307–320). Boston: Allyn & Bacon.

Torrance, E. P. (1984). *Mentor relationships: How they aid creative achievement, endure, change, and die.* Buffalo, NY: Bearly.

Yamamoto, K. (1988). To see life grow: The meaning of mentorship. *Theory Into Practice, 27,* 183–189.

CHAPTER 8

UNIVERSITY-BASED PROGRAMS

Talented students find academic and social benefits in university-based programs designed for them. These programs may take place in the summer, on Saturdays, or during the academic year; they are both residential and commuter. However, the common denominator is the opportunity to take challenging academic courses, to cultivate interests, and to develop friendships.

WHAT WE KNOW

Universities across the country offer an array of options for talented students who are not yet of college age. A number of programs are nonresidential, commuter courses held on Saturdays or during the summer; others are residential programs ranging from a few days to several weeks during the summer. Some university offerings are in partnership with local schools, and still others involve residential high schools where students take undergraduate college courses. A commonality of all these varied university-based programs is the attention given to providing students with challenging academic courses, the option of tele-scoping semester- or year-long courses into a few weeks, a variety of enrich-ment experiences, and opportunities to make close friendships (Enersen, 1993; Feldhusen & Sokol, 1982; Feldhusen & Robinson-Wyman, 1980; Robinson & Stanley, 1989).

Students who wish to participate in such programs usually submit a teacher or parent recommendation and some form of academic assessment. Students who apply to take part in the Saturday and daily summer programs usually provide nationally normed standardized test scores from their schools or an ability measure in addition to other documentation. Students ready for sub-ject-area acceleration are served nationally by university-based talent search programs in each geographical area of the country (Brody & Mills, 2005). These programs are often summer residential offerings serving the top 5% of students in several subject areas. Talent search applicants take the ACT or SAT college entrance exams. Designed for high school juniors and seniors, the tests are taken by middle school and early high school students to meet specific requirements for subject-area courses. In the elementary-level talent searches, students take the EXPLORE test (Swiatek & Lupkowski-Shoplik, 2000). For some programs, there is also an audition, portfolio, essay, or other additional information needed for the application. Because university-based courses can grant high school credit (Lynch, 1990; Olszewski-Kubilius, 1989, 2007; Olszewski-Kubilius & Laubscher, 1996) or prepare a student to take an exam to test out of a scheduled homeschool course, necessary documenta-tion may be provided to the local school. (Further information concerning the effects of participating in university-based talent searches is found in the chapter on acceleration in this volume.)

Students who return to their local schools after several Saturday sessions or a summer of participation in university-based programs need and desire more advanced classes and experiences. Some schools provide accelerated course-work, grade advancement, placement in classes above the student's grade level for certain subjects, mentors, and counseling support to respond to student needs, but others do not. Olszewski-Kubilius and Grant (1994) found that students who participated in a university-based summer program continued to achieve throughout high school and college. The effects were particularly strong for girls who took mathematics rather than other subject-area classes. When compared with girls who didn't take mathematics classes, the girls who did reported higher educational aspirations.

Motivation for Attending University-Based Programs

Students who attend university-based programs, particularly the fast-paced courses associated with talent searches, differ in their motivation for participa-tion (Brounstein, Holahan, & Sawyer, 1988). Some students reported a primary interest in academic concerns; others were less interested in the academic context and more interested in the social value of university-based experiences. A few students appear to be equally motivated by both. In a study based on interviews, Enersen (1993) noted that peer relationships were an especially potent attraction for students.

Success of University-Based Programs

University-based programs have a positive impact in several areas. There is strong evidence that the challenging coursework of these programs is motivating and intriguing for students and that the students learn and retain the material taught in the intense, telescoped format (Feldhusen, Enersen, & Sayler, 1992; Hapai, 1994; Hess, 1991; Lupkowski-Shoplik & Kuhnel, 1995; Miserandino, Subotnik, & Ou, 1995). University-based programs also encourage students, especially females, to take more advanced math and science courses (Barnett & Durden, 1993; Olszewski-Kubilius & Grant, 1994; Subotnik & Strauss, 1995) and provide for individual interest and talent (Flack & Friedberg, 1997). Focused enrichment programs also encourage confidence and motivation to study science, although some students also report feeling a "splashdown effect" when they return to their home schools (Stake & Mares, 2001, 2005). Less encouraging are the reports that students who do achieve at levels normally allowing them to acquire academic credit in their home schools can return to find that credit and placement do not always follow. Lynch (1990) noted that 80% of the students who requested credit ultimately received it. However, students were often required to take a school exam to demonstrate proficiency. She reported that schools were more likely to make an appropriate subsequent placement than to award credit. Olszewski-Kubilius (1989) reported the much lower rate of 50% and noted that credit and placement were more likely for mathematics and foreign language than for writing or literature. After securing accreditation by the North Central Association of Colleges and Schools, one university reported increases in the percentage of summer students whose home schools accepted credit for these experiences (Olszewski-Kubilius & Lee, 2004).

Many universities follow the students who attend programs on campus and then enroll in the university for their college education. It appears that the programs promote greater interest in higher education among all students, especially those who are considered at risk for economic reasons (Flack & Friedberg, 1997; Lynch & Mills, 1990; Olszewski-Kubilius & Laubscher, 1996; Thomas, 1993). The campus experience demystifies college life and gives students confidence that they can be successful. Follow-up studies of students who attend residential programs demonstrate that participation, especially over a number of years, plays a significant role in helping students select careers (Enersen, 1996). An important benefit is the social opportunity for students who may have difficulties in their own schools in the realm of interpersonal relationships, finding friends, and validating their feelings of uniqueness (Dauber & Benbow, 1990; Enersen, 1993). The effects of campus-based programs are small, variable, or negligible on the self-concepts of students (Kolloff & Moore, 1989; Olszewski, Kulieke, & Willis, 1987).

Most university-based programs have an evaluation system to report feedback from students, teachers, and parents. Typically, high satisfaction is reported for the programs, academically, as well as socially. Often the students' comments communicate their excitement with challenging learning situations, teachers who are experts in their fields and who love to teach, high expectations, in-depth investigations of topics, and the pleasure of being with their peers (Enersen, 1993, 1996; Feldhusen & Koopman-Daytons, 1987).

WHAT WE CAN DO

At Home

∾ Consider the benefits available to students who attend university-based programs: high-level coursework, campus experience, models and mentors in academic and professional career fields, social growth, and development of friendships. Evaluations of university-based programs document a high degree of satisfaction from participants and parents (Enersen, 1993, 1996; Olszewski-Kubilius & Lee, 2004).

∾ Parents and schools can contact local colleges and universities to inquire about programs designed for high-ability students. Use reference materials in public libraries to locate sites across the country; program directories are published annually. Contact the state department of education and the state advocacy organizations for their listing of programs. Web site listings are also available from national advocacy organizations.

At School

∾ Involve schools, parents, and businesses in providing funding for students who need financial aid to attend university-based programs. Many programs offer scholarships based on financial need. Some programs target talented low-income youth for services, and they report positive effects on subsequent college experiences (Olszewski-Kubilius & Laubscher, 1996).

∾ Encourage university-based programs and the local schools to develop credit and placement policies to recognize the academic achievements of students in summer and Saturday programs when they return to their home school. Credit and placement practices are frequently uneven in the schools (Lynch, 1990; Olszewski-Kubilius, 1989, 1996).

ð› Share information with school counselors and administrators and encourage them to disseminate information about the availability and impact of these programs to students and their families. Thousands of talented students participate in university-based programs each year. The results of participation impact students throughout their school and career and personal lives (Enersen, 1993, 1996; Olszewski-Kubilius & Grant, 1994).

REFERENCES

Barnett, L. B., & Durden, W. G. (1993). Education patterns of academically talented youth. *Gifted Child Quarterly, 37,* 161–168.

Brody, L. E., & Mills, C. J. (2005). Talent search research: What have we learned? *High Ability Studies, 16,* 97–111.

Brounstein, P. J., Holahan, W. A., & Sawyer, R. (1988). The expectations and motivations of gifted students in a residential academic program: A study of individual differences. *Journal for the Education of the Gifted, 11*(3), 36–52.

Dauber, S. L., & Benbow, C. P. (1990). Aspects of personality and peer relations of extremely talented adolescents. *Gifted Child Quarterly, 34,* 10–15.

Enersen, D. L. (1993). Summer residential programs: Academics and beyond. *Gifted Child Quarterly, 37,* 169–176.

Enersen, D. L. (1996). Developing talent in Saturday and summer programs. *Gifted Education International, 11,* 159–163.

Feldhusen, J. F., Enersen, D. L., & Sayler, M. F. (1992). Challenging the gifted through problem solving experiences: Design and evaluation of the COMET program. *Gifted Child Today, 15*(4), 49–54.

Feldhusen, J. F., & Koopman-Daytons, J. (1987). Meeting special needs of the gifted through Saturday programs: An evaluation study. *Gifted International, 4,* 82–93.

Feldhusen, J. F., & Robinson-Wyman, A. (1980). Super Saturday: Design and implementation of Purdue's special program for gifted children. *Gifted Child Quarterly, 24,* 15–21.

Feldhusen, J. F., & Sokol, L. (1982). Extra-school programming to meet the needs of gifted youth: Super Saturday. *Gifted Child Quarterly, 26,* 51–56.

Flack, J., & Friedberg, J. (1997). When children go to college on Saturday. *Teaching Pre-K–8, 27,* 44–46.

Hapai, M. N. (1994). Super science Saturdays: Developing Hawaii's natural treasures. *Science Scope, 17,* 42–44.

Hess, J. (1991). The arts as a resource. *Communicator, 21,* 141.

Kolloff, P. B., & Moore, D. A. (1989). Effects of summer programs on the self-concepts of gifted children. *Journal for the Education of the Gifted, 12,* 268–276.

Lupkowski-Shoplik, A. E., & Kuhnel, A. (1995). Mathematics enrichment for talented elementary students. *Gifted Child Today, 18*(4), 28–31.

Lynch, S. (1990). Credit and placement issues for the academically talented following summer studies in science and mathematics. *Gifted Child Quarterly, 34,* 27–30.

Lynch, S., & Mills, C. J. (1990). The Skills Reinforcement Project (SRP): An academic program for high potential minority youth. *Journal for the Education of the Gifted, 13,* 364–379.

Miserandino, A. D., Subotnik, R. F., & Ou, K. (1995). Identifying and nurturing mathematical talent in urban school settings. *Journal of Secondary Education, 6,* 245–257.

Olszewski, P., Kulieke, M., & Willis, G. B. (1987). Changes in the self-perceptions of gifted students who participate in rigorous academic programs. *Journal for the Education of the Gifted, 10,* 287–303.

Olszewski-Kubilius, P. (1989). Development of academic talent: The role of summer programs. In J. VanTassel-Baska & P. M. Olszewski-Kubilius (Eds.), *Patterns of influence on gifted learners: The home, the self and the school* (pp. 214–230). New York: Teachers College Press.

Olszewski-Kubilius, P. (1996). Issues and factors involved in credit and placement for accelerated summer coursework. *Journal of Secondary Gifted Education, 8,* 5–15.

Olszewski-Kubilius, P. (2007). The role of summer programs in developing the talents of gifted students. In J. VanTassel-Baska (Ed.), *Serving gifted learners beyond the traditional classroom: A guide to alternative programs and services* (pp. 13–32). Waco, TX: Prufrock.

Olszewski-Kubilius, P., & Grant, B. (1994). Academically talented females in mathematics: The role of special programs and support from others in acceleration, achievement, and aspiration. In K. D. Noble & R. F. Subotnik (Eds.), *Remarkable women: Perspectives on female talent development* (pp. 281–291). Cresskill, NJ: Hampton Press.

Olszewski-Kubilius, P., & Laubscher, L. (1996). The impact of a college counseling program on economically disadvantaged gifted students and their subsequent college adjustment. *Roeper Review, 18,* 202–208.

Olszewski-Kubilius, P., & Lee, S-Y. (2004). Parent perceptions of the effects of the Saturday enrichment program on gifted students' talent development. *Roeper Review, 26,* 156–165.

Robinson, A., & Stanley, T. D. (1989). Teaching to talent: Evaluating an enriched and accelerated mathematics program. *Journal for the Education of the Gifted, 12,* 253–267.

Stake, J. E., & Mares, K. R. (2001). Science enrichment programs for gifted high school girls and boys: Predictors of program impact on science confidence and motivation. *Journal of Research in Science Teaching, 38,* 1065–1088.

Stake, J. E., & Mares, K. R. (2005). Evaluating the impact of science-enrichment programs on adolescents' science motivation and confidence: The splashdown effect. *Journal of Research in Science Teaching, 42,* 359–375.

Subotnik, R. F., & Strauss, S. M. (1995). Gender differences in classroom participation and achievement: An experiment involving AP calculus classes. *Journal of Secondary Gifted Education, 6,* 77–85.

Swiatek, M. A., & Lupkowski-Shoplik, A. (2000). Gender differences in above-level EXPLORE scores of gifted third through sixth graders. *Journal of Educational Psychology, 92,* 718–723.

Thomas, T. A. (1993). *The achievement and social adjustment of accelerated students: The impact of academic talent search after seven years.* Sacramento: California State University at Sacramento.

PART II
CLASSROOM

CHAPTER 9

ENCOURAGING CREATIVITY

Despite the fact that creativity is difficult to define, identify, and evaluate, we must not ignore this trait in talented children. The world depends on creative people for contributions in all areas of life, from technology, travel, and medicine, to movies, music, and literature.

If that were not reason enough, the most compelling motive for our attention is that we are committed to enabling individuals to live fulfilled lives. Parents and teachers need to know that they have a powerful influence on the development of creativity.

WHAT WE KNOW

Although much of the recent research concerning creativity has not been centered in the field of gifted education, numerous studies have important things to say about the development of creative talent in children. Feldman and Benjamin (1998) gave examples of some of the newest areas of investigative research, which include artificial intelligence (creative process in computers), historiometry (i.e., why clusters of creative genius occur at the same time), developmental psychology (searching the lives of extreme achievers for characteristics), and inventive and innovative thinking (pp. 83–84). This broadening of the concept of creativity opens possibilities for students to be recognized in many fields other than art, drama, or music. The new developments also legitimize the creative process as necessary for success in industry, academia, and other careers.

It is revealing that each study, article, chapter, and book about creativity begins with a detailed description of the way the author views the construct. At first, creativity was considered to be the study of genius, then the study of imagination (Rugg, 1963). Finally, the word *creativity* appeared in the dictionary, and it was defined as the ability to make something new (Piirto, 1992). Definitions today range from Winner and Martino's (1993) ". . . inventiveness within a domain. A creative individual revolutionizes a domain of knowledge" (p. 253), to Treffinger, Sartore, and Cross's (1993) "Creativity is one among a number of important skills people use to reason, solve problems, make decisions, and add meaning and value to life" (p. 557), to Piirto's (1992) "Creativity is a swampy concept" (p. ii). There are areas of general agreement: Creativity is complex; it can be nurtured or lost; parents, teachers, coaches, and mentors have tremendous power to influence and shape its development; there are stages in its development; it is visible in its production; and creative people exhibit characteristics that must be understood by those who desire to enable its fulfillment.

Creativity derives its complexity from individual differences in personality, knowledge, environment, motivation, and receptivity, as well as creative abilities (Davis, 1997). All of these components are shaped by societal values at large (Shore, Cornell, Robinson, & Ward, 1991; Tannenbaum, 1983), and family and school values locally. Isaksen (1987) states that there is not one definition, because creativity appears differently, in differing degrees, and with different kinds of productivity in individuals. Perhaps the most noticeable differences are seen in the emerging creativity or "germinal creativity" of a child who is not yet skilled (Fishkin, 1988), as compared to the mature productivity of an adult (Fishkin & Johnson, 1998).

Murdock and Puccio (1993) believe that the meaning of creativity can best be captured by studying the interactions among MacKinnon's (1961) four perspectives of personality, process, press (environment), and product. Yet, Sawyer (1992) and Martindale (1990) found that a significant portion of creative processing happens on an unconscious level. Each person brings to the process his or her own history and experiences that impact creative thought even at this unconscious level.

Csikszentmihalyi (1998) raises the discussion about personal creativity—small "c"—and cultural creativity—big "C." Many who have characteristics that should lead them to creative pursuits do not become successful. He believes creativity to be a multidimensional interaction amid the person, the social system, and the cultural system, with all three synchronized for "C" to occur.

There has long been debate about defining creativity by a connection to intelligence. Wallach (1985) reported numerous studies in the arts, sciences, architecture, mathematics, writing, and leadership that showed IQ scores to be poor predictors of creative accomplishment in any field. The one intellectual ability that appeared to operationalize divergent thinking was ideational fluency, which served as an index of creativity in many contexts in preschool to high school students. The attempt to separate intelligence and creativity may have originated with the 1972 Marland Report, which listed creativity as one type of giftedness rather than as a feature of all giftedness (Piirto, 1992). Guilford's (1970) Structure of the Intellect, Torrance's (1974) Tests of Creative Thinking, Gardner's (1983) theory of multiple intelligences, and Renzulli's (1977) Enrichment Triad Model were among the theories offered to explain the relationship of IQ and creativity. Today, the "evolving idea is that creativity is necessary for giftedness, and not separate from it" (Piirto, 1992, p. 24).

Han and Marvin (2002) review the discussion of general creativity versus domain-specific creativity, and suggest from their study of second-grade students that creativity may be more domain-specific than thought. Their subjects exhibited an interesting range of creative abilities tied to certain domains rather than a pervasive, uniform ability that showed up in diverse domains.

Even as we admit that the complexity of creativity makes defining it difficult, there is agreement that creativity can be nurtured and developed in a person, or it can be repressed and even lost. For all children, creativity training and recognition of production is important; here, we look at the necessity of addressing the needs of gifted children by understanding their creative characteristics.

Characteristics of Creative Individuals

Dabrowski's theory of emotional development suggests that creative, gifted individuals have high levels of emotional overexcitability, expanded awareness, and heightened responses, which result in above-average types and degree of expression (as discussed in O'Connor, 2002, and in Silverman, 1993). It may be these same intense emotions and sensitivities, coupled with introversion and the usual school-related rejections and boredom, that cause some students to be at risk for mental illness and suicide (Silverman). Jamison (1993) looked at the timing and depth of mood changes that appeared to open or inhibit creative thought. Nickerson (1999) spoke of the crippling fear some creative children suffer when faced with failure or ridicule. Gardner's (1993) in-depth, retrospective case studies of seven famous creative people such as Picasso, Einstein, and Gandhi showed more vulnerability and marginalization evident in them than in the general population. Other case studies of creative students, especially adolescents, show that because of these characteristics, there is a need for counselors who are trained to work with gifted teens to facilitate the right educational plan at a critical time (Hébert, 1998; Renzulli, Reis, Hébert, & Diaz, 1995).

A list of specific traits of creative individuals was given by VanTassel-Baska (1998):
- independence in attitude and social behavior;
- dominance;
- introversion;
- tolerance for ambiguity;
- openness to stimuli, wide interests;
- self-acceptance;
- intuitiveness;
- flexibility;
- an asocial attitude, unconcern for social norms, risk-takers;
- social presence and poise;
- radicalism, rejection of external constraints;
- ability to fantasize and toy with ideas; and
- aesthetic and moral commitment to work (pp. 383–384).

To this list, Amabile (1989) added the following thinking styles that are typical of creative people:
- able to break out of patterns of thinking,
- understand complexity,
- suspend judgment while generating as many ideas as possible,
- see relationships between ideas,
- remember well and accurately,
- see things in ways others do not, and
- use tricks to prompt thinking (make the familiar strange and the strange familiar; pp. 48–49).

Neihart and Olenchak (2002) reiterated that creative people are:
- open to new ideas and experiences,
- persevering,
- nonconforming,
- intellectually and emotionally mature, and
- self-confident and aware of their abilities.

On the other hand, Davis (1997) reminded us that there are less-esteemed traits, as well. Creative people often challenge rules, and can be indifferent to formalities, careless, sloppy with details or unimportant matters, and intolerant or temperamental.

One area of consensus is the direct influence of parents, teachers, and mentors on the development of a child's creativity. Retrospective studies of highly creative people continually identified the critical importance, and in some cases, the life-saving effects of having at least one adult who saw beyond nonconforming behavior and nurtured and championed the child's creative efforts (Kemple & Nissenberg, 2000; Piirto, 1992, 1998; Silverman, 1993; Treffinger et al., 1993; VanTassel-Baska, 1998). These adults were willing to devote time, resources, and leadership to the children's development. Field and laboratory studies (Amabile, 1989) netted the following ways in which parents, in particular, support their children's creative inclination:

- They are authoritative and give their children freedom without excessive worry about risks.
- They respect their children as individuals and as creative persons and see them as capable.
- They are moderately close as a family, not dependent, but accepted.
- They are not permissive, but share values instead of levying rules.
- They emphasize achievement over grades, and they appreciate and cultivate creativity.
- They observe the children to see where interests lie, and then capitalize on those.
- They are active and have many interests themselves.
- They exhibit humor and family fun.
- They provide and take part in experiences that are stimulating.
- They are often models of creative thinking and behavior (pp. 103–112).

Over the years, there has even been some suggestion that less positive family characteristics may encourage a rebellious attitude, leading to more independent, divergent thinking (i.e., Siegelman, 1973). However, most researchers see as desirable home and school environments that allow children time to explore and experiment and that are supportive and nurturing; environments that are characterized by pressure, control, and criticism are detrimental to creative development (Hirsh-Pasek, 1991).

In a related study concerning home support, Isenberg and Jalongo (2001) found that some parents are skeptical of play and creative expression, seeing them as frivolous and a waste of instructional time in school. Yet, Csikszentmihalyi and Sawyer (1995) classified this as an incubation time of "idling and leisure" (p. 359), and said that an always-busy schedule does not permit the necessary opportunity for reflection and insight. Their case study subjects (who were adults) reported rich and creative insight occurring at those "frivolous" times throughout their lives.

In the same way that characteristics of academically talented children translate into academic needs, the characteristics of creatively gifted children indicate curricular needs. Researchers are in accord that creativity can be developed through attention to skills and to providing an environment of acceptance and encouragement. For many years, dissension was heard in whether to instruct students in creative thinking skills in a context, such as writing class or mathematics, or to give instruction of skills in isolation for concentrated effort on learning the properties of the skills. Wallach (1985) said that "[c]reative work takes place in a context, and that context cannot be ignored" (p 381). Davis (1997) disagreed and saw self-actualized creativity—the goal of a creative life—as content free and able to be enhanced by instruction in techniques and attitudes without tying it to content. As others lined up on both sides, it appears that a combination of drawing attention to the metacognitive aspects of creative thinking skills *and* linking them to specific domains results in the best transfer and integration of creative strategies (Feldhusen, 1993; VanTassel-Baska, 1996).

The school's responsibility to provide an environment where potential is realized means including a child's creative, as well as academic, potential. This is often at odds with today's tight classroom schedules and substantial curricular goals that must be met. In fact, Atkinson (2000) found in a "real-world" situation of technology design, teachers may structure learning experiences to reduce creativity because they do not value creative thinking and find it difficult and time consuming to evaluate. The feeling that creative thinking is not welcome is experienced by children in some classrooms where their creative ideas take discussions and projects off in new directions not anticipated and not appreciated by the teacher.

Nickerson (1999) gave recommendations for enhancing creativity, but cautioned that personality traits and environmental factors combine to produce or inhibit growth in creativity and creative endeavors. He listed the necessity of *purpose* first, and said it is "essential to creative expression—nobody carves a statue without intending to do so" (p. 408). He encouraged developing basic and domain-specific skills and knowledge, engaging in playfulness, the rewarding of exploration, and the building of motivation for hard work and positive beliefs about one's abilities. He also advocated the learning of self-management skills (especially helpful when the person gains notoriety) and strategies for productive thinking.

Several researchers have organized the creative process into stages to help understand the path of its development. Kirschenbaum's (1998) Creativity Classification System showed that novices, just learning and developing expertise, are in the first phase of Contact (approaching new situations with eagerness), Consciousness (maintaining a thoughtful, questioning attitude), Interest (working to meet own high standards), and Fantasy (using imagination). After a time of Incubation (remaining internally open) and Creative Contact (experiencing insight), those who are creatively more mature move into Inspiration (feeling empowered to work), Production (making the product), and Verification (evaluating the effectiveness of the creation). VanTassel-Baska (1996) offered four life stages in the developing of writing talent that may hold true for other creative growth: (a) born into a family that values the literary and intellectual life; (b) informal early development of the craft of writing; (c) active experimentation with various forms of writing; and (d) progressive development of mature form and idea in successive works.

WHAT WE CAN DO

It is not that creative children are fragile, volatile people who require hot-house treatment. However, it is important to learn and care about children as individuals who deserve opportunities to develop their talents to the highest levels possible. Parents and teachers can provide many kinds of support to nurture children and creative talents alike.

At Home

❧ Reach beyond the school for development of creative talent for those students who require more advanced instruction, mentoring, and challenges in their fields (Haroutounian, 1995). Look for summer programs and special public or private schools that offer arts or sciences or other areas of focus that more closely match the talents and needs of certain students.

❧ Allow a place at home and at school where some work can remain "in progress" for a time, focusing on the process of the task instead of finishing and the potential reward (i.e., grade, praise). Provide materials and free up time to use them. Display projects, writings, paintings—any fruit of creative labor.

❧ Provide lessons, instruments, guest authors, dancers, scientists, and other experts from a wide array of fields, as well as trips to concerts and lectures (and then to the stage door to meet the artists).

❧ Model and teach that hard work, practice, and persistence are all part of being creatively successful.

In the Classroom

❧ Teach students through concepts and relationships, in context and meta-cognitively. Many areas of the curriculum should provide strategy lessons and strategy application (Mumford, 1998; Starko, 2005; VanTassel-Baska, 1998). The discovery method is less effective at the beginning, because students' lack of knowledge about strategies interferes with learning, but can be utilized as expertise grows.

❧ Teach students to recognize and clarify problems and new ideas, reorganize knowledge, purposely seek alternatives, evaluate ideas and solutions, and monitor their own activity. Encourage them to find problems instead of always providing them with problems (Runco & Nemiro, 1994). Build in them a tolerance for ambiguity and deferred judgment.

❧ Evaluate and praise creative production honestly (children know if the praise is false), specifically ("I like the way you used blue to set the mood," vs. "That is the most beautiful picture in the world."), and positively (show you appreciate the effort). Runco (1992) noted that creative people are more naturally self-evaluative, but that support and positive, honest evaluation from others is crucial.

❧ Use biographies and fiction of creative people to inspire and provide a point of identification for children. This can be especially effective for females, children of minority groups, nonathletic males, and any child who has experienced rejection and misunderstanding because of his or her giftedness (VanTassel-Baska, 1996).

At School

❧ Use multiple ways of identifying creative talent and what a student needs, and include instruments that measure skills; self-report data on feelings, interests, and aspirations; observations by parents and teachers; and evaluation of productivity and performance.

❧ Provided flexible scheduling so that students can enroll in classes that meet their specific needs (perhaps two art classes and band).

❧ Set expectations that both the home and the classroom will be places that value creative thinking and work. Let children see their parents and teachers do creative work of their own, talk positively about people who create, give girls and boys equal opportunities in all creative endeavors, and give children time to think, experiment, and resolve the disequilibrium of creative work.

❧ Support creatively gifted children with counseling, if needed, as they search for their identities and places in their schools, families, and careers. Torrance's (1962, 1988) work over the decades confirmed the necessity of these kinds of supports. He believed that children who lacked them could become physically and psychologically ill.

If creativity is a swampy concept, as Piirto says, it is worth braving the alligators. Creative works enhance all our lives and bring fulfillment to those who create.

REFERENCES

Amabile, T. M. (1989). *Growing up creative: Nurturing a lifetime of creativity.* New York: Crown.

Atkinson, S. (2000). Does the need for high levels of performance curtail the development of creativity in design and technology project work? *International Journal of Technology and Design Education, 10,* 255–281.

Csikszentmihalyi, M. (1998). Self and evolution. *NAMTA Journal, 23,* 204–233.

Csikszentmihalyi, M., & Sawyer, K. (1995). Creative insight: The social dimension of a solitary moment. In R. J. Sternberg & J. E. Davidson (Eds.), *The nature of insight* (pp. 329–363). Cambridge, MA: The MIT Press.

Davis, G. A. (1997). Identifying creative students and measuring creativity. In N. Colangelo & G. A. Davis (Eds.), *Handbook of gifted education* (2nd ed., pp. 269–281). Boston: Allyn & Bacon.

Feldhusen, J. F. (1993). A conception of creative thinking and creative training. In S. C. Isaksen, M. C. Murdock, R. L. Firestien, & D. J. Treffinger (Eds.), *Nurturing and developing creativity: The emergence of a discipline* (pp. 31–50). Norwood, NJ: Ablex.

Feldman, D. H., & Benjamin, A. C. (1998). Letters from the field. *Roeper Review, 21,* 78–88.

Fishkin, A. S. (1998). Issues in studying creativity in youth. In A. S. Fishkin, B. Cramond, & P. Olszewski-Kubilius (Eds.), *Investigating creativity in youth: Research and methods.* Cresskill, NJ: Hampton Press.

Fishkin, A. S., & Johnson, A. S. (1998). Who is creative? Identifying children's creative abilities. *Roeper Review, 21,* 40–46.

Gardner, H. (1983). *Frames of mind.* New York: BasicBooks.

Gardner, H. (1993). *Creating minds: An anatomy of creativity seen through the lives of Freud, Einstein, Picasso, Stravinsky, Eliot, Graham, and Gandhi.* New York: BasicBooks.

Guilford, J. P. (1970). Traits of creativity. In P. E. Vernon (Ed.), *Creativity* (pp. 167–188). Baltimore: Penguin.

Han, K., & Marvin, C. (2002). Multiple creativities? Investigating domain-specificity of creativity in young children. *Gifted Child Quarterly, 46,* 98–109.

Haroutounian, J. (1995). Talent identification and development in the arts: An artistic/educational dialogue. *Roeper Review, 12,* 112–117.

Hébert, T. P. (1998). DeShea's dream deferred: A case study of a talented urban artist. *Journal for the Education of the Gifted, 22,* 56–79.

Hirsh-Pasek, K. (1991). Pressure or challenge in preschool? How academic environments affect children. *New Directions for Child Development, 53,* 39–46.

Isaksen, S. G. (1987). Introduction: An orientation to the frontiers of creativity research. In S. G. Isaksen (Ed.), *Frontiers of creativity research: Beyond the basics* (pp. 1–26). Buffalo, NY: Bearly.

Isenberg, J. P., & Jalongo, M. R. (2001). *Creative expression and play in the early childhood curriculum* (3rd ed.). Upper Saddle River, NJ: Prentice Hall.

Jamison, K. R. (1993). *Touched with fire: Manic depressive illness and the artistic temperament.* New York: Free Press.

Kemple, K. M., & Nissenberg, S. A. (2000). Nurturing creativity in early childhood education: Families are part of it. *Early Childhood Education Journal, 28,* 67–71.

Kirschenbaum, R. J. (1998). *Understanding the creative activity of students.* Mansfield Center, CT: Creative Learning Press.

MacKinnon, D. W. (1961). The study of creativity. In D. W. MacKinnon (Ed.), *The creative person* (pp. I-1–I-15). Berkeley: University of California, Institute of Personality Assessment Research.

Marland, S. P., Jr. (1972). *Education of the gifted and talented: Report to the Congress of the United States by the U.S. Commissioner of Education and background papers submitted to the U.S. Office of Education,* 2 vols. Washington, DC: U.S. Government Printing Office. (Government Documents, Y4.L 11/2: G36)

Martindale, C. (1990). *The clockwork muse: The predictability of artistic change*. New York: BasicBooks.

Mumford, M. D. (1998). Creative thought: Structure, components, and educational implications. *Roeper Review, 21*, 14–19.

Murdock, M. C., & Puccio, G. J. (1993). A contextual organizer for conducting creativity research. In S. G. Isaksen, M. C. Murdock, R. L. Firestien, & D. J. Treffinger (Eds.), *Understanding and recognizing creativity: The emergence of a discipline* (pp. 249–280). Norwood, NJ: Ablex.

Nickerson, R. S. (1999). Enhancing creativity. In R. J. Sternberg (Ed.), *Handbook of creativity*. New York: Cambridge University Press.

Neihart, M., & Olenchak, F. R. (2002). Creatively gifted children. In M. Neihart, S. M. Reis, N. M. Robinson, & S. M. Moon (Eds.), *The social and emotional development of gifted children: What do we know?* (pp. 165–175). Waco, TX: Prufrock Press.

O'Connor, K. J. (2002). The application of Dabrowski's theory to the gifted. In M. Neihart, S. M. Reis, N. M. Robinson, & S. M. Moon (Eds.), *The social and emotional development of gifted children: What do we know?* (pp. 51–60). Waco, TX: Prufrock Press

Piirto, J. (1992). *Understanding those who create*. Dayton, OH: Ohio Psychology Press.

Piirto, J. (1998). Themes in the lives of successful contemporary women creative writers. *Roeper Review, 21*, 60–70.

Renzulli, J. S. (1977). *The enrichment triad model: A guide for developing defensible programs for the gifted*. Mansfield Center, CT: Creative Learning Press.

Renzulli, J. S., Reis, S. M., Hébert, T. P., & Diaz, E. I. (1995). The plight of high-ability students in urban high schools. In M. C. Wang & M. C. Reynolds (Eds.), *Making a difference for students at risk* (pp. 61–98). Thousand Oaks, CA: Corwin Press.

Rugg, H. (1963). *Imagination*. New York: Harper & Row.

Runco, M. A. (1992). The evaluative, valuative, and divergent thinking of children. *Journal of Creative Behavior, 25*, 311–319.

Runco, M. A., & Nemiro, J. (1994). Problem finding, creativity, and giftedness. *Roeper Review, 16*, 235–241.

Sawyer, K. (1992). Improvisational creativity: An analysis of jazz performance. *Creativity Research Journal, 5*, 253–264.

Shore, B. M., Cornell, D. G., Robinson, A., & Ward, V. S. (1991). *Recommended practices in gifted education: A critical analysis*. New York: Teachers College Press.

Siegelman, M. (1973). Parent behavior correlates of personality traits related to creativity in sons and daughters. *Journal of Counseling and Clinical Psychology, 40*, 43–47.

Silverman, L. K. (1993). The gifted individual. In L. K. Silverman (Ed.), *Counseling the gifted and talented* (pp. 3–28). Denver: Love.

Starko, A. J. (2005). *Creativity in the classroom: Schools of curious delight* (3rd ed.). Mahwah, NJ: Lawrence Erlbaum Associates.

Tannenbaum, A. (1983). *Gifted children: Psychological and educational perspectives*. New York: Macmillan.

Torrance, E. P. (1962). *Guiding creative talent*. Englewood Cliffs, NJ: Prentice-Hall.

Torrance, E. P. (1974). *Torrance tests of creative thinking*. Bensenville, IL: Scholastic Testing Services.

Torrance, E. P. (1988). The nature of creativity as manifest in its testing. In R. W. Sternberg (Ed.), *The nature of creativity* (pp. 43–75). New York: Cambridge University Press.

Treffinger, D., Sartore, D., & Cross, J. (1993). Programs and strategies for nurturing creativity. In K. A. Heller, F. J. Mönks, & A. H. Passow (Eds.), *International handbook of research and development of giftedness and talent* (pp. 555–567). Oxford, England: Pergamon.

VanTassel-Baska, J. (1996). The process of talent development. In J. VanTassel-Baska, D. T. Johnson, & L. N. Boyce (Eds.), *Developing verbal talent* (pp. 3–22). Boston: Allyn & Bacon.

VanTassel-Baska, J. (1998). Creativity and the gifted. In J. VanTassel-Baska (Ed.), *Excellence in educating gifted and talented learners* (pp. 381–398). Denver, CO: Love.

Wallach, M. (1985). Creativity testing and giftedness. In F. Horowitz & M. O'Brien (Eds.), *The gifted and the talented: Developmental perspectives* (pp. 99–132). Washington, DC: American Psychological Association.

Winner, E., & Martino, G. (1993). Giftedness in the visual arts and music. In K. A. Heller, F. J. Mönks, & A. H. Passow (Eds.), *International handbook of research and development of giftedness and talent* (pp. 253–281). New York: Pergamon Press.

CHAPTER 10

MULTIPLE INTELLIGENCES

G ardner's theory of multiple intelligences provides an articulate and easily remembered view of human abilities in which different strengths are valued. Therefore, it is well suited to explorations of more egalitarian identification procedures for gifted programs. Its links to curriculum development are more tenuous, possibly very general, such as ensuring that different domains generate activities in the curriculum. This creates a special challenge in matching identification techniques to curricular practice. Multiple intelligences theory offers considerable promise in sensitizing parents and educators to diversity at the level of intellectual strengths. It needs to be combined with curricular theories and models to have an impact on education in general and gifted education in particular. The potential for multiple intelligences theory to contribute in such combinations is not yet explored in the literature.

WHAT WE KNOW

The Multiple Intelligences (MI) Theory

Gardner's (1983) MI theory offered an alternative way to perceive intelligence. He proposed that "narrow assessment (IQ testing) was wrong in scientific terms and has seriously damaging social consequences" (Gardner, p. 22). IQ assessment also fails to predict success outside of school (Morris & Leblanc, 1996). "MI offers a potentially more viable theory of cognitive functioning, particularly because it is based on and takes into account the nature of real-world intelligent behavior" (Matthews, 1988, p. 100).

The theory "defines an intelligence as the capacity to solve problems or fashion products which are valued in one or more cultural settings" (Blythe & Gardner, 1990, p. 35). Gardner's theory also "postulates intelligence as a profile showing an individual's relative strengths and weaknesses across seven domains, or intelligences" (Matthews, 1988, p. 100) or an "identifiable core operation or set of operations" (Gardner, 1983, p. 64).

Gardner's theorizing drew upon studies of brain damage, prodigies, developmental patterns, cross-cultural comparison, and various types of subtests that led him to originally identify seven main intelligences: linguistic-verbal, logical-mathematical, visual-spatial, bodily-kinesthetic, musical-rhythmic, social-interpersonal, and intrapersonal (Morris & Leblanc, 1996). More recently, Gardner (1996) introduced one-and-a-half other intelligences. He used the term naturalist, which is the ability to be sensitive to the ecological environment, for the first. The half intelligence (because he is not certain that it consists of a full-blown intelligence) is called moralist, which is the ability to be sensitive to ethical concerns (Sarouphim, 1999).

The criteria for an intelligence to be recognized as independent according to Gardner are:
1. potential isolation by brain damage;
2. existence of savants, prodigies, and other exceptional individuals;
3. an identifiable core set of operations;
4. a distinctive developmental history along with a definable set of expert "end-state" performance;
5. an evolutionary history and plausibility;
6. support from experimental and psychological tasks;
7. support from psychometric findings; and
8. susceptibility to encoding from a symbol system. (Gardner, 1983, pp. 63–66)

Gardner stated that all intelligences can be enhanced, that they may develop almost independently, and that there is no specific order of priority (Morris & Leblanc, 1996). Each of the recognizable intelligences is characterized by a pattern of neurological organization and a unique cluster of abilities (Strahan,

Summey, & Bowles, 1996). These are domain-specific intelligences (Matthews, 1988), meaning that they are recognizable in the context of domains of activity (e.g., mathematics, dance, or poetry). Similarly, according to Sternberg's (1986) triarchic model of intellectual giftedness, "giftedness is found in a multiplicity of forms, and varies from one person to another" (Matthews, p. 101). This view of intelligence can be seen as multidimensional reasoning. It is also a useful foundation for understanding more about individual differences (Strahan et al.). "MI offers a theoretical framework . . . that is inherently adaptive to a wide spectrum of individual cognitive differences" (Matthews, p. 100). MI is regarded by some as contributing to a paradigm shift by changing the way we perceive students and their potential, and our roles and responsibilities as educators (Hoerr, 1996). It can serve to remind teachers to guide students and help them learn using their individual strengths.

What educators like about the theory is that it emphasizes individual diversity and encourages teachers to discover new means of making learning easier for each individual student. Multiple intelligences permit teachers to personalize instruction (Strahan et al., 1996) and give each child the opportunity to use his or her strengths. In order to identify giftedness, we now have the option to use alternative assessment criteria based on multiple intelligences. It is regarded as a viable alternative because it includes more areas of knowledge, abilities, and expertise than general intelligence testing. Traditionally, "a person's giftedness basically is determined by results on a standardized, norm-referenced measure of general intellectual ability or achievement" (Rogers, 1998, p. 131).

Some critics argue that the theory of multiple intelligences does not make a new contribution to our understanding of exceptional human abilities. For example, Morgan (1996) proposed that MIs were just cognitive styles under another name, but the domain-specific focus somewhat belies that criticism. Multiple intelligence theories have been described in one form or another by Carrol (1993) and Cattell (1971), and both Guilford (1956, 1967) and Hudson (1970) have explored links between different intellectual strengths and domains of intellectual activity. Nevertheless, even if Gardner's theory has clear antecedents, its arrival may be well timed, and it does strike a balance between excessive simplicity (Hudson primarily addressed convergent versus divergent abilities) and excessive complexity (Guilford's three-dimensional model of some 120 cells may not be broadly useful to classroom teachers, even though curricular materials to develop the specific abilities are available). Even if Gardner did not intend his theory for educational purposes in the first place, it has inspired many teachers to examine their ways of teaching.

In recent years, publishers of curricular materials have issued dozens of school texts based on MI principles, including many designed as enrichment materials or promoted for use in gifted programs (e.g., Zephyr Press listed more than 50 titles in its 1999 catalog), although we could not find any research on the effectiveness of these materials or curricula. Schools have been created following the principles of the theory (Lockwood, 1993), but the formal research we have located has addressed the question of identification, that is, whether or not the use of MI-based identification techniques increases the likelihood that underrepresented groups of children will more likely be identified for gifted education programs. A judgment of the appropriateness of MI for gifted education will therefore be somewhat tentative.

Assessment of Intelligence Profiles and Abilities of Gifted Students

The verb *to assess* comes from the Latin verb *assidere*, which translates as "to sit with." Assessment should be something we do with the child, not *to* the child. Rogers (1998) criticized identification practices in gifted education as being different in title only, not in underlying substance. In attempting to guide new thinking in this regard, Gardner (1992) advocated new assessment methods that:

- are simple, natural, and occurring on a reliable schedule;
- have ecological validity;
- incorporate instruments that are intelligence-fair;
- use multiple measures;
- are sensitive to individual differences, developmental levels, and forms of expertise;
- use intrinsically interesting and motivating materials; and
- are applied for the student's benefit. (pp. 91–94)

Kornhaber (1999), working in Gardner's Project Zero laboratory, has added two other MI-specific conditions to this list. Assessment methods should assess "abilities beyond those traditionally tested" and they should be "domain-based" (p. 153).

The majority of research conducted on MI has been to identify giftedness in children of low-socioeconomic or culturally diverse backgrounds. One approach to identifying giftedness through multiple intelligences is to seek children who are superior problem solvers in two or more activities or domains (Rogers, 1998). For example, Leibowitz and Starnes (1993) evaluated children aged 3 to 9 "to uncover the strengths and gifts of traditionally underserved gifted youngsters" (p. 28). Twice a year, teachers used a checklist to identify learning strengths based on MI theory, and they received feedback and suggestions from the researchers on Gardner's team at Project Spectrum. Portfolios of children's work were used to monitor progress and strengths in each intelligence. The program changed the way children were discussed and perceived by their teachers. Teachers and their attitudes changed; they became teacher-researchers.

Strahan et al. (1996) recorded two sixth-grade teachers' recollections of their efforts to create a more inclusive school with the use of Gardner's theory. With help from the research team, teachers encouraged students to develop awareness about the way they acquire knowledge and introduced into the curriculum activities that tapped their seven ways of knowing. Researchers found that learning about MI provided the teachers with a framework to analyze and organize their perception of individual students. It also made them aware of the need for personalized instruction. Testing revealed improvement in the mathematical and reading abilities of the students, but the complex set of interventions makes it impossible to ascribe these gains to any particular element. Univariate analyses using *t*-tests (not a powerful technique and incapable of uncovering interactions among the variables) indicated that the students' gains were significant—almost two grade equivalents in reading and three grade equivalents in mathematics. Not only did the use of *t*-tests fail to adequately partition the sources of variability, but no control group was used for comparison. Further interviews with 13 of the 15 students showed their enjoyment of the program and their desire for its continuation the next year.

Similar outcomes were reported by Tomlinson, Callahan, and Lelli (1997), who observed students in their classroom settings and interviewed their parents to "develop identification procedures based upon Howard Gardner's (1983) multiple intelligences theory" and "identify high-potential primary age students from culturally diverse and/or low economic backgrounds through use of this framework" (p. 6). Four students judged successful and four judged unsuccessful by their teachers were interviewed and observed. The students were equally distributed in grades 2 and 3. Researchers made extensive observations, took field notes, and kept reflective journals. Interviews were also conducted with the parents and the teachers. Unlike Strahan et al. (1996), who only addressed judgments by teachers and students, Tomlinson et al. also included parents. The program resulted in positive and important differences for students and families. Parents were more involved, and the team approach was seen as a powerful asset.

Another program that tried to identify socioeconomically disadvantaged gifted children using MI was evaluated by Baldwin (1994) with questionnaires, interviews, observations, and program documents. The research involved 399 students from kindergarten to grade 3 and two special education classes, 17 teachers, 5 paraprofessionals, and the administration of the schools. Teachers were immersed in the MI theory in order to facilitate their assessment of the students' abilities and an assessment model was developed. It emphasized experience and performance for each intelligence. Researchers designed a Likert-type scale of behavior characteristics to assess change in students. Preliminary findings were taken from 75 cases with matched pretest and posttest rating scale data. The administration noticed that changes occurred in the students' self-confidence, general knowledge, sophistication, and communication skills. Parents described the program as "a spiritual oasis" (p. 83) for their children and felt the students were empowered by it. Like many other studies, this project did not have a control or comparison program, so it is difficult to identify whether it was the MI content or the involvement in a school improvement project in general that led to the positive results.

Sarouphim (1999) used Gardner's theory to verify whether a child identified as gifted using DISCOVER (Discovering Intellectual Skills and Capabilities while Observing Varied Ethnic Responses), a performance-based model derived from the theory of multiple intelligences, would also be considered to be gifted by teachers and independent observers using activities that reflect six intelligences. A 5-year-old Hispanic girl, Anna, was identified as gifted in spatial and mathematical intelligences using the DISCOVER process. Teachers and observers agreed with DISCOVER about Anna's abilities in mathematical-logical, linguistic, and spatial intelligences. However, teachers and observers detected strengths in personal and kinesthetic intelligence when the formal assessment did not. DISCOVER needs to develop activities that tap into those intelligence to be capable of assessing them. The author also suggested that the study had limitations due to the small size of the sample. Rogers (1998) evaluated an assessment method the DISCOVER team developed to document students' problem-solving abilities in several of Gardner's intelligences. Observers followed students in grades 6–8 involved in activities requiring spatial, mathematical-logical, and linguistic abilities. Students who showed higher levels of problem solving in two or more activities were identified as gifted. Teachers noted that the process gave them insight into strengths in multiple intelligences when observing the students and their work. It also helped them readjust their perception of their students.

Kornhaber (1999) compared the identification outcomes of three MI-based identification models, including DISCOVER, and found that DISCOVER was intelligence-fair in that it opened the doors to gifted behavior characteristics of different groups, but that it was weak in assessing abilities that were not addressed by traditional IQ and achievement tests, and it did not tap domain-based talents (these three criteria being those that she selected as particularly stressed as assessment conditions by MI theory). A second program, based on DISCOVER, met none of these three conditions, and a third, the Gifted Model Program in Montgomery County, MD, met all three. On the other hand, the first two led to increases in minority representation in gifted programs, and the third did not, perhaps because minority representation was already equitable in that jurisdiction.

Guskin, Peng, and Simon (1992) examined the influence that teachers' beliefs and perceptions can have on the identification of and the programming for the gifted. They asked 95 undergraduate education students, 13 experienced teachers in a graduate course, and 50 teachers in an urban middle school to rate case descriptions of students and predict the degree of success for each case. In order to do the ratings, evaluators had to use five categories or intelligences to identify the strengths and abilities of their subject cases (motor, creative arts, verbal, analytic, and social abilities). The study revealed that teachers were more sensitive to MI when they had sufficient information about a student. Experienced teachers tended to rate the students higher than their less-experienced colleagues. Teachers predicted that students with verbal, analytic, or social skills would be more successful than students with motor and creative arts skills. They did not recommend much special programming or resources for students with strengths in social and motor abilities, while little agreement was apparent for students with artistic talent.

The identification literature is therefore still inconclusive. Fasko (2001) reviewed the Guskin et al. (1992) study and several others not described here, and similarly concluded that "there are no data reported that indicate that this approach does identify more gifted and talented students than do the more traditional methods" (pp. 126–127). MI has not yet been demonstrated to be either a necessary or sufficient condition for increasing the participation of underrepresented children in gifted programs, but it does appear to be capable of being embraced by teachers and thereby able to serve as an incentive to action on this front.

The Use of Domain-Specific Intelligences by Gifted Students

At the core of the criticism surrounding multiple intelligences, one theme prevails: the assumption that there is more that one intelligence and that intelligences are domain specific.

Maker (1993) and her students studied the relationships among the seven (then identified) intelligences and the processes that two gifted pupils and two gifted adults used when solving problems. The perceptions of outstanding performance in a domain were consistent with Gardner's MI model. The research underlined the need to focus on the individual before the group. Distinct patterns of intellectual strengths and weaknesses are also visible in traditional assessment data that can be linked to MI theory. For example, Gardner and Hatch (1989) studied 20 young students from upper middle-income families on 10 different activities and the Stanford-Binet Intelligence Scale, Fourth Edition. Fifteen students showed a strength in at least one subject, and 12 demonstrated one or more weaknesses, while one had neither weaknesses nor strengths. Children exhibited strengths and weaknesses in the seven different multiple intelligences.

Plucker, Callahan, and Tomchin (1996) explored whether activities based on MI assess different intelligences or solely linguistic and mathematical-logical intelligences (the two that are favored in traditional testing). They assessed 1,813 children enrolled in kindergarten and grade 1 from 16 different schools in a district using a multiple intelligences assessment approach. They found four factors or intelligences portrayed in the activities (mathematical-logical, linguistic, spatial, and interpersonal).

The literature does not yet contain studies that demonstrate how different MI-based intelligences are brought to bear on common problems, nor how persons who are able to use any one intelligence to a lesser or greater degree may differ in thinking processes and performance on common tasks within recognized domains. The use of multiple intelligences by gifted pupils is effectively unexplored, but open for exploration.

Does MI Theory Have a Place in Gifted Education?

The answer is a highly qualified yes. There are four potential ways in which MI might be useful in gifted education:

- MI sensitizes educators and parents to individual differences in a culturally acceptable way and to different kinds of talents in terms that are readily understood and applied. The sensitization has been described in several studies and general observation; the resulting identification tasks are still rather complex and variable in their success regarding diversity in gifted programs.
- MI theory has formed the basis for general curricular innovations. These materials are increasingly available, but there have been no published accounts of their appropriateness or effectiveness in general education or for the gifted in particular.
- It provides a framework for enhancing learning opportunities for gifted learners in the inclusive classroom. This potential also awaits elaboration and documentation.
- It offers alternative working definitions for giftedness, for example, having a higher level of problem-solving ability in two or more intelligences. Doing so has been shown to be associated with increased minority identification, but the studies have generally lacked controls.

Empirical research in support of affirmative answers is primarily descriptive and heavily weighted toward identification of the gifted students from underserved populations. MI may be a useful tool in general education settings that offers some specific benefit for the student. There has not yet been a controlled evaluation of the effectiveness of the approach.

Most critically, MI is a template, not a curriculum. It guides teachers' decisions at a general level, but even though some programs report children making their own MI profiles, none yet reports students using this knowledge to construct curriculum. This is possible, and research on the outcomes in absolute and comparative terms would be a welcome addition to the literature.

WHAT WE CAN DO

This advice is speculative, because the contribution of MI to gifted education is not clearly established, with one possible exception, namely its association with positive action toward broader ethnic and socioeconomic representation in gifted education. Even if the effect is indirect, MI theory can appropriately guide action in this respect. In addition, the theory is not generating a substantial amount of outcome-based research.

At Home

Multiple intelligences theory is generally more relevant to school than home, but some suggestions can be drawn from it:

 Parents can be sensitized to the existence of different patterns of strengths in different children, thereby broadening the base of their advocacy for their children.

 Thinking in MI terms or in the broad framework can also increase the opportunities for parents to praise and support their children's activities in and out of school. This alone can have a salubrious effect.

MI terminology may not be essential to parents' efforts in this regard, but it can help at meetings and in written materials to provide consistent examples of what it means to celebrate different kinds of successes in different children or at different times in the same child, because as the domains of children's interests change with time, the specific intelligences that best apply may also change.

In the Classroom

This is the most difficult category in which to assess the potential impact of MI theory. Because MI is not primarily a curriculum model, its application may be limited in the classroom but for one major exception:

 By reminding teachers that there is more than one way to excel intellectually, classroom activities such as readings, assignments, tests, and homework can be applied individually to ensure that opportunities are being provided for students to use their various strengths to learn and to flourish in the classroom environment. This impact could be studied directly, and that would be a welcome addition to the literature.

One of the tests of the success of MI as a companion to the curricular process would be that it helps include children and create programs or activities that would not otherwise exist. However, it would be important to evaluate the success not only in terms of MI, but also by external criteria such as Maker's (1982) ideas about depth and breadth of the curriculum; Renzulli's (1977) emphasis on a curiosity-driven component with real audiences, high-level questions, and realistic products; and children' and teachers' co-construction of at least some part of the total curriculum.

At School

School districts in several parts of the U.S. have demonstrated by their actions that MI theory can serve as an inspiration and guide to action in reforming identification practices that increase minority and low-SES representation in gifted programs. The successes have been variable, but theory-driven action is rare in educational policy and should be applauded.

MI has not yet been demonstrated to be as useful a basis for curriculum construction. The most influential current curriculum-reform theory, known as social constructivism, which is based on Piaget's and Vygotsky's concerns that children need to construct their own knowledge under favorable conditions of guidance, has not been incorporated into MI theory. They can be connected, especially through the concerns for ecological validity and links to expert thinking processes. There may, therefore, be limits to the primary impact of MI theory, and it may be appropriate that the initial attention has been given to identification questions. It will be interesting to see if attention is given to defining curriculum-based assessment in a constructivist curriculum and how that might be linked to differential potential. MI theory may then prove more useful, but perhaps more so for the focus on domain specificity. Children construct their knowledge in domains, though some of the processes (e.g., metacognition) are domain-general. MI theory may help schools to focus on what is learned and how it is learned, and reduce the focus on ideas such as IQ and general achievement wherein accomplishments across domains are averaged and blurred.

That MI theory may be useful in this respect is a welcome addition to educational thinking, but it is not unique in creating this focus.

Multiple intelligences theory is extremely articulate, compact, and memorable. This is a useful contribution to enlightening thinking about abilities. It is not, however, a comprehensive theory that links assessment and curriculum development. Neither was it designed as a theory of giftedness. This connection needs to be made by others, and that process has barely begun.

REFERENCES

Baldwin, A. Y. (1994). The seven plus story: Developing hidden talent among students in socioeconomically disadvantaged environments. *Gifted Child Quarterly, 38,* 80–84.

Blythe, T., & Gardner, H. (1990). A school for all intelligences. *Educational Leadership, 47*(7), 33–37.

Carrol, J. B. (1993). *Human cognitive abilities: A survey of factor analytic studies.* New York: Cambridge University Press.

Cattell, R. B. (1971). *Abilities: Their structure, growth and action.* Boston: Houghton-Mifflin.

Fasko, D., Jr. (2001). An analysis of multiple intelligences theory and its use with the gifted and talented. *Roeper Review, 23*, 126–130.

Gardner, H. (1983). *Frames of mind: The theory of multiple intelligences.* New York: BasicBooks.

Gardner, H. (1992). Assessment in context: The alternative to standardized testing. In B. R. Gifford & M. C. O'Conner (Eds.), *Changing assessment: Alternative views of aptitude, achievement, and instruction* (pp. 77–120). Boston: Kluwer.

Gardner, H. (1996). Probing more deeply in the theory of multiple intelligences. *NASSP Bulletin, 80*(583), 1–7.

Gardner, H., & Hatch, T. (1989). Multiple intelligences go to school: Educational implications of the theory of multiple intelligences. *Educational Researcher, 18*(8), 4–9.

Guilford, J. P. (1956). Structure of intellect. *Psychological Bulletin, 53*, 267–293.

Guilford, J. P. (1967). *The nature of human intelligence.* New York: McGraw-Hill.

Guskin, S. L., Peng, C. J., & Simon, M. (1992). Do teachers react to "multiple intelligences"? Effects of teachers' stereotypes on judgments and expectancies for students with diverse patterns of giftedness/talent. *Gifted Child Quarterly, 36*, 32–37.

Hoerr, T. R. (1996). Introducing the theory of multiple intelligences. *NASSP Bulletin, 80*(583), 8–10.

Hudson, L. (1970). *Frames of mind: Ability, perception and self-perception in the arts and sciences.* Harmondsworth, England: Penguin.

Kornhaber, M. (1999). Enhancing equity in gifted education: A framework for examining assessments drawing on the theory of multiple intelligences. *High Ability Studies, 10*, 143–161.

Lockwood, A. T. (1993). Multiple intelligences theory in action. *Research and the Classroom, 4*, 1–12.

Leibowitz, D. G., & Starnes, W. T. (1993). Unmasking young children's gifts. *Gifted Child Today, 16*(5), 28–32.

Maker, C. J. (1982). *Curriculum development for the gifted.* Rockville, MD: Aspen.

Maker, C. J. (1993). Creativity, intelligence, and problem solving: A definition and design for cross-cultural research and measurement related to giftedness. *Gifted Education International, 9*, 68–77.

Matthews, D. (1988). Gardner's multiple intelligence theory: An evaluation of relevant research literature and a consideration of its application to gifted education. *Roeper Review, 11*, 100–104.

Morgan, H. (1996). An analysis of Gardner's theory of multiple intelligences. *Roeper Review, 18*, 263–269.

Morris, C., & Leblanc, R. (1996). Multiple intelligences: Profiling dominant intelligences of grade eight students. *McGill Journal of Education, 31*, 119–141.

Plucker, J. A., Callahan, C. M., & Tomchin, E. M. (1996). Wherefore art thou, multiple intelligences? Alternative assessments for identifying talent in ethnically diverse and low-income students. *Gifted Child Quarterly, 40*, 81–92.

Renzulli, J. S. (1977). *The enrichment triad model: A guide for developing defensible programs for the gifted and talented.* Mansfield Center, CT: Creative Learning Press.

Rogers, J. A. (1998). Refocusing the lens: Using observation to assess and identify gifted learners. *Gifted Education International, 12*, 129–144.

Sarouphim, K. M. (1999). Discovering multiple intelligences through a performance-based assessment: Consistency with independent ratings. *Exceptional Children, 65*, 151–161.

Sternberg, R. J. (1986). A triarchic theory of intellectual giftedness. In R. J. Sternberg & J. E. Davidson (Eds.), *Conceptions of giftedness* (pp. 223–243). Cambridge, England: Cambridge University Press.

Strahan, D., Summey, H., & Bowles, N. (1996). Teaching to diversity through multiple intelligences: Student and teacher responses to instructional improvement. *Research in the Middle Level Education Quarterly, 19*(2), 43–65.

Tomlinson, C. A., Callahan, C. M., & Lelli, K. M. (1997). Challenging expectations: Case studies of high-potential, culturally diverse young children. *Gifted Child Quarterly, 41*, 5–17.

CHAPTER 11

HIGHER LEVEL THINKING

I n teaching for thinking, the concern is not how many answers students know, but what they do when they do not know; the goal is not merely to reproduce knowledge, but to create knowledge and grow in cognitive abilities. These were tenets of the first programs for gifted children, and the field led the way for general education to embrace the agenda of greatly improving the quality of thinking in all children.

WHAT WE KNOW

A thinking skill is a competency that contributes to some type of reasoning, which means that there are thinking skills involved in reading, problem solving, creativity, and all other forms of thinking. It is more than a technical skill or practice; it is one factor upon which good contemplation, study, reflection, examination, resolution, decision, evaluation, appraisal, and other types of reasoning are based (Swartz & Perkins, 1990).

Most thinking skills develop in the first few years of a child's life, which points to the crucial variable of interactions with significant adults, primarily parents, grandparents, older siblings, caregivers, and teachers. Because children's mental development is highly correlated with the complexity of language in their environment, it should not be a surprise to see a decline in development in homes where passive television watching and minimal time for family conversation is the norm (Costa & Lowery, 1989).

Teachers, in particular, shape children's thinking through effective instruction and classroom climate (Coleman & Cross, 2005; Costa & Lowery, 1989). Teachers must have a deep respect for students, listen to them to understand their ideas and thought processes, value their effort to think by allowing time for it, encourage open discussion and active learning, accept errors that will come as thinking experimentation occurs, and give supportive and specific feedback to the students (Udall & Daniels, 1991; VanTassel-Baska, 1994). In this environment and with quality instruction, improvement can be seen in the following broad areas of thinking: awareness (noticing how thinking and resolution feels); effort (investing in the process); attitude (feeling responsible for thinking); organization (learning strategies); subskills (learning the components of skills); and smoothness (making new patterns of thinking more efficient; Swartz & Perkins, 1990, pp. 21–23). Because of the complex merger of these components with an individual's prior knowledge of the topic, general mental capacity, and personality, improving thinking begins at the level of reorganization in the person's mind through the integration of new strategies and then practice.

During the 1970s and 1980s, investigations into the thinking processes of gifted children led to the question of whether instruction in thinking skills was needed. Gifted students appeared to be superior in their thinking, and in fact, it was often that characteristic that prompted identification of a child as gifted (Anderson, 1986; Feldhusen, 1989; Spitz, 1982; Ward, 1979). More recently, attention has been focused on how thinking varies among individuals. Shore and Kanevsky (1993) reported seven ways in which gifted individuals differ in their thinking processes:

- they have more extensive knowledge and use it more effectively;
- they utilize metacognition more efficiently and more often;
- they spend more time on the cognitively complex parts of problem solving and then quickly solve and report solutions;
- they understand problems better especially in terms of commonalties and transfer;
- they employ assumptions that they systematically evaluate;
- they are flexible in choosing strategies and points of view; and
- they enjoy and create complexity and challenge around their tasks (pp. 137–139).

Sternberg and Grigorenko (1993) considered how thinking styles impact the identification of children for gifted programs and the instruction procedures that are employed in those programs—everything from matching styles with the teacher, to benefiting from the components of the programs. Each child responds differently to discussions, independent studies, games, drill, and the like. Sternberg and Grigorenko used the metaphor of mental self-government to explain their theory: The legislative function creates, imagines, and plans; the executive function implements; and the judicial function evaluates. They believed individuals favor one of these functions over the others and that it matters in how thinking develops.

In the last two decades, researchers began to delve into cognitive science and development (Feldman, 1982; Gardner, 1985; Sternberg, 1985), and emphasis was directed to improving curriculum for gifted students through thinking skills. The phrase *higher level thinking* became the hallmark of gifted programs, and moving students into the more advanced skills such as those of Bloom's taxonomy (1956) was the goal. Students were to do less work at the knowledge and comprehension levels, and more at the application, analysis, synthesis, and evaluation levels. Although it was developed for the purpose of classifying teaching objectives and student outcomes, the taxonomy quickly became the basis for gifted programming (Feldhusen, 1994). Leaders in the field of gifted education identified the principles of instruction as including more complex and abstract concept/theme/issues-based curriculum, in-depth investigations, problem solving, decision making, and reflection and understanding of self and the learning process (Clark, 1983; Feldhusen, 1989; Maker, 1982; VanTassel-Baska, 1988). These necessitated more integrative and productive kinds of thinking. Although there is a dearth of research specifying the benefits of thinking skills instruction for gifted students (Shore, Cornell, Robinson, & Ward, 1991; Shore & Kanevsky, 1993), the recommendations for higher level thinking skills were and are still present in virtually every source of curriculum for talented learners.

With the present-day focus in education on standards in all disciplines, the place of higher level thought processes takes on renewed importance. Many of the standards focus on increasing higher order skills for all students. VanTassel-Baska (2003) cautioned educators of the gifted to look carefully at the standards, seeing how broad and deep they are and conscientiously planning for how they will be met by able learners.

Curriculum for Thinking

Believing that thinking can be developed and strengthened, and understanding that advanced level of ability in thinking skills requires high-level instruction, teachers of gifted students choose and create curricula that provide complexity and deep-thinking opportunities. Endorsed instruction for students prescribes infusion of the following broad categories of thinking into daily teaching:

- critical thinking (Ennis, 1985; Winocur & Maurer, 1997);
- creative thinking (Pyryt, 1999; Rostan & Goertz, 1999);
- problem finding (Starko, 1999) and problem solving (Isaksen & Treffinger, 1985);
- metacognition (Swartz & Perkins, 1990);
- domain-specific patterns and forward reasoning (VanTassel-Baska, 1992);
- correlational reasoning (Ross & Smyth, 1995);
- reflective inquiry (Shermis, 1992);
- questioning created for memory, divergence, convergence, aesthetics, and ethics (Thompson, 1996);
- inquiry and investigation (VanTassel-Baska, 2003);
- dialectical thinking skills (Paul, 1990); and
- Socratic discussion (Paul; Thompson, 1996).

Coleman and Cross (2005) wrote that the

> overwhelming majority of teaching methods reported in the literature on gifted education are variations on creativity and problem-solving themes. Their major characteristics involve suspension of judgment, practice in generating responses, and opportunities for children to consider how they think (metacognition). (p. 400)

Evaluating complex thinking processes allows teachers to see how students understand and define problems and how they organize and interpret information. This is not a simple task, and it is one that awaits research and credible instruments (McDaniel, 1994). Different disciplines require different kinds of thinking, and the thinker's level of expertise and maturity complicate the process of understanding children's thinking (Feldhusen, 1998). Teachers who instruct students in these pervasive thinking skills must be able to model their use, as well as convey knowledge about them and measure student responses. Teachers must have appropriate training to understand how children think, and then be taught how to use that wisdom as they plan for their students' learning experiences (Hansen & Feldhusen, 1994; McDaniel; Shore & Kanevsky, 1993).

Because of the complexity of thinking, none of the programs available to teachers is, in and of itself, a complete thinking course for talented learners. It is tempting to purchase one of the hundreds of kits or books of ideas that are advertised to teachers as the formula for teaching thinking skills. The dangers range from reliance on a too-narrow set of thinking skills, to an indefensible stream of disconnected activities that have no longevity for students to use outside of the activity. A balanced approach to thinking instruction includes: (a) thinking and content learned together (thinking does not need to wait until the child has acquired a large base of knowledge about a field); (b) learning about thinking as the students are learning to do thinking ("learning about" teaches metacognitive skills, and "learning to do" teaches the ways of organizing thinking and provides practice); (c) giving students opportunities to become more and more autonomous (teacher introduction, small group work, solo activities); and (d) providing attention to transfer (deliberate awareness and teacher modeling of using strategies in varied contexts; O'Tuel & Bullard 1993; Swartz & Perkins, 1990).

Swartz and Perkins (1990) also recommended three planning methods for teaching thinking: (a) direct instruction of a particular strategy in a noncurricular context; (b) use of a strategy that promotes thinking in a curricular context; and (c) infusion, or restructuring traditional content-area lessons for direct instruction in specific thinking skills. They believed that infusion is the preferable mode, because it helps students develop and integrate effective thinking into both their academic and nonacademic lives. Good thinking development and use of thinking skills cut across all grade levels from kindergarten to graduate school, as well as across all subject areas of instruction. This allows many opportunities for meshing thinking skills materials and programs with the classroom content. Teaching thinking according to a well-articulated, comprehensive plan and effective pedagogical techniques maximizes the students' incorporation of the skills—and habit—into all of their thinking (Renzulli, 1994; VanTassel-Baska, 2003).

Shore and Kanevsky (1993) pointed out the difficulty of "researching" thinking programs and practices for the gifted: The field needs classroom research instead of clinical research. Students and teachers must be observed over time and in varying school and out-of-school settings to discover what is effective. Because of the complexity of the thinking process and the variables that impact the process, short-term studies are not reliable venues for policy statements about what is best for gifted students.

WHAT WE CAN DO

Using what is known from research and practical experience, educators and parents can make a difference in the development of gifted children's thinking skills.

At Home

❧ Adults must model reflective behavior for children. "Think-aloud" modeling that allows children to witness adults' commitment to the processes of good reasoning is powerful, especially when it is done in the home and at school.

❧ A climate of acceptance and respect of children's thinking that opens the possibilities of discussion and idea exploration will show children that thinking is valued.

In the Classroom

ॐ Emphasis in classrooms, with the support of the school administration, should be on rewarding thinking, inquiry, reflection, and the consideration of alternatives in lieu of memorization, drill, reliance on lower level recall, and tight control of content and class work.

ॐ Thinking skills should be taught within a context that is substantial and motivating for students. Teach for transfer to all thinking by the infusion method, across grades and subjects. Do not leave the learning of these skills to chance.

ॐ Students' thinking should be expanded into more complex, higher level mental operations and reasoning by using questions, problems, and conceptual issues. Help students build a strong knowledge and conceptual base from which to develop relationships and connections (VanTassel-Baska, 1998).

ॐ Teachers should become aware of their interaction patterns with students, and seek ways to respond more reflectively and less judgmentally. This requires listening and watching themselves teach (through audio- and videotaping), using self-assessment tools such as a checklist to analyze their teaching (looking for responses that limit or inhibit thinking and those that encourage thinking), and training in the areas as needed.

At School

ॐ Evaluation methods, especially standardized tests, that tap students' ability to think well and productively should be developed. These new instruments for evaluating growth in students' thinking must be integrated into teacher preparation. Rubrics, process measurement, and tests that require students to construct answers rather than recognize them, as well as conduct long-term observations, will provide more information about children's thinking skills.

ॐ Preservice and in-service teachers should have professional preparation in the differences in gifted students' thinking patterns and in defensible, appropriate curriculum differentiation designed to meet those students' needs. Rather than just talking to students about thinking, teachers must actively engage students in thinking in areas such as the writing process, scientific experimentation, reading comprehension and analysis, computation, and study skills.

Practical experience teaches that thinking skills that result in the creation of ideas and intelligent problem solving help gifted students develop their unique abilities. Yet, schools graduate young people who are experts at memorizing and recalling factual information, but who lack proficiency in using that information to make informed judgments. They drive for certainty, are uncomfortable with new problems, and have a need to know the "right answers" from their teachers. Textbooks and classroom resource materials are slow to change.

Teachers must use what they learn about their gifted students from reflective teaching to build a solid, defensible thinking skills curriculum and the climate needed in which to teach it.

References

Anderson, M. A. (1986). Protocol analysis: A methodology for exploring the information processing of gifted students. *Gifted Child Quarterly, 30,* 29–32.

Bloom, B. (Ed.). (1956). *Taxonomy of educational objectives: The classification of educational goals. Handbook I: Cognitive domain.* New York: McKay.

Clark, B. (1983). *Growing up gifted: Developing the potential of children at home and at school.* Columbus, OH: Merrill.

Coleman, L. J., & Cross, T. L. (2005). *Being gifted in school: An introduction to development, guidance, and teaching* (2nd ed.). Waco, TX: Prufrock Press.

Costa, A. L., & Lowery, L. F. (1989). *Techniques for teaching thinking.* Pacific Grove, CA: Midwest.

Ennis, R. H. (1985). A logical basis for measuring critical thinking skills. *Educational Leadership, 43*(2), 44–48.

Feldhusen, J. F. (1989). Thinking skills for the gifted. In J. F. Feldhusen, J. VanTassel-Baska, & K. Seeley (Eds.), *Excellence in educating the gifted* (pp. 239–259). Denver, CO: Love.

Feldhusen, J. F. (1994). Thinking skills and curriculum development. In J. VanTassel-Baska (Ed.), *Comprehensive curriculum for gifted learners* (2nd ed., pp. 301–324). Boston: Allyn & Bacon.

Feldhusen, J. F. (1998). Thinking skills for the gifted. In J. VanTassel-Baska (Ed.), *Excellence in educating gifted and talented learners* (3rd ed., pp. 399–418). Denver, CO: Love.

Feldman, D. H. (1982). A developmental framework for research with gifted children. In D. H. Feldman (Ed.), *Developmental approaches to giftedness and creativity* (pp. 31–45). San Francisco: Jossey-Bass.

Gardner, H. (1985). *The mind's new science: A history of the cognitive revolution.* New York: BasicBooks.

Hansen, J. B., & Feldhusen, J. F. (1994). Comparison of trained and untrained teachers of gifted students. *Gifted Child Quarterly, 38,* 115–121.

Isaksen, S., & Treffinger, D. (1985). *Creative problem solving: The basic course.* Buffalo, NY: Bearly.

Maker, C. J. (1982). *Curriculum development for the gifted.* Rockville, MD: Aspen.

McDaniel, E. (1994). *Understanding educational measurements.* Dubuque, IA: Brown.

O'Tuel, F. S., & Bullard, R. K. (1993). *Developing higher-order thinking in content areas K–12.* Pacific Grove, CA: Critical Thinking Press and Software.

Paul, R. W. (1990). *Critical thinking: What every person needs to survive in a rapidly changing world.* Rohnert Park, CA: Center for Critical Thinking and Moral Critique.

Pyryt, M. C. (1999). Effectiveness of training children's thinking: A meta-analytic review. In A. S. Fishkin, B. Cramond, & P. Olszewski-Kubilius (Eds.), *Investigating creativity in youth: Research and methods* (pp. 351–365). Cresskill, NJ: Hampton Press.

Renzulli, J. S. (1994). *Schools for talent: A practical plan for total school improvement.* Mansfield Center, CT: Creative Learning Press.

Ross, J. A., & Smyth, E. (1995). Thinking skills for gifted students: The case for correlational reasoning. *Roeper Review, 17,* 238–243.

Rostan, S. M., & Goertz, J. (1999). Creators thinking and producing: Toward a developmental approach to the creative process. In A. S. Fishkin, B. Cramond, & P. Olszewski-Kubilius (Eds.), *Investigating creativity in youth: Research and methods* (pp. 97–113). Cresskill, NJ: Hampton Press.

Shermis, S. S. (1992). *Critical thinking: Helping students learn reflectively.* Bloomington, IN: EDINFO Press.

Shore, B. M., Cornell, D. G., Robinson, A., & Ward, V. S. (1991). *Recommended practices in gifted education.* New York: Teachers College Press.

Shore, B. M., & Kanevsky, L. S. (1993). Thinking processes: Being and becoming gifted. In K. A. Heller, F. J. Mönks, & A. H. Passow (Eds.), *International handbook of research and development of giftedness and talent* (pp. 133–147). Oxford, England: Pergamon.

Spitz, H. H. (1982). Intellectual extremes, mental age, and the nature of human intelligence. *Merrill-Palmer Quarterly, 28,* 167–192.

Starko, A. J. (1999). Problem finding: A key to creative productivity. In A. S. Fishkin, B. Cramond, & P. Olszewski-Kubilius (Eds.), *Investigating creativity in youth: Research and methods* (pp. 75–96). Cresskill, NJ: Hampton Press.

Sternberg, R. J. (1985). *Beyond IQ: A triarchic theory of human intelligence.* New York: Cambridge University Press.

Sternberg, R. J., & Grigorenko, E. L. (1993). Thinking styles and the gifted. *Roeper Review, 16,* 122–130.

Swartz, R. J., & Perkins, D. N. (1990). *Teaching thinking: Issues and approaches.* Pacific Grove, CA: Midwest.

Thompson, M. C. (1996). Mentors on paper: How classics develop verbal ability. In J. VanTassel-Baska, D. T. Johnson, & L. N. Boyce (Eds.), *Developing verbal talent: Ideas and strategies for teachers of elementary and middle school students* (pp. 56–74). Boston: Allyn & Bacon.

Udall, A. J., & Daniels, J. E. (1991). *Creating the thoughtful classroom: Strategies to promote student thinking.* Tucson, AZ: Zephyr.

VanTassel-Baska, J. (1988). *Comprehensive curriculum for gifted learners.* Boston: Allyn & Bacon.

VanTassel-Baska, J. (1992). *Planning effective curriculum for gifted learners.* Denver, CO: Love.

VanTassel-Baska, J. (1994). Development and assessment of integrated curriculum: A worthy challenge. *Quest, 5*(2), 1–6.

VanTassel-Baska, J. (Ed.). (1998). *Excellence in educating gifted and talented learners.* Denver, CO: Love.

VanTassel-Baska, J. (2003). *Curriculum planning and instructional design for gifted learners.* Denver, CO: Love.

Ward, M. G. (1979). Differences in the ability levels and growth gains in three higher cognitive processes among gifted and non-gifted students. *Dissertation Abstracts International, 39,* 3960-A.

Winocur, S. L., & Maurer, P. A. (1997). Critical thinking and gifted students: Using IMPACT to improve teaching and learning. In N. Colangelo & G. A. Davis (Eds.), *Handbook of gifted education* (2nd ed., pp. 308–317). Boston: Allyn & Bacon.

CHAPTER 12

INQUIRY-BASED LEARNING AND TEACHING

I n inquiry-based learning, the student plays a major role in defining the content through curiosity-driven questions and in defining the pedagogy needed to actively pursue the answers to these questions. Unfortunately, neither teachers nor students have sufficient experience with authentic inquiry-based learning to make it a common reality in either general education classrooms or specialized experiences for talented students. Well-implemented, inquiry-based learning is applicable to a broad range of students, but the expectations for talented students' accomplishments can be suitably differentiated. The skills involved may best be directly taught and practiced.

WHAT WE KNOW

The majority of empirical research on inquiry-based learning has been at the classroom level, but only occasionally with specific attention to students with high ability. For example,

DiGisi and Willett (1995) surveyed 184 high school biology teachers about their use of text readings with regular and Advanced Placement (AP) students. They then interviewed a representative sample of 16 of these teachers in greater depth. Teachers responded that AP students were more often given texts for independent reading and that they had more independent responsibility for learning from their texts. On the matter of inquiry, however, only the AP students were also shown how to construct new knowledge from the texts. Raudenbush, Rowan, and Cheong (1993) had also noted this differential adaptation by teachers. They sent questionnaires to 303 teachers of 1,205 classes in 16 secondary schools located in Michigan and California. The questionnaires probed the teaching of higher order thinking skills in those classes. Teachers set a greater number of higher order thinking goals for college-bound classes.

Studies of students, rather than teachers, reveal similar results. Moar and Taylor (1995) made an important general point, based on studies of two 11th-grade classrooms in Western Australia having teachers with diverse epistemologies: The teacher whose pedagogical approach promoted inquiry through both personal and social processes of constructing knowledge, in contrast to a direct teaching approach, more successfully engaged students in inquiry. How the two teachers came to differ on this important variable was not discussed, nor is it clear if the students' abilities were directly comparable. Shepardson (1996) examined much younger students, two randomly selected groups of four first-grade children in the same rural Indiana school. Each group of four was teacher-selected to vary by gender, as well as academic and verbal ability. Shepardson showed that teachers taught for understanding in individual children rather than promoting interaction or collaboration among the children, that negotiating and sharing of materials contributed to science learning, and that the heterogeneity of the groups (an icon in some models of cooperative learning) did not result in the negotiation of meaning. In contrast, a very detailed qualitative study of eight highly able fifth-grade students working in groups of four, but more closely matched for ability and comprising two pairs of more assertive and docile children, clearly engaged in both cognitive and social moves related to their cognitive gains (Barfurth, 1994). Barfurth's relatively open-ended task, to design a Lego-LOGO machine that demonstrates the principle of mechanical advantage, may have been more appropriate than the more limited goals set for the younger children. Teachers do, however, clearly establish the academically and socially expected and accepted ways for pupils to interact in learning groups. Student ability differences seem to play a role, but this role is not fully discernible as a result of the designs used.

Similar outcomes have been reported at the college level. King (1995) examined and taught critical thinking skills in her own psychology courses at California State University, San Marcos. Compared to experts in their discipline, college students ask questions that call upon relatively low levels of knowledge and factual understanding unless they are specifically trained to ask thoughtful questions. This training includes two key components: good examples and feedback while practicing. Wineburg (1991) used protocol analysis to examine the process of historical inquiry in eight historians and eight high school students as they evaluated documentary and pictorial evidence. He also concluded that the high school students were able to learn many facts as well as the experts, but did not wonder about discrepancies or attempt to match different kinds of evidence, and sometimes extrapolated beyond the evidence; they did not understand how new historical knowledge is constructed. Unlike King, who demonstrated that training could change the performance, Wineburg only speculated about the impact of training in asking questions.

Inquiry With Talented Learners

The gifted education literature has begun to pose similar questions. The best-known example of an inquiry-based learning context in gifted education is probably a Type III Enrichment Triad Model activity as enunciated and developed by Renzulli (1977). The literature on Type III activities is extensive, and it is dominated by prescriptive and descriptive studies. As a corpus of work, however, it shows rather convincingly that highly able students exposed to such curricular options enjoy them and produce some remarkable products (cf. Baum, Renzulli, & Hébert, 1995). Lest anyone anticipate, however, that Type III forms of inquiry experiences abound in schools, it needs to be recalled that a massive national survey of nearly 3,400 regular classroom teachers conducted by the National Research Center on the Gifted and Talented found that, at best, only minor changes to the regular curriculum were occasionally made to accommodate the needs of highly able pupils (Archambault et al., 1993), and Type III adaptations are much rarer than Type I or other general enrichment activities.

Nonetheless, when given the opportunity, gifted students are able to engage in inquiry-driven learning in a variety of subjects ranging from art (Kay, 1994) to social studies, as well as the more often studied science cited in the general literature. In Cramond, Martin, and Shaw (1990), two groups of school-identified gifted children were trained either in a Creative Problem Solving control group (n = 28) in which memory training skills were added, or in which specific transfer skills were incorporated (n = 25). The inquiry-related transfer skills generalized across domains. Kaniel and Reichenberg (1992) worked with 140 talented and culturally disadvantaged 10- to 12-year-old children in Israel, all of whom were academically underachieving. Half received training in Feuerstein's Instrumental Enrichment (IE), plus metacognition and other thinking training. Half learned only the IE programming. The group that also received higher order thinking skills training generalized these skills to verbal and nonverbal tasks, but, strangely, not immediately to school performance. Four years later, this group's school performance was also enhanced. The reasons for the delay were not explored, but this does suggest the need for patience in awaiting educational benefits. Gallagher and Stepien (1996) countered a frequently expressed fear that children who engage in inquiry will miss basic content. Their study of 167 sophomores at an Illinois state residential secondary school for mathematically and scientifically gifted students found that students whose instruction was initiated with an ill-structured problem and continued with significant student control of the content and pace of instruction did just as well on basic information as gifted pupils in more conventional, expository programs. Friedman and Lee (1996) studied seven small-city Kansas teachers of 137 children in grades 4 and 5. None of the teachers had more than a single-day workshop exposure to gifted education as such, but all had been assigned identified gifted children to their classrooms. The teachers were given further coaching in three gifted education models (including the Enrichment Triad), but the differences among these were overshadowed by the importance of specific, focused instruction on how to pose high-level questions in order to develop students' questioning techniques. These studies, and others like them, clearly demonstrated that talented learners can be directly equipped with component skills that favor inquiry-based leaning. None of these studies, however, explicitly included a nongifted control group nor investigated if or how this situation might be different for children of average ability.

In a larger study with a similar sample, Hansen and Feldhusen (1994) found results similar to those reported in the general education literature for the importance of training. They compared 54 gifted education teachers who had three to five courses in gifted education to those without such training but who also had responsibility for gifted pupils. Trained teachers created more opportunities for gifted children to determine their learning activities and to exercise self-direction. Because the teachers were included in the study on the basis of their having been trained in gifted education or not, there is a risk that teachers predisposed to inquiry-favorable relationships with pupils may seek gifted education training. It seems fair to agree that teachers make a difference, but the impact of specific independent variables needs more controlled examination. The same applies to the study by Baum et al. (1995) that closely followed the work of 12 Enrichment Triad trained teachers with 17 gifted underachieving students aged 8–13 who were doing Type III projects. Once again, the students developed worthy projects, but it is not possible to conclude whether the positive outcome is the result of their ability, their having been congregated for instruction, the specific actions of the teachers, or the content of the instruction; the authors fully acknowledged this limitation. It was also not clear how much explicit training the students had in asking questions.

A key unanswered question remains whether or not inquiry-based learning is in any way uniquely appropriate to high-ability students. Two empirical studies gave contradictory preliminary answers to this question. Meador (1994) found that training in synectics, using analogies to make original connections among apparently unrelated ideas, and helping students to value their own ideas (as opposed to textbooks or teachers as primary authorities—cf. Gabella, 1994, who has examined this authority question among older pupils) helped 107 gifted and nongifted Texas kindergarten pupils to ask higher level questions. From this, we might expect the evidence to swing toward a nonspecific outcome with respect to ability. On the other hand, Roberts, Ingram, and Harris (1992) showed that higher order cognitive processes were most enhanced in gifted Utah pupils in grades 3–5 who received special programming consisting of the Schoolwide Enrichment Model (cf. Renzulli & Reis, 1985), Triad activity Types I and II, creative problem solving, and independent research. The contrasts included less able pupils (*n* = 56) in both of the special programs and high-ability pupils (*n* = 30) in regular schools. Roberts et al. acknowledged the still partly unexplained contribution of merely bringing the more able pupils together. An issue they did not address was the appropriateness of the special programming. Renzulli Type I and II activities are generally given to the whole class (as noted explicitly by Friedman & Lee, 1996), and unmodified creative problem solving, without additional transfer components, was not effective for Cramond et al. (1990). The remaining element of their program was training in independent research. The conclusion then returns to a very straightforward one implied elsewhere: In order to get students to do independent research, teach them to do independent research; this objective may be especially appropriate to highly able pupils. The remaining uncertainty arises from the Roberts et al. criterion measure, the Ross Test of Higher Cognitive Processes, rather than a performance outcome with higher ecological validity, such as an independent research project as used by Baum et al. (1995).

In addition, no study to date fully answers the important "chicken and egg" question. Do the students respond differently because they are taught differently, or are they taught differently because they perform differently? And, where they are taught differently, how has this come about? This dilemma may require study of inquiry in a general education setting where the teacher and program are blind to the abilities of the children, and these abilities should then be examined in retrospect. One hint, but just a hint, comes from a study by Moss (1990), who found that mothers of 2- and 3-year-olds who scored high on a preschool intelligence test were more likely to guide and question their children through puzzle and construction tasks (e.g., asking what they'd like to build or asking how the child might decide that pieces fit together) than to prompt them directly toward solutions (e.g., suggesting what to build, or saying to look for matching colored edges). Cause and effect are thoroughly entwined, but the prospect that the shape of early parental interaction could create precursors for inquiry is ideal for a longitudinal follow-up study.

WHAT WE CAN DO

Research on inquiry-based learning so far points to its being effective in classrooms across ability levels to varying degrees, and that it can be taught by teachers experienced in teaching students to ask inquiry-related questions and facilitating their small group interaction. Inquiry-driven learning is not the unique domain of gifted pupils, but it is likely that there will be qualitative differences in the outcomes, and that inquiry can be given special expression in differentiated programming for highly able pupils. The precise nature of this differentiation remains to be determined.

At Home

❧ None of the research so far published connects inquiry-based learning at school in relation to home experience. The fact that some of the studies found differences as young as kindergarten, however, suggests that home experiences can play an important preparatory role. At this point, it is a matter for research waiting to be done, but children who are given the opportunity to make choices in daily events in their lives, who are asked for input on family decisions, and whose inquisitiveness is encouraged rather than suppressed may, at home and in school, be at an advantage in an inquiry-based curriculum.

In the Classroom

❧ A defensible hypothesis at this point may well be that students need to be directly taught the specific components of inquiry-based learning—from asking high-level and interesting questions, to valuing their own judgments, to criticizing arguments, to presenting reports—and given practice in bringing these components together.

❧ Research reported to date has not adequately addressed the extent to which teachers need specific training and experience in inquiry-based learning before they can engage effectively in inquiry-based teaching. The success of Type III activities, however small in relative numbers, points to the possibility of eventually bringing closure to this question. Working in a computer environment for data presentation with students in grades 5, 6, and 8, as well as their teachers, Hancock, Kaput, and Goldsmith (1992) have identified a need for both teachers and students to acquire and practice defining problems, negotiating priorities, synthesizing findings, resolving contradictions, and monitoring data for relevance, and surmised that it may take years to master these skills. Such an outcome would not be a surprise to university doctoral program supervisors.

At School

❧ Schoolwide decisions can clearly affect the opportunity for inquiry-based learning in the classroom, but this too is more an issue of educated guessing than the outcome of specific study. Many schools adopt educational missions that affect the overall curriculum, and nearly every major curricular reform initiative in the past decade, from mathematics, to social studies and language arts, to science, has stressed the central nature of inquiry. The same is true across levels from the youngest learners to university students. It is not generally happening, and very few teachers-in-training, not alone among other university students, have experienced a true inquiry experience in their educational histories (Aulls & Luconi, 1997). The role of educational leadership and teachers' prior experience is only beginning to be explored. The general and gifted literatures show a high concordance on what works when it is implemented, but so far it is rarely implemented.

References

Archambault, F. X., Jr., Westberg, K. L., Brown, S. W., Hallmark, B. W., Emmons, C. L., & Zhang, W. (1993). *Regular classroom practices with gifted students: Results of a national survey of classroom teachers* (Research Report No. 93101). Storrs: National Research Center on the Gifted and Talented, University of Connecticut.

Aulls, M. W., & Luconi, F. (1997, May). *Participation in inquiry instruction: Pre-service teachers' exposure to inquiry instruction and beliefs about the nature of inquiry and who can successfully participate in it.* Paper presented at the midyear meeting of the National Association for Gifted Children, Montreal, QC, Canada.

Barfurth, M. A. (1994). *The collaborative process as seen through children's disagreements while learning science.* Unpublished doctoral dissertation, McGill University, Montreal, QC, Canada.

Baum, S. M., Renzulli, J. S., & Hébert, T. P. (1995) Reversing underachievement: Creative productivity as a systematic intervention. *Gifted Child Quarterly, 39,* 224–235.

Cramond, B., Martin, C. E., & Shaw, E. L. (1990). Generalizability of creative problem solving procedures to real life problems. *Journal for the Education of the Gifted, 13,* 141–155.

DiGisi, L. L., & Willett, J. B. (1995). What high school biology teachers say about their textbook use: A descriptive study. *Journal of Research in Science Teaching, 32,* 123–142.

Friedman, R. C., & Lee, S. W. (1996). Differentiating instruction for high-achieving/ gifted children in regular classrooms: A field test of three gifted education models. *Journal for the Education of the Gifted, 19,* 405–436.

Gabella, M. S. (1994). Beyond the looking glass: Bringing students into the conversation of historical inquiry. *Theory and Research in Social Education, 22,* 340–363.

Gallagher, S. A., & Stepien, W. J. (1996). Content acquisition in problem-based learning: Depth versus breadth in American studies. *Journal for the Education of the Gifted, 19,* 257–275.

Hancock, C., Kaput, J. J., & Goldsmith, L. T. (1992). Authentic inquiry with data: Critical barriers to classroom implementation. *Educational Psychologist, 27,* 337–364.

Hansen, J. B., & Feldhusen, J. F. (1994). Comparison of trained and untrained teachers of gifted students. *Gifted Child Quarterly, 19,* 115–123.

Kay, S. (1994). From theory to practice: Promoting problem-finding behavior in children. *Roeper Review, 16,* 195–197.

Kaniel, S., & Reichenberg, R. (1992). Instrumental enrichment: Effects of generalization and durability with talented adolescents. *Gifted Education International, 8,* 128–135.

King, A. (1995). Designing the instructional process to enhance critical thinking across the curriculum. Inquiring minds really do want to know: Using questions to teach critical thinking. *Teaching of Psychology, 22,* 13–17.

Meador, K. S. (1994). The effect of synectics training on gifted and nongifted kindergarten students. *Journal for the Education of the Gifted, 18,* 55–73.

Moar, D., & Taylor, P. C. (1995). Teacher epistemology and scientific inquiry in computerized classroom environments. *Journal of Research in Science Teaching, 32,* 839–854.

Moss, E. B. (1990). Social interaction and metacognitive development in gifted preschoolers. *Gifted Child Quarterly, 34,* 16–20.

Raudenbush, S. W., Rowan, B., & Cheong, Y. F. (1993). Higher order instructional goals in secondary schools: Class, teacher, and school influences. *American Educational Research Journal, 30,* 523–553.

Renzulli, J. S. (1977). *The enrichment triad model: A guide for defensible programs for the gifted and talented.* Mansfield Center, CT: Creative Learning Press.

Renzulli, J. S., & Reis, S. M. (1985). *The Schoolwide Enrichment Model: A comprehensive plan for educational excellence.* Mansfield Center, CT: Creative Learning Press.

Roberts, C., Ingram, C., & Harris, C. (1992). The effects of special versus regular classroom programming on higher cognitive processes of intermediate elementary aged gifted and average ability students. *Journal for the Education of the Gifted, 15,* 332–343.

Shepardson, D. P. (1996). Social interactions and the mediation of science learning in two small groups of first graders. *Journal of Research in Science Teaching, 33,* 159–178.

Wineburg, S. S. (1991). History problem solving: A study of the cognitive processes used in the evaluation of documentary and pictorial evidence. *Journal of Educational Psychology, 83,* 73–87.

CHAPTER 13

COMPACTING THE CURRICULUM

A s much as 50% of the general curriculum can be eliminated for high-ability elementary students in the regular classroom with no differences in achievement test scores in reading, mathematics concepts, and social studies, even when students are tested at one grade level above class placement. When provided with professional development, teachers accurately can identify students whose curriculum should be compacted and report a willingness to engage in the strategy, although they also acknowledge a lack of time to prepare appropriate instructional material.

WHAT WE KNOW

Whether it is called curriculum compacting (Renzulli, Smith, & Reis, 1982), diagnostic-prescriptive instruction (Stanley, 1978), or compression of content (VanTassel-Baska, 1989), the intent of the strategy, instructional technique, or curricular process is the same. The idea is to assess high-ability students' knowledge and skill development in particular content areas prior to instruction, to identify what they already know and can do, and to provide them with instruction and curricula that meets their academic needs. Especially for high-ability students in heterogeneous classrooms, compacting alters the curricula to avoid rehashing already mastered material.

A major component in curriculum compacting is pretesting or preassessment. It is essential that the pretest materials reflect the goals and objectives regarding the skills and content to be mastered during instruction. Teachers need to be cognizant of those goals and objectives in order to select or develop pretest materials matched to the curriculum being considered for compacting. Another vital component is prescription for instruction in areas still to be developed or mastered, but at a rate and with curricular experiences more appropriate to the high-ability learner. For students, the benefits of compacting include time and opportunity for acceleration and enrichment activities such as free reading or alternative reading assignments, projects, and math puzzles and problems (Reis & Purcell, 1993).

The Need for Compacting

In studies reported by Archambault and colleagues (1993), Reis and Purcell (1993), and Reis and Westberg (1994), high-ability students are served primarily in heterogeneous classrooms, especially at the elementary and middle school levels. Serving them in this setting presents a challenge (VanTassel-Baska & Stambaugh, 2005). They largely spend a good deal of their school year practicing skills they have already mastered, reviewing content they already know, or reading materials insufficient to challenge them; little is done to differentiate their instructional experience (Archambault et al.). Reis and Purcell supplied a list of experts decrying the lack of challenge in textbooks in general and in specific content areas such as reading (Chall & Conrad, 1991) and mathematics (Usiskin, 1987). In addition to the lack of challenging textbooks, evidence also suggests that many learners already know what they are being taught. For example, Taylor and Frye (1988) reported that 78–88% of fifth- and sixth-grade average and above-average readers passed the pretests before they encountered the skill development activities in the basal reader. Both of these examples—textbook limitations and prior achievement—are of concern in general, but especially for academically advanced students in the heterogeneous, traditional classroom. Reliance on textbooks is common in such settings, and presenting students with information they already know or skills they already have is a waste of time. Compacting—the elimination of already mastered material—is one aspect of what should be a comprehensive set of services for high-ability students, including culturally diverse high-ability learners (Renzulli & Reis, 2004).

Student Achievement

The question on the minds of teachers, administrators, and parents may be, "How does curriculum compacting affect achievement?" Reis and her colleagues (1998) noted that one of the reasons teachers may be unwilling to compact is their fear that students whose curriculum is compacted are at risk for doing poorly on state accountability tests or standardized achievement batteries. The effects of compacting on student achievement were investigated in a study of 436 students in grades 2–6 (Reis et al., 1998). Using out-of-level testing with the Iowa Tests of Basic Skills, the authors reported that students' achievement test scores did not suffer in comparison with an equally able group of students whose curriculum was not compacted. The results were consistent for mathematics, reading, and social studies. The authors noted that even though 40–50% of the curriculum was eliminated for these students, the high-ability learners still maintained their high end-of-year scores. Specifically, the median percentile in the mathematics concepts and in the reading subtests was 93 on an out-of-level test. In other words, the high-ability elementary students whose curriculum was compacted scored as well as equally academically talented students served by the traditional grade-level curriculum. Parents, teachers, and school administrators should not fear a drop in achievement if the elementary curriculum is compacted for a high-ability learner.

Teacher Skill in Compacting

Teachers can identify students in need of curriculum compacting with proper training. Reis and Purcell (1993) reported that 95% of a sample of teachers who received professional development in compacting were able to select high-achieving students in need of the strategy. Teachers also understand what curriculum needs to be compacted and tend to compact most frequently in mathematics and language arts (Reis & Purcell; Reis & Westberg, 1994). In two related studies of teachers from 27 and 20 school districts, respectively, researchers reported that elementary teachers were able to eliminate "between 24–70% of the curriculum across content areas for more capable students" (Reis & Purcell, p. 147) and on average "between 42% and 57% of the content for the high-ability students they selected" (Reis & Westberg, p. 127). Stamps (2004) partially replicated the national compacting study on a smaller scale with four randomly selected classrooms of first-grade students in two schools. She found that teachers who received professional development and the support of a gifted resource room teacher compacted for students and reported that they would continue to do so in the future. Reis and Purcell investigated the strategies teachers used to eliminate content and found that teachers tended to compact at the unit level rather than in larger blocks of time such as grading periods or semesters. In this regard, the strategies of teachers implementing curriculum compacting with enrichment replacement activities may differ from the diagnostic-prescriptive instruction approach conceptualized by Stanley, which emphasizes preassessment to identify specific gaps in student learning and individually tailors instruction to move students ahead in semester or course blocks (Brody & Mills, 2005; Stanley, 1978).

The challenge of compacting may not be in identifying what should be compacted, but rather what to do with the released time and how to manage it. In studies reported by Reis and Purcell (1993) and Reis and Westberg (1994), teachers with the most intensive professional development, including peer coaching, provided the most opportunities for compacting. In terms of the quality of the forms used to document the process, teachers who received the staff development treatment that included peer coaching produced more elaborated plans and more replacement strategies to meet the needs of their students than did teachers with less intensive support. In general, teachers who engaged in compacting report their greatest frustrations were finding appropriate replacement materials and the time to plan for meeting individual needs. They were also concerned about the logistics of implementing and managing the compacting process.

WHAT WE CAN DO

In the Classroom

ಶ Allay the fears of parents and school personnel who worry that compacting may adversely affect high-ability students' performance on high-stakes tests. Elementary students whose curriculum has been compacted do not lose ground.

ಶ Classroom teachers need continuous support from peer coaches to implement and sustain curriculum compacting.

ಶ Classroom teachers need continuous support from professional staff such as reading and mathematics specialists and gifted resource personnel who are able to provide replacement materials and curricular guidance.

ಶ Classroom teachers need time to locate or to develop replacement activities for individual students. Administrators should carve out time for their faculty to engage in such curricular work.

ಶ Classroom teachers need alternative materials for replacement activities, and administrators should allocate instructional dollars to acquire such materials.

At School

🙢 Because compacting can move students ahead in the curriculum, schools should adopt policies that permit students and teachers access to materials from advanced grade levels.

There is research to indicate the value of professional development regarding curriculum compacting in the elementary grades. Teachers are successful at identifying students who need compacting, and they are willing to engage in the practice. In terms of student effects, the single large-scale national study on compacting indicates students lose no ground on measures of achievement (Reis et al., 1998). There is also evidence that when embedded in a comprehensive set of services, compacting contributes to improved attitudes toward learning for elementary learners because it creates time for students to pursue self-selected interests (Olenchak, 1990). We can hypothesize that if students who have already mastered content knowledge and skills are not required to review it repeatedly, they will be more involved and fulfilled learners.

REFERENCES

Archambault, F. X., Westberg, K. L., Brown, S., Hallmark, B. W., Zhang, W., & Emmons, C. (1993). Regular classroom practices with gifted students: Findings from the classroom practices survey. *Journal for the Education of the Gifted, 16,* 103–119.

Brody, L. E., & Mills, C. J. (2005). Talent search research: What have we learned? *High Ability Studies, 16*(1), 97–111.

Chall, J. S., & Conrad, S. S. (1991). *Should textbooks challenge students? The case for easier or harder textbooks.* New York: Teachers College Press.

Olenchak, F. R. (1990). School change through gifted education: Effects on elementary students' attitudes toward learning. *Journal for the Education of the Gifted, 14,* 66–78.

Reis, S. M., & Purcell, J. (1993). An analysis of content elimination and strategies used by elementary classroom teachers in the curriculum compacting process. *Journal for the Education of the Gifted, 16,* 147–170.

Reis, S. M., & Westberg, K. L. (1994). The impact of staff development on teachers' ability to modify curriculum for gifted and talented students. *Gifted Child Quarterly, 38,* 125–135.

Reis, S. M., Westberg, K. L., Kulikowich, J. M., & Purcell, J. H. (1998). Curriculum compacting and achievement test scores: What does the research say? *Gifted Child Quarterly, 42,* 123–129.

Renzulli, J. S., & Reis, S. M. (2004). Curriculum compacting: A research-based differentiation strategy for culturally diverse talented students. In D. Boothe & J. C. Stanley (Eds.), *In the eyes of the beholder: Critical issues for diversity in gifted education* (pp. 87–100). Waco, TX: Prufrock.

Renzulli, J. S., Smith, L., & Reis, S. M. (1982). Curriculum compacting: An essential strategy for working with gifted students. *The Elementary School Journal, 82*, 185–194.

Stamps, L. S. (2004). The effectiveness of curriculum compacting in first grade classrooms. *Roeper Review, 27*, 31–42.

Stanley, J. C. (1978). SMPY's DT-PI mentor model: Diagnostic testing followed by prescriptive instruction. *Intellectually Talented Youth Bulletin, 4*(10), 7–8.

Taylor, B. M., & Frye, B. J. (1988). Pretesting: Minimize time spent on skill work for the intermediate readers. *The Reading Teacher, 42*, 100–103.

Usiskin, Z. (1987). Why elementary algebra can, should and must be an eighth-grade course for average students. *Mathematics Teacher, 80*, 428–438.

VanTassel-Baska, J. (1989). Appropriate curriculum for the gifted. In J. F. Feldhusen, J. VanTassel-Baska, & K. Seeley (Eds.), *Excellence in educating the gifted* (pp. 175–191). Denver, CO: Love.

VanTassel-Baska, J., & Stambaugh, T. (2005). Challenges and possibilities for serving gifted learners in the regular classroom. *Theory Into Practice, 44*, 211–217.

CHAPTER 14

FLEXIBLE GROUPING

F lexible grouping of students within elementary classrooms promotes achievement, especially in mathematics and reading. The achievement effects are positive for high-ability students, as well as average and low-achieving students. Cross-graded grouping in reading (often called the Joplin Plan) is also effective in promoting achievement. Other kinds of flexible grouping such as pull-out programs for talented children, cooperative learning in the heterogeneous classroom, and cluster grouping of talented students in a grade-level classroom show differing effects depending upon the classroom context and the curriculum accompanying the grouping strategy. Schools that group by ability between classes display a range of adaptations but tend to make decisions based on prior achievement in a particular school subject rather than on general ability.

WHAT WE KNOW

Few instructional practices generate more discussion than grouping. Some studies have produced some consistent patterns, but others are frequently ambiguous and influenced by the historical period in which the study took place (Kulik, 1992). In many of the studies, high-ability or high-achieving students are not the focus of concern; however, there are points of agreement among various reviews (Kulik & Kulik, 1992; Loveless, 1998; Rogers, 1991; Slavin, 1987). These areas of agreement are the basis for current best practices.

Flexible Grouping in the Elementary Classroom

As reported in meta-analyses from multiple authors (Kulik & Kulik, 1991; Rogers, 1991; Slavin, 1987), within-class grouping of students in elementary classrooms results in higher achievement than whole-class instruction in the heterogeneous classroom. Loveless (1998) compared the effect sizes for the Kulik and Slavin meta-analyses and found that both reported increased achievement for all students whether they are high-, medium-, or low-achieving in the within-class grouping pattern. In the comparative summary provided by Loveless, the effect size reported by the Kuliks was +.30 for high-achieving students, + .18 for medium-achieving students, and +.26 for low-achieving students. The overall size of the effect reported by the Kuliks for this type of flexible grouping was +.25. The effect size reported by Slavin (1987) was +.41 for high-achieving students, +.27 for medium achieving students, and +.65 for low-achieving students. The overall size of the effect reported by Slavin (1987) for this type of flexible grouping was +.34. Within-class grouping is generally done in reading and mathematics; these are the school subjects for which most research exists. Studies also tend to focus on the upper elementary grades, although there are investigations of flexible within-class grouping as early as second grade and as late as eighth grade.

In a study of grouping practices on mathematics achievement of students in grades 4 and 5, Tieso (2005) found that within-class grouping with curricular adjustments resulted in higher achievement for high- and middle-achieving learners with no differences for low achievers. Her study compared students in traditional whole-group textbook instruction, whole-group instruction with revised and upgraded curriculum, a between-class Joplin plan with a revised and upgraded curriculum, and within-class flexible grouping with a revised and upgraded curriculum. The upgraded curriculum produced positive benefits for all students; the upgraded curriculum implemented with flexible small groups resulted in the greatest achievement gains for all groups with effect sizes ranging from +.29 to +.83. Tieso's results for the Joplin Plan grouping pattern were less positive than the flexible within-class groups, but still effective for high- and middle-achieving students. Previous research on Joplin Plan grouping has been generally favorable for all groups of students, and Tieso hypothesized that implementation problems and erratic schedules for the Joplin treatment may have affected the results.

The Joplin Plan in Elementary and Middle Grades

The Joplin Plan, named after Joplin, MO, where it was devised, focuses on reading. Students are regrouped on the basis of their reading level for reading instruction. Sometimes the regrouping occurs across three to five grade levels and includes as many as nine different reading level groups. After instruction in the flexibly grouped setting, students return to their homerooms and participate in approximately half an hour of free reading. Classrooms are stocked with a variety of reading materials, and students are able to choose whatever they wish to read. As with within-class grouping, research on the Joplin Plan is more prevalent at the upper elementary and middle school grades (see Kulik, 1992, Table 3, p. 29). However, studies also include learners in primary grades and last from 1 to 3 years in duration. Kulik reported a median effect size of +.30, and Slavin (1987) reported +.45.

Other Flexible Grouping Plans

Other flexible grouping plans that have been used with talented students include pull-out enrichment grouping patterns in which students are grouped outside the classroom for time periods ranging from one half hour a week to one day per month and within-class models such as cooperative learning and cluster grouping in the heterogeneous classroom. In a comparison of programs that varied by grouping arrangements, Delcourt, Lloyd, Cornell, and Goldbert (1994) found that achievement levels for talented children in grades 2 and 3 were higher in pull-out grouping arrangements when compared with within-class models and with children who had no services. Achievement was assessed with the Iowa Tests of Basic Skills. Vaughn, Feldhusen, and Asher (1991) also reported favorable results for the pull-out grouping arrangement in a meta-analysis of a small number of controlled studies investigating this type of grouping arrangement. The outcomes were achievement, critical thinking, creative thinking, and self-concept measures; individual studies assessed some, but not all of the outcomes. When combined, the large-scale comparative study by Delcourt and her colleagues and the meta-analysis by Vaughn and her colleagues indicated that pull-out grouping arrangements result in higher achievement and do not result in lowered self-esteem.

Cooperative learning is also a form of within-class grouping recommended for talented students (Slavin, 1990a). In the heterogeneous classroom, groups are formed by pairing or grouping three to five students of varying abilities to accomplish a common task. A key feature of cooperative learning is a group goal; advocates differ on the ways to implement a reward structure (Johnson

& Johnson, 1992; Slavin, 1990b). Talented students are rarely the focus of concern in cooperative learning research; however, some patterns emerge that can guide practice (Robinson, 1990, 2003). Some studies that analyzed for ability differences reported that high-ability learners performed better in homogeneous groups (Fuchs, Fuchs, Hamlett, & Karns, 1998) or achieve similarly on common tasks, but accomplish more tasks when grouped with other high-ability learners (Kenny, Archambault, & Hallmark, 1995). Students respond differently to cooperative grouping and can withdraw and become passive, thereby relinquishing their opportunity to learn (Mulryan, 1992). The nature of the task, as well as the partner, influenced high-ability learners working on complex mathematics (Diezmann & Watters, 2001). Finally, middle school educators report widespread use of cooperative learning and believe it to meet the needs of high-ability learners, but do not necessarily implement its features with fidelity (Moon, Tomlinson, & Callahan, 1995). Particularly at risk for implementation are the features of individual accountability that reduce free-rider effects (Antil, Jenkins, Wayne, & Vadasy, 1998). As a grouping pattern, cooperative learning should be monitored for overuse with high-ability learners and for faithful implementation.

Finally, two studies have investigated cluster grouping in which 3–10 high-ability learners are placed in a grade-level classroom with a teacher trained to differentiate curriculum to meet their needs. The research is limited, but Gentry and Owen (1999) found that cluster grouping, when combined with regrouping for reading, improved reading achievement for students in grades 3–5. Qualitative data from Gentry and Owen and a survey study by Hoover, Sayler, and Feldhusen (1993) indicate that teachers believe that cluster grouping benefits high-ability learners and grade-level students.

WHAT WE CAN DO

In the Classroom

❧ Adopt flexible within-class grouping for reading and mathematics instruction at the elementary level. For maximum achievement effects, the grouping should be accompanied by adapting curriculum and instruction to student needs (Tieso, 2005).

❧ Adopt cross-grade grouping reading programs like the Joplin Plan in the elementary and early middle school grades.

❧ Use cooperative learning with caution. Reports of student perceptions of unfairness (Clinkenbeard, 1991, Matthews, 1992), fears of free-rider effects, and individual differences in response to cooperative learning (Mulryan, 1992) should be monitored. For complex mathematics problems, cooperative learning in homogeneous dyads is preferable for high-ability learners (Fuchs et al., 1998).

At School

∂♥ Be wary of policies that disband advanced curricular opportunities. A better strategy is to retain them and offer support so that greater numbers of students may participate in them (Epstein & MacIver, 1992). Rogers and Span (1993) have crafted guidelines for the use of various flexible grouping arrangements with high-ability learners.

The political debates surrounding grouping are long-standing and frequently heated. Adopting federal, state, or even district-wide policies is unlikely to address the day-to-day educational concerns of parents, teachers and administrators. Because grouping decisions are affected by subject matter, as well as classroom and school characteristics, broad policies are interpreted and implemented differently by schools. It is possible for several grouping patterns to coexist in a single elementary, middle, or high school building (Loveless, 1999).

REFERENCES

Antil, L. R., Jenkins, J. R., Wayne, S. K., & Vadasy, P. F. (1998). Cooperative learning: Prevalence, conceptualizations, and the relation between research and practice. *American Educational Research Journal, 35*, 419–454.

Clinkenbeard, P. R. (1991). Unfair expectations: A pilot study of middle school students' comparison of gifted and regular classes. *Journal for the Education of the Gifted, 15*, 56–63.

Delcourt, M. A. B., Lloyd, B. H., Cornell, D. G., & Goldbert, M. D. (1994). *Evaluation of the effects of programming arrangements on student learning outcomes* (Monograph No. 94018). Storrs: National Research Center on the Gifted and Talented, University of Connecticut.

Diezmann, C. M., & Watters, J. J. (2001). The collaboration of mathematically gifted students on challenging tasks. *Journal for the Education of the Gifted, 25*, 7–31.

Epstein, J. L., & MacIver, D. J. (1992). *Opportunities to learn: Effects on eighth graders of curriculum offerings and instructional approaches* (Report No. 34). Baltimore: Center for Research on Elementary and Middle Schools.

Fuchs, L. S., Fuchs, D., Hamlett, C. L., & Karns, K. (1998). High-achieving students' interactions and performance on complex mathematical tasks as a function of homogeneous and heterogeneous pairings. *American Educational Research Journal, 35*, 227–267.

Gentry, M., & Owen, S. V. (1999). An investigation of the effects of total school flexible cluster grouping on identification, achievement, and classroom practices. *Gifted Child Quarterly, 43*, 224–243.

Hoover, S., Sayler, M., & Feldhusen, J. F. (1993). Cluster grouping of elementary students at the elementary level. *Roeper Review, 16*, 13–15.

Johnson, D. W., & Johnson, R. T. (1992). Positive interdependence: Key to effective cooperation. In R. Hertz-Lazarowitz & N. Miller (Eds.), *Interaction in coopera-*

tive groups: The theoretical anatomy of group learning (pp. 174–199). New York: Cambridge University Press.

Kenny, D. A., Archambault, F. X., & Hallmark, B. W. (1995). *The effects of group composition on gifted and talented elementary students in cooperative learning groups.* Storrs: National Research Center on the Gifted and Talented, University of Connecticut.

Kulik, J. A. (1992). *An analysis of the research on ability grouping: Historical and contemporary perspectives* (Research Monograph No. 9204). Storrs: National Research Center on the Gifted and Talented, University of Connecticut.

Kulik, J. A., & Kulik, C.-L. C. (1991). Ability grouping and gifted students. In N. Colangelo & G. A. Davis (Eds.), *Handbook of gifted education* (pp. 178–196). Boston: Allyn & Bacon.

Kulik, J. A., & Kulik, C.-L. C. (1992). Meta-analytic findings on grouping programs. *Gifted Child Quarterly, 36,* 73–77.

Loveless, T. (1998). *The tracking and ability grouping debate.* Washington, DC: Thomas B. Fordham Foundation. (ERIC Document Reproduction Service No. ED422445)

Loveless, T. (1999). *The tracking wars: State reform meets school policy.* Washington, DC: Brookings Institution Press.

Matthews, M. (1992). Gifted students talk about cooperative learning. *Educational Leadership, 50*(2), 48–50.

Moon, T. R., Tomlinson, C. A., & Callahan, C. M. (1995). *Academic diversity in the middle school: Results of a national survey of middle school administrators and teachers* (Research Monograph No. 95124). Storrs: National Research Center on the Gifted and Talented, University of Connecticut.

Mulryan, C. M. (1992). Student passivity during cooperative small groups in mathematics. *Journal of Educational Research, 85,* 261–273.

Robinson, A. (1990). Cooperation or exploitation? The argument against cooperative learning for talented students. *Journal for the Education of the Gifted, 14,* 9–27.

Robinson, A. (2003). Cooperative learning and high ability students. In N. Colangelo & G. A. Davis (Eds.), *Handbook of gifted education* (3rd ed., pp. 282–292). Boston: Allyn & Bacon.

Rogers, K. B. (1991). *The relationship of grouping practices to the education of the gifted and talented learner* (Research Monograph No. 9101). Storrs: National Research Center on the Gifted and Talented, University of Connecticut.

Rogers, K. B., & Span, P. (1993). Ability grouping with gifted and talented students: Research and guidelines. In K. A. Heller, F. J. Mönks, & A. H. Passow (Eds.), *International handbook of research and development of giftedness and talent* (pp. 585–592). Oxford, England: Pergamon.

Slavin, R. E. (1987). Ability grouping: A best-evidence synthesis. *Review of Educational Research, 57,* 175–213.

Slavin, R. E. (1990a). Ability grouping, cooperative learning and the gifted. *Journal for the Education of the Gifted, 14,* 3–8.

Slavin, R. E. (1990b). Research on cooperative learning: Consensus and controversy. *Educational Leadership, 47*(4), 52–54.

Tieso, C. L. (2005). The effects of grouping practices and curricular adjustments on achievement. *Journal for the Education of the Gifted, 29,* 60–89.

Vaughn, V. L., Feldhusen, J. F., & Asher, J. W. (1991). Meta-analyses and review of research on pullout programs in gifted education. *Gifted Child Quarterly, 35,* 92–98.

CHAPTER 15

INSTRUCTIONAL TECHNOLOGY

Computer technology in education is exploding in terms of the range and capability of available equipment and software. Pedagogically, however, there is a long way to go in connecting these with the most sophisticated types of learning and teaching experiences, and there is no evidence as yet that directly supports the differentiated use of instructional technology in gifted education. On the other hand, it has excellent potential to be a useful tool in developing and practicing intellectual skills of inquiry, debate, and exploration. Technology can benefit from the experiences of talented students who may sooner and more enthusiastically push its boundaries, but there are elements of privilege in the degree of access to educational technology, inside and outside the school, and it is not without potential dangers. Teachers and parents also need the opportunity to experience inquiry-driven learning through technology.

WHAT WE KNOW

In its broadest context, instructional technology includes a wide spectrum of media, especially electronic media, complementary to the teacher. This can include everything from books to the Internet. Most of these technologies are, in fact, merging, with television and radio easily available through a tuner or Web software on a personal computer, and books and music available on easily accessed compact disks or from Web-based virtual libraries. However, it is very easy to be overwhelmed by the literature about the technology itself and diverted from the relatively limited central question that needs to be posed here. Is the education of gifted, creative, or talented children differentially affected by instructional technology? We shall limit our definition of technology to that which can be experienced at the interface with a personal computer connected or not to the Internet. That, perhaps, is a very small limitation, but it excludes television or radio as mass media, books as printed materials, and the like.

The impact of technology should be felt at two levels: first on teaching and the organization of the teaching experience—what is normally thought of as teaching at the classroom level. We located no research that directly and explicitly addressed how teachers should change the way they deal with groups of gifted versus other students as the result of the introduction of technology. Such questions are beginning to be addressed in the general literature with only incidental differentiation regarding the abilities of the students. In addition to the opportunity for increased individualization, some of the technical language of these studies is finding its way into general educational conversation, such as the important shift from teacher-centered monologue as a source of information and an instruction on how to think, to cognitive apprenticeships, expert systems, and intelligent tutoring (cf. Lajoie & Derry, 1993; Schofield, 1997). These address the second level of impact, namely the level of the individual learner, and there is some general discussion (e.g., Mann, 1994) and research (summarized below) that address the special case of highly able learners. The question to be pursued is whether or not to regard technology as a special question in gifted education or simply to incorporate whatever is generally appropriate for the whole class. The challenge is illustrated by Liu (2004), whose introduction of a problem-based learning environment in a sixth-grade classroom improved the scaffolding for all students, boys and girls, English-speaking or not, and gifted or not. Computer technology, matched to appropriate pedagogy, can enhance learning and teaching—for everyone.

In an overview of promising practices, Jones (1995) suggested that computers offer gifted students three potential advantages: accommodation of learning-style differences, taking responsibility for one's own learning, and enabling new kinds of social interaction. Research does show that the latter two characteristics are observed in bright students, but not necessarily to the exclusion of observing it in others. With regard to taking charge of learning situations, Hativa (1992) reported that second- through fourth-grade students with above-average IQs "beat the computer system" (p. 61) and used several problem-solving skills (e.g., analogy, synthesis of previously acquired knowledge, means-ends analysis to make sense of unfamiliar language in the instructions, heuristics or subroutines, probabilistic inference, and seeking appropriate assistance outside the computer environment), and learned unfamiliar concepts they did not fully understand. This was accomplished even though the software was primarily a drill-and-practice program not intended for independent learning. Barfurth and Shore (in press) showed that able (but not formally identified as gifted) fifth-grade students assigned in teams of four to create a machine that demonstrated the principle of mechanical advantage using Lego-LOGO software and apparatus engaged in dialogue wherein solutions were distinguished by both social and cognitive moves that would not be apparent in a teacher-centered lesson. The technology, however, while central to the tasks in both experiments, is probably only a medium in which these learning processes are readily but not exclusively visible. On the other hand, Cohen (1997a, 1997b) observed gifted pupils over their first full year in a technology-rich junior high school and found that the use of computers was inconclusive regarding any observable changes in learning styles, but it fostered an environment that encouraged exploration and discourse. In an example of more traditional applications of both computer use and instructional adaptation, Ravaglia, Suppes, Stillinger, and Alpert (1995) demonstrated that a computer-delivered accelerated mathematics and physics curriculum successfully enabled high school students to move ahead quickly at their own pace with challenging material. These studies give the strong impression that students of lesser ability would not perform in these ways, but this has not been tested under optimum learning conditions and sufficiently long time frames.

In a study that involved teacher use but not direct student experience of instructional technology, Ysseldyke, Tardrew, Betts, Thill, and Hannigan (2004) observed uniquely strong gains in mathematics by gifted pupils whose teachers used a commercially available learning-management program. Although it controlled for student group variables, the fact that gifted students' performance in mathematics surpassed that of others, even when their teachers used the management system for all pupils, demonstrates the need for good learning management, computerized or not. Thus, the technology did not so much better differentiate learning for the gifted as it removed a barrier; this is certainly a worthy undertaking, nonetheless.

Also in favor of the use of technology specifically with gifted students, Peck and Hughes (1996) collected interviews, teacher logs, and student projects from eight first-grade students, their parents, and teachers over the first 2 years of their exposure to inquiry-based learning using computers. Attitude, collaboration, and student thinking processes all benefited, apparently directly from the use of the technology. Trotter (1991) tapped into the inquiry-driven learning component when he described how a few high schools were given the opportunity to link their more able students online with researchers using supercomputers on sophisticated research projects. Ziegler and Terry (1992) compared a computer education unit, creative problem solving, and a computer literacy course on problem solving. The computer education group significantly outscored the other two, affirming the value of hands-on, technology-dependent tasks for bright students but still demonstrating a differential pattern for such students.

In another form of software programming as curriculum, gifted sixth-grade students wrote a tutorial that taught first-grade students to tell time from an analog clock. The program received a first-place award at a software development contest and was displayed at the 1997 National Educational Computing Conference (Hoffman, 1997). The absence of a control group in this study is not fatal because other studies have compared high- and average-ability students on more or less open-ended programming tasks. Maniatis, Cartwright, and Shore (1998) found that high-IQ pupils working in teams on LOGO design tasks differed from lower IQ students in the complexity of the projects they undertook and in their higher use of integral subroutines and global error searching strategies. The differences in favor of the higher IQ pupils were found in the process of the design of effective, real software, and in the quality of the product from the perspective of a user. From such a user's perspective, Bowen, Shore, and Cartwright (1992) demonstrated that more able students prefer greater complexity in their software environments. High on their list of priorities for enhancing programs they worked with would be to increase various kinds of complexity of learning and playing opportunities.

Another interesting, but speculative, application is for gifted students with learning disabilities (Howard, 1994). This potential lies in the multichannel capability of computers, allowing learning-disabled students, gifted or not, to find or create alternative paths to understanding based on their metacognitive strengths. In such a task, but not in a computer context, students with learning disabilities who are also gifted have been shown to perform like gifted students without disabilities and differently from both children who fit neither category or who have learning disabilities (Hannah & Shore, 1995).

A major need in the incorporation of instructional technology in education at all levels is the preparation of teachers. In addition to skills in using different media, teachers need to become familiar and competent with inquiry-driven, student-centered, developmentally and cognitively based constructivist models of teaching and learning. The successful insertion of instructional technology in classrooms, with success defined in the context of inquiry-driven learning by students, is probably impossible until the teachers themselves have experienced and value such learning experiences (Bracewell, Le Maistre, Lajoie, & Breuleux, in press). A study of 175 student teachers, mostly from Quebec and Ontario, but also representing eight other Canadian provinces, four U.S. states, and four European countries, reports the mean number of inquiry experiences they recalled from their entire elementary and secondary education as 5, but the range was from 0 to 27 (Aulls & Luconi, 1997). Also, student teachers who had a mentor in the inquiry process recalled significantly more inquiry events from their school years. Such teacher mentoring also appears critical in incorporating instructional technology in pedagogically valuable ways.

The opportunities created by technology in education are not yet fully imagined. Less than a decade after the invention of the Internet, a pupil can search the contents of many of the worlds' greatest libraries and museums, and take an inquiry-driven journey that supersedes the greatest encyclopedias from which students once copied large chunks, causing the teacher's common lament about it not being research. Of course, how the pupil uses the greater technology is not predetermined. We do not yet know if gifted, creative, or talented students, however defined, search differently (although the question has been asked under the broader heading of expertise—cf. Luconi & Tabatabai, 1999).

It is reasonable to expect that gifted students' potential to use the Internet, like any other tool, will be impressive, but we do not know how widely these abilities and experiences can be distributed in the population as a whole until the opportunity to do so is given a powerful test. The warning signs are up: Schofield (1997) flagged an important school-level caveat regarding the implementation of technology in schools when she titled Chapter 5 of her book "The Computer Room for Gifted Students: A (Bright, White Boys') Lunch Club." And, Cartwright, Finkelstein, and Maenling (in press) pointed out some of the psychological dangers lurking on the Internet and to children at risk of emotional and social difficulties, especially among the highly able who are especially drawn to exploration of cyberspace. For example, what is the emotional impact on a lonely child with a vivid imagination and fear of dark places who gets fully involved and lost in a dark alley in a virtual reality game? Finally, Olszewski-Kubilius and Lee (2004) observed that gifted students using computer technology to take an Advanced Placement course by distance education were dissatisfied with two related parts of their experience, namely, the opportunities for interaction with other students and also with teachers. In short, instructional technology may have important limitations as a stand-alone educational provider and if one's expectations for its benefits are cast too generally.

Conclusion

Computer technology is becoming ubiquitous in education in North America and other prosperous societies. There is increasing evidence that it can play a role in enhancing inquiry-driven learning, especially since the advent of the Internet. It is not proven, however, that such technology is necessary for intellectual skills to flourish, and it is very clear that it is not a sufficient condition. Gifted students have demonstrated in technology-rich environments, as in others, that they are capable of qualitatively different and superior performance, but (once again) the extent to which these differences are the result of additional exposure to technology or to superior teaching or curriculum is not known. Technology also poses risks: at the general level through disparity in its availability and appeal to boys and girls from different cultural groups, and in the unexplored worlds of the uses made of information gleaned from the Internet and the impact on psychic well-being of youngsters whose exposure is excessive and unmonitored.

The bottom line seems to be that technology is and will remain a part of gifted education, but (a) it is generally not fully exploited in terms of potential to develop thinking abilities, (b) we do not yet know how and to what extent its use should be differentiated for use with gifted students, and (c) we do not know what we can learn from its gifted students that can enhance the education of all students in technologically rich or poor settings. It is a rich field for research in the years ahead.

WHAT WE CAN DO

If it were ever shown that technology is essential rather than just useful, then there would be an immediate danger of a schism between those who have it readily available and those who do not. This is not to say that every school child should not learn to use computers for direct purposes such as writing and searching the Internet and learn about their uses in modern society, but that is computer literacy and not the same topic we are addressing here. If technology is useful, as it seems to be, then we need to learn what it is useful for and need to explore whether those goals, such as inquiry-driven learning, can be effectively mastered with or without expensive technology.

At Home

There is no evidence at this time that parents should place computer technology ahead of necessities or other growth experiences such as social, athletic, and creative endeavors outside the house, family travel, and the like. Internet access is available without charge at a rapidly increasing number of public libraries, and a trip there together could be at least as valuable an experience as time spent at a computer in the basement or the living room. However, parents should:

- insist that children have equitable access to technology at school, and

- that they are given a chance to learn along with their children.

Whatever parents do to encourage children to enjoy learning, to interact respectfully with others (both listening and contributing), to explore, and to pursue the answers to questions that occur to them will serve children well when technology supplements the school curricula. In many ways, working with technology is an extension of literacy and intelligence, and there is probably nothing more valuable parents can do in the academic domain than read daily to their child and send him or her to school literate and inquisitive.

In the Classroom

The great advantage of technology, already present in the world outside the school, will be to communicate and to respond to self-directed inquiry. If the classroom does not have these as primary goals and have them built into the implementation of the curriculum, then adding technology will be like adding driver education—just another way of getting somewhere, if that is where you want to go. At this time, there is no basis for differential use of technology with gifted versus other students, but, as with anything,

❧ it is reasonable to adjust the goals to foster success for all and to keep raising those aspirations as much as possible.

Gifted students appear to be drawn to technology, and this is especially the case for boys from Western or Westernized cultures.

❧ Girls and boys from other cultures can be drawn to computers through content that appeals to them, the chance to communicate with people they want to be in touch with, and the chance to fumble without being overseen by more technology-savvy pupils.

Unless every student is "wired," and maybe even after they are,

❧ small groups working together on topics of interest is an effective means to encounter technology.

As with any other resource,

❧ students may need some help getting up and running and the teacher can assist by helping each group plan the use it could make of technology in relation to its learning goals.

Such an approach will ensure that technology is an able and willing servant of the teaching and learning process, as well as a guaranteed ubiquitous one.

At School

Technology is expensive and not available privately to every child. Because it is going to be around as long as electricity flows, schools have a responsibility to ensure that:

❧ all children are given opportunities to use and enjoy it,

❧ teachers are similarly engaged, and,

❧ given the importance of informed home support, parents are invited to learn to work with technology, as well. Working with parents could be combined with literacy programs where this is an issue.

One of the key decisions is whether to centralize or decentralize computers and Web access in a school. We found no evidence of research on the learning advantages of one or the other. Using technology in creative ways means that

❧ teachers need to have experienced the processes they are to guide. This should be expected to take years, not days or weeks to accomplish.

Most importantly,

❧ administration, teachers, and parents need to decide why they want technology in their school. This will avoid serious waste of expensive resources. Schools need to think carefully about plans for the use of technology, and these plans need to be updated every few years.

REFERENCES

Aulls, M. W., & Luconi, F. (1997, May). *Participation in inquiry education: Pre-service teachers' exposure to inquiry instruction and beliefs about the nature of inquiry and who can successfully participate in it.* Paper presented at the midyear meeting of the National Association for Gifted Children, Montreal, QC, Canada.

Barfurth, M. A., & Shore, B. M. (in press). White water during inquiry learning: Understanding the place of disagreements in the process of collaboration. In B. M. Shore, M. W. Aulls, & M. A. B. Delcourt (Eds.), *Inquiry in education: Overcoming barriers to successful implementation.* Mahwah, NJ: Erlbaum.

Bowen, S., Shore, B. M., & Cartwright, G. F. (1992). Do gifted children use computers differently? A view from "The Factory." *Gifted Education International, 8,* 151–154.

Bracewell, R. J., Le Maistre, C., Lajoie, S. P., & Breuleux, A. (in press). The role of the teacher in opening worlds of inquiry-driven learning with technology. In B. M. Shore, M. W. Aulls, & M. A. B. Delcourt (Eds.), *Inquiry in education: Overcoming barriers to successful implementation.* Mahwah, NJ: Erlbaum.

Cartwright, G. F., Finkelstein, A., & Maenling, M. (in press). *Caught in the web: Internet risks for children.* In B. M. Shore, M. W. Aulls, & M. A. B. Delcourt (Eds.), *Inquiry in education: Overcoming barriers to successful implementation.* Mahwah, NJ: Erlbaum.

Cohen, V. L. (1997a). Implications for learning in a technology-rich school. *Journal of Interactive Learning Research, 8,* 153–174.

Cohen, V. L. (1997b). Learning styles in a technology-rich environment. *Journal of Research in Computing in Education, 29,* 338–350.

Hannah, C. L., & Shore, B. M. (1995). Metacognition and high intellectual ability: Insights from the study of learning-disabled gifted students. *Gifted Child Quarterly, 39,* 95–109.

Hativa, N. (1992). Good students beat the computer system: Strategies for self learning from computerized practice in arithmetic. *Mathematics Education Research Journal, 4,* 61–82.

Hoffman, B. (1997). The wonder world of time. *Hypernexus, 8*(1), 10–11.

Howard, J. B. (1994). Addressing needs through strengths: Five instructional practices for gifted/learning disabled students. *Journal of Secondary Gifted Education, 5,* 23–34.

Jones, G. (1995). Personal computers and gifted students. *Teaching Exceptional Children, 27,* 80–81.

Lajoie, S. P., & Derry, S. J. (Eds.). (1993). *Computers as cognitive tools.* Hillsdale, NJ: Erlbaum.

Liu, M. (2004). Examining the performance and attitudes of sixth graders during their use of a problem-based hypermedia learning environment. *Computers in Human Behavior, 20,* 357–379.

Luconi, F., & Tabatabai, D. (1999, May). *Searching the Web: Expert-novice differences in a problem-solving context.* Paper presented at the annual meeting of the American Educational Research Association, Montreal, QC, Canada.

Maniatis, E., Cartwright, G. F., & Shore, B. M. (1998). Giftedness and complexity in a self-directed computer-based task. *Gifted and Talented International, 13,* 83–89.

Mann, C. (1994). New technologies and gifted education. *Roeper Review, 16,* 172–176.

Olszewski-Kubilius, P., & Lee, S-Y. (2004). Gifted adolescents' talent development through distance learning. *Journal for the Education of the Gifted, 28,* 7–35.

Peck, J. K., & Hughes, S. V. (1996). *The impact of an inquiry approach to learning in a technology-rich environment.* Unpublished manuscript. (ERIC Document Reproduction Service No. ED375796)

Ravaglia, R., Suppes, P., Stillinger, C., & Alpert, T. M. (1995). Computer-based mathematics and physics for gifted students. *Gifted Child Quarterly, 39,* 7–13.

Schofield, J. W. (1997). *Computers and classroom culture.* New York: Cambridge University Press.

Trotter, A. (1991). The sky's the limit when super students meet supercomputers. *Executive Educator, 13,* 17–18, 39.

Ysseldyke, J., Tardrew, S., Betts, J., Thill, T., & Hannigan, E. (2004). Use of an instructional management system to enhance math instruction of gifted and talented students. *Journal for the Education of the Gifted, 27,* 293–310.

Ziegler, E. W., & Terry, M. S. (1992). Instructional methodology, computer literacy, and problem solving among gifted and talented students. *International Journal of Instructional Media, 19,* 45–51.

CHAPTER 16

USING PRIMARY SOURCES IN HISTORY

omplex learning in history occurs when teachers incorporate primary sources and provide students with opportunities to think and write like historians. Students learn strategies for interpretation in historical problem solving and increase their ability to write from primary documents. Talented students must be taught explicitly about the use of evidence and how to corroborate, source, and contextualize documents.

WHAT WE KNOW

Historians analyze sources to interpret the past. They use documents to piece together evidence to corroborate facts and events and to permit them to suggest causes and consequences. Students can also engage in complex thinking in history when provided with a rich array of opportunities and resources in the classroom. Learning to practice the methods and skills of historians has been suggested as desirable for gifted learners (Reis & Hébert, 1985). Lee and Ashby (2000) have investigated the development of historical understanding in learners from elementary to high school. Ashby, Lee, and Shemilt (2005) have provided an in-depth discussion of teaching and learning in history, including a model for the ways students develop their thinking about historical evidence. Two types of classroom sources are often used to analyze history: primary and secondary. Generally, primary sources are documents or other kinds of evidence written or created at the time of the event. First-person accounts, artifacts, data, or people who possess specific knowledge or expertise are examples of primary sources (Michigan State University, 1999). Textbooks that interpret findings are secondary (in some cases tertiary) sources, and these are the most common resources used to teach history in the classroom. A survey in the 1980s indicated that 90% of all social studies teachers used textbooks in the classroom and that approximately half reported they relied on one textbook (Patrick & Hawke, 1982). Sadly, a review of history texts concluded they have changed little in their emphasis on low-level understanding (Shermis & Clinkenbeard, 1981). Students tend to acknowledge history textbooks as the foremost authority on historical content (Wineburg, 1991). Thus, the kinds of source materials presented in the classroom are important determinants of student thinking about historical problems.

Two approaches characterize the teaching of history; these are the transmission and transformation approaches. Stahl, Hynd, Britton, McNish, and Bosquet (1996) refer to the transmission approach as one that emphasizes the text, the teacher, and the acquisition of a body of factual historical knowledge. Transformation approaches emphasize higher level thinking about the conditions leading to events, cause and effect relationships, and the analysis and evaluation of source material. While the acquisition of knowledge in history is undeniably important, talented students are more likely to develop the historical habits of mind when presented with complex problems, primary sources that illuminate those problems, and the skills to think about them (Gallagher & Stepien, 1996).

Learning to Think Historically: A Focus on Complex Understanding

According to Spoehr and Spoehr (1994), students learn to think historically by studying the relationships among facts and events from different sources, generating a hypothesis about the events, and developing an argument based on evidence. The ability to hold multiple sources in mind (Stahl et. al., 1996), to evaluate their credibility, and to write convincingly about the primary sources (Baker, 1994; Young & Leinhardt, 1998) are key attributes of complex learning in history.

In a study comparing the differences between practicing historians and academically talented students, Wineberg (1991) noted that historians used three processes not generally employed by the students: corroboration, sourc-ing, and contextualization. Wineberg observed eight historians and eight Advanced Placement (AP) history students as they examined historical texts about a Revolutionary War battle. He noted that historians corroborated their sources. In other words, they explicitly compared and contrasted the multiple documents available on the battle. They also engaged in "sourcing" by looking first at the source of the document before they read it in order to consider the bias or perspective of the writer. Finally, historians contextualized the docu-ments or placed them in time and space in order to understand them. For example, an eyewitness account that commented on the sunlight glinting on weapons when the reported time of the battle was early evening could be chal-lenged for its lack of credibility. The students in Wineberg's study, academically talented though they were, did not frequently or spontaneously use these same processes when evaluating historical texts.

Early studies of students' historical thinking based on theories about the development of abstract thought (Hallam, 1967, 1970) were not promising. Researchers concluded that students did not acquire these abilities until later adolescence, if then. However, later investigations indicated that students can engage in genuine historical thinking when provided with a curriculum that stresses the nature of history, the use of varied source materials, and active learning (Ashby et al., 2005; Booth, 1983, 1994; Shemilt, 1987).

Primary Sources and Multiple Documents in History

Complex learning in history is more likely when students and teachers use multiple and primary sources. The stuff of history is found in primary docu-ments, thus the assumption is that students are better served if they have access to primary sources and opportunities to manipulate them in the classroom (Holt, 1990; Korbin, 1996). Research generally supports the recommendation, but also illustrates the challenge of teaching and learning history as historians practice it.

Writing From Historical Documents

Young and Leinhardt's study (1998) of five AP history students traced their development in writing using primary documents in the context of prac-tice problems for the document-based question portion of the examination. Students were given general coaching by a history teacher identified as exem-plary on the basis of AP examination scores of her students and referrals by other teachers, students, and parents. Over the course of a year, students were presented with four different questions that required them to interpret and synthesize primary documents and write an essay responding to a problem-based prompt. Each problem included between 8 and 11 primary documents for students to consider. The researchers analyzed the students' historical writing on the basis of its overall organization and use of the primary documents. These advanced students were able to move from enumerating discrete bits of knowledge to more coherent persuasive essays. However, the growth was not smooth. Initially, students were reasonably good schoolhouse writers—they were academically literate. However, as they tried to incorporate primary documents in their essays, they lost control of their prose. For some of the students, writing became awkward as they tried to manage across multiple sources. As Greene (1994) suggested, writing history is neither familiar to students nor easy to accomplish. The use of sets of documents that included conflicting points of view coupled with a strategy for teaching corroboration and persuasive writing was investigated with 12 learning-disabled, 39 normally achieving, and 4 talented middle school writers. Following instruction, students gained on a measure of persuasive writing with the papers written by the talented students receiving the highest scores, but few students demonstrated complex historical understanding (De La Paz, 2005).

WHAT WE CAN DO

In the Classroom

◈ Provide complex, open-ended problems as part of the history curriculum. The research on problem-based learning indicates that content acquisition does not suffer (Gallagher & Stepien, 1996). The practice of inserting ill-structured problems into a more traditional textbook-driven curriculum throughout the year provides a reasonable structure for teachers who are bound by district or state curricular guides.

◈ Teach the processes of historical thinking directly. Comparisons between practicing historians and academically talented students indicate that the use of these processes distinguishes between the two groups (Wineberg, 1991). Students can learn to detect bias in sources effectively (Perfetti, Britt, & Georgi, 1995). They can construct more consistent understandings when they read two historical documents, but tend not to integrate conflicting opinions unless guided carefully (De La Paz, 2005; Stahl et. al., 1996). Recommended skill sequences are available (Hall, 1987; Henry, 1990).

◈ Increase the opportunity for writing from primary documents. There are specific rhetorical characteristics of historical writing. Young and Leinhardt (1998) recommend explicit teaching of rhetorical devices in historical writing even when the students are advanced and the teacher openly models historical thinking. Outlets for publication of student historical writing are available (Reecer, 1993/1994).

At School

&❧ Equip history classrooms with adequate access to primary documents. If teachers and students are to use primary sources rather than secondary texts, they need multiple copies of multiple sources. Documents from the National Digital Library, a project of the Library of Congress, are available electronically. The Internet provides a wealth of primary sources for teachers and students to access. Packets of written and pictorial documents are commercially available from publishers like Jackdaw Publications. Finally, practice questions that incorporate primary sources are available from past AP examinations (Spoehr & Fraker, 1995).

REFERENCES

Ashby, R., Lee, P. J., & Shemilt, D. (2005). Putting principles into practice: Teaching and planning. In M. S. Donovan & J. D. Bransford (Eds.), *How students learn history, mathematics, and science in the classroom* (pp. 79–178). Washington, DC: National Academies Press.

Baker, E. L. (1994). Learning-based assessments of history understanding. *Educational Psychologist, 29*(2), 97–106.

Booth, M. B. (1983). Skills, concepts and attitudes: The development of adolescent children's historical thinking. *History and Theory, 22*, 101–117.

Booth, M. B. (1994). Cognition in history: A British perspective. *Educational Psychologist, 29*(2), 61–69.

De La Paz, S. (2005). Effects of historical reasoning instruction and writing strategy mastery in culturally and academically diverse school classrooms. *Journal of Educational Psychology, 97*, 139–156.

Gallagher, S., & Stepien, W. (1996). Content acquisition in problem-based learning: Depth versus breadth in American studies. *Journal for the Education of the Gifted, 19*, 257–275.

Greene, S. (1994). The problems of learning to think like a historian: Writing history in the culture of the classroom. *Educational Psychologist, 29*(2), 89–96.

Hall, D. C. (1987). Developing historical writing skills: A scope and sequence. *Magazine of History, 3*, 20–24.

Hallam, R. N. (1967). Logical thinking in history. *Educational Review, 19*, 183–202.

Hallam, R. N. (1970). Piaget and thinking in history. In M. Ballard (Ed.), *New movements in the teaching of history* (pp. 162–178). London: Temple Smith.

Henry, M. S. (1990). A skill sequence for honors classes in high school social studies. *Social Education, 54*, 45–46.

Holt, T. (1990). *Thinking historically.* New York: The College Board.

Korbin, D. (1996). *Beyond the textbook: Teaching history using documents and primary sources.* Portsmouth, NH: Heinemann.

Lee, P. J., & Ashby, R. (2000). Progression in historical understanding among students ages 7 to 14. In P. Seixas, P. Stearns, & S. Wineburg (Eds.), *Knowing, teaching and learning history: National and international perspectives* (pp. 192–222). New York: University Press.

Michigan State University (1999). *About primary sources. The Primary Sources network.* Retrieved on June 13, 2006, from http://www.msu.edu/home

Patrick, J. J., & Hawke, S. (1982). Social studies curriculum materials. In Project Span Staff (Eds.), *The current state of social studies: A report of Project Span* (pp. 105–185). Boulder, CO: Social Science Education Consortium.

Perfetti, C. A., Britt, M. A., & Georgi, M. C. (1995). *Text-based learning and reasoning: Studies in history.* Hillsdale, NJ: Erlbaum.

Reecer, M. (1993/1994). Getting carried away with history. *American Educator, 17*(4), 19–23.

Reis, S. M., & Hébert, T. P. (1985). Creating practicing professionals in gifted programs: Encouraging students to become young historians. *Roeper Review, 8,* 101–104.

Shemilt, D. (1987). Adolescent ideas about evidence and methodology in history. In C. Portal (Ed.), *The history curriculum for teachers* (pp. 39–61). Lewes, England: Falmer.

Shermis, S. S., & Clinkenbeard, P. R. (1981). History texts for the gifted: A look at the past century. *Roeper Review, 4,* 19–21.

Spoehr, L., & Fraker, A. (1995). *Doing the DBQ: Teaching and learning with the document-based question.* New York: The College Board.

Spoehr, K., & Spoehr, L. (1994). Learning to think historically. *Educational Psychologist, 29*(2), 71–77.

Stahl, S., Hynd, C., Britton, B., McNish, M., & Bosquet, D. (1996). What happens when students read multiple source documents in history? *Reading Research Quarterly, 31,* 430–456.

Wineberg, S. (1991). Historical problem solving: A study of the cognitive processes used in the evaluation of documentary and pictorial evidence. *Journal of Educational Psychology, 83,* 73–87.

Young, K., & Leinhardt, G. (1998). Writing from primary documents: A way of knowing history. *Written Communications, 15*(1), 25–68.

CHAPTER 17

LANGUAGE ARTS INSTRUCTION

E ven before 2 years of age, some children exhibit indications of advanced language development. Throughout their school years, they excel in language arts: they read widely, write well, and understand and appreciate the nuances of literary works. Students who receive appropriate instruction and support for their talents produce quality pieces of writing, find outlets for expression in theater, debate, and other speaking forums, and use literature and poetry to enhance their lives.

WHAT WE KNOW

Some children seem to love words from a very early age. Children who have an environment where books are readily available, where someone reads to them often, and where opportunities to interact with books and words are abundant, develop a special interest in all things about language (Smutny & von Fremd, 2004). Their parents report unusual attention to books and early reading, remarkable memory for stories and rhymes, and precocious vocabulary attainment that includes the delight of the way words "feel" in their mouths and ears (Silverman, 1997). By the time the children are in school, they are still ahead of their age peers by at least 2 years, involved with and enjoying literature, verbal puzzles, writing, and word relationships (Gardner, 1983; VanTassel-Baska, Johnson, & Boyce, 1996), and showing sensitivity to authors' intent (Piirto, 1992). They develop different, more sophisticated strategies for writing, reading, and comprehending, partly through their quick and deep learning abilities and partly by their knowledge and competence. For example, a study of senior high school students (Fehrenbach, 1991) found that those who have verbal talent use a set of reading strategies that is substantially different from that used by average readers. They independently employ the strategies of rereading, inferring, analyzing structure, predicting, evaluating, and relating to content areas. Because all of these students read widely, interface with texts on a deep level, and savor the sound and feel of words that are spoken and written, they are able to build connections and meanings and interpretations that, in turn, make them even more effective learners. Black (2005) spoke of the "language-sensitive child" (p. 109) who is able to store impressions from the senses. These children not only excel in language arts classes in school, but become gifted storytellers. Storytelling develops the imagery and music of language. When performance skills for storytelling are taught, Sasser and Zorena (1991) showed that children's creative and expository writing, awareness of and expertise in language, and personal involvement and motivation improve and increase.

Language Arts in the Classroom

In all situations, talent must be nurtured and developed. Children who have mastered the basic skills of reading and writing—in many cases 2 or more years ahead of curricular projections—must be provided with high-level applications of the skills (Robinson, 1986; VanTassel-Baska, Johnson, Hughes, & Boyce, 1996). The usual basal text-driven language arts instruction that focuses on recall comprehension and fragmented reading skills has the effect of diminishing motivation for reading and writing (Lockwood, 1992). The evaluation efforts of Aldrich and McKim (1992) and Aldrich (1996) found all of the basal texts lacking in sufficient challenge for gifted learners. Their data also revealed that even the best students' verbal achievement was lower than it was 20 years ago. The National Assessment of Educational Progress (1990) pointed to similar deficits in students at all levels. The group's report also highlights practices within classrooms such as the heavy use of workbook and skill-sheet assignments, the infrequency with which students are asked to examine their understanding of reading by writing or discussion, and the prevalent use of a single basal text for an entire classroom. These findings hold true even for classes of high-ability students.

Increasing Achievement

Students who show precocity in the area of English and the language arts require specialized instruction. Edmunds and Noel (2003) found this to be true in their in-depth study of an exceptional and precocious child, Geoffrey, who at the age of 5 was a sophisticated and prolific writer. Their analysis of his 129 books (many of them more than 50 pages long) and the environment in which he created his books made it clear that mainstream first-grade reading and writing would not be reasonable for Geoffrey. While he is an exceptional case among exceptional cases, there are other children who show great promise in reading and writing and who also need curriculum that nurtures and develops this promise.

It is generally accepted that a complex, integrated curriculum based on concepts and crossing disciplines is an appropriate method of instruction for higher level thinking and meaning. VanTassel-Baska, Johnson, and Boyce (1996), studied seven experimental and three control classes of gifted fourth- through sixth-grade students across the country. The experimental classes received instruction using a specially created, integrated language arts curriculum (Integrated Curriculum Model; ICM), that included high-level literary analysis and interpretation, persuasive writing, and linguistic competency (VanTassel-Baska, 1986, 1995). The results showed that each of the experimental groups made significant gains on all assessments, while the comparison groups showed no significant growth on the assessments. Subsequent development of units using the ICM retained the successful components of knowledge, higher order processing, and interdisciplinary issues and themes (VanTassel-Baska, Johnson, Hughes, et al., 1996). Further research on the units with 2,189 gifted learners in grades 2–8 in 46 schools across the country during a 5-year period brought similar results (VanTassel-Baska, Zuo, Avery, & Little, 2002). Significant and important gains were made in literary analysis and interpretation for persuasive writing by all students, males and females, economically advantaged and disadvantaged, in all grouping models. The achievement gains continue over time as found by Feng, VanTassel-Baska, Quek, Bai, and O'Neill (2005) in a study of 973 gifted students in grades 3–9, who had been instructed using the ICM units during a 3-year period. Not only had student learning in language arts been enhanced, but data on the perceptions of students, parents, and teachers showed that they considered the instruction highly beneficial. An important part of this study highlighted the dependence of the curriculum delivery on the expertise of the teachers and called for more professional development and more materials suitable for unit support.

Lessons From Adult Writers

Examining the lives of talented writers (poets, novelists, journalists, playwrights) and orators (actors, politicians, certain categories of media personalities) showed several factors that allowed their gifts to emerge and become productive (Barron, 1972; Bloom, 1985; Feldman, 1986; Goertzel & Goertzel,

1962; MacKinnon, 1978; Piirto, 1992; Radford, 1990). The common threads among the researchers' findings were a combination of the individual's inner drive and the environment's sensitivity to the needs of the individual. Numerous famous writers, orators, actors, and others report that they read early, that they read almost obsessively (often to escape a dull education or to find solace for loneliness and introversion), that they were fascinated by words and expressions, and that they were exposed to adult literature early—especially Shakespeare, Kipling, Goethe, Milton, and Thackeray, among others. This advanced and continuous immersion into substantial words and thoughts developed the early interest into a passion, as well as taught these individuals structure and mechanics through the words of great writers. For children to have this kind of preparation, schools must make considerably different arrangements as early as kindergarten. To illustrate the need for special attention, the following partial list of qualities of writing done by very young, gifted writers stands in sharp contrast to the writing of other elementary school children. These young writers applied paradox, parallel structure, rhythm, and visual imagery; figures of speech and adjectives and adverbs; sophisticated syntax, prose lyricism, and movement; and gave evidence of a sense of humor, a philosophical bent, and playfulness with words (Piirto). Elementary students who already employ these kinds of sophisticated literary skills will need to be instructed at a vastly different level than their age peers. The inclusion of poetry, principled rhetoric, impassioned speeches, and historically important language events such as debates become necessary components of the language arts curriculum for gifted learners (Halsted, 2002; Ravitch, 1991).

Children who read widely, speak with an advanced vocabulary, and write their inner thoughts are often characterized by their age peers as different and strange. If the talents are not recognized positively and nurtured, these children suffer blows to their self-esteem. This is especially true in the junior high or middle school years, and neglecting these talents often results in the concealment of talent (Alvino, 1991; Silverman, 1995). For these students, programs such as university-based summer and Saturday courses that bring talented young people together for fast-paced, challenging courses are lifesavers and give them positive experiences that make their regular school days more successful (Silverman, 1998). High school students who have access to accelerated Advanced Placement (AP) courses in English and opportunities through school activities to be recognized for their writing or oratory skills, and who are able to connect with a teacher or mentor, can set goals for their higher education and professional development (Kennedy, 1993/1994; Ochse, 1990). These types of experiences are invaluable for verbally talented students.

Student-Centered Approaches

The field of English education has a history of innovation and retreat, but during the last 30 years, the call for a student-centered approach remained loud and clear. The Personal Growth Model asserts that students grow as individuals and persons of character toward productive careers through English (Tchudi, 1991). The central features of the model include using the students' language and experience as the starting point for instruction; allowing for natural progression of language skill development instead of prescribed sequences; connecting language and literature; and treating language as a whole instead of dividing instruction into skill components and separate courses (Tchudi, p. 12). The model provides for writing instruction to be focused on process—how to make compositions—and leaves the structure of completed pieces to be discovered by the students, or at least learned during the process of writing (Graves, 1983). Process is the goal of the model's emphasis in reading, focusing on the child's engagement with the text and the meaning that is made at the junction of the text and the child's experience. The range and content of literature strive to be increasingly multicultural and relevant in contemporary themes, and in response, the field of specialty books and adolescent literature has grown rapidly. The idea that English/language arts is naturally interdisciplinary, and that it is best learned when it is "about something else," answers the model's demand for relevance to the student's life. In this light, grammar becomes a facet of editing; skills are taught as students encounter problems in their writing, and grammar, punctuation, spelling, and syntax are part of preparing the finished product (Tchudi).

The Personal Growth Model has possibilities for sustaining development of verbally gifted children's talents. Using a student's experiences (interests) and personal starting point for instruction are components of individualization and lead to compacting the curriculum to eliminate instruction in skills already learned. The emphasis on process and interdisciplinary integration of language arts meets the needs of "big-picture" thinkers. The use of multiple kinds of literature appeals to many good readers. However, all depends on the teachers' skills and preparation in identifying and understanding verbally gifted students, on the flexibility of options and pacing, and the atmosphere of support for the pursuit of excellence. Westberg and Archambault (1997) conducted a multicase study of classrooms considered exemplary in differentiating instruction for high-ability students. Across the sites, teachers' advanced training and knowledge, their willingness to change and collaborate, their beliefs and strategies for differentiating instruction for gifted students, their leadership, and their autonomy and support through the changes were the crucial factors in successfully teaching gifted learners. The Personal Growth Model will work well in an environment where teachers are knowledgeable and receptive to accepting gifted children and meeting their needs.

Gifted Second Language Learners

A relatively new aspect of language arts instruction is the identification of gifted children who do not speak English as their primary language. Some students show verbal giftedness in their ability to learn English quickly and with unusual depth, and then go on to high-level performance in one or more areas of the language arts (Kitano & Espinosa, 1995; Malave, 1994). Matthews and Matthews (2004) recommended heritage language classes for students who have English as a second language. The students can demonstrate their academic potential in these classes, they find the classes motivating, and achievement in other courses often follows success in the heritage class. The authors specifically showed these advantages occurring in Spanish heritage classes. As classrooms become more multicultural, studies that provide valid identification measures for gifted students developing proficiency in two languages will be important.

WHAT WE CAN DO

Westberg and Archambault's (1997) study reiterated and gave urgency to studies of the last 25 years (i.e., Feldhusen, 1985; Renzulli, 1981; Seeley, 1985) that call for teachers to be well prepared in the knowledge of characteristics and needs of gifted children and how to translate those into curriculum options. The recommendation that may be the lynchpin in providing gifted learners with appropriate educational interventions is to require preservice teachers, inservice teachers, administrators, and guidance counselors to take coursework in gifted education. From a better understanding of able learners and knowledge of successful strategies for use in the classroom will come more partnership with the students' parents, more confidence in the ability to meet students' needs, and more acceptance of and affection for gifted students.

At Home

ﾔ Encourage students to take advantage of university-based programs that offer accelerated courses in writing, literature, and speaking.

In the Classroom

ﾔ Develop or use inquiry-based, interdisciplinary units that integrate the language arts. The ICM units developed around central concepts, such as *Journeys and Destinations* (College of William and Mary, 1998a), *Literary Reflections* (College of William and Mary, 1998b), and *The 1940s: A Decade of Change* (College of William and Mary, 1998c), are commercially available.

ﾔ Introduce complex topics, problems, and issues for reading, discussion, and writing responses.

ﻬ Provide abundant time and incentive for reading and writing.

ﻬ Use reading, writing, and oral presentation across the curriculum.

ﻬ Provide verbally gifted learners with a literary group of students who share interests for discussions and projects in conjunction with their shared reading.

ﻬ Develop writing using process-based instruction in all areas, such as narrative, expository, poetry, argument, report, and performance pieces.

ﻬ Teach grammar, spelling, and syntax in the context of real writing.

ﻬ Provide opportunities such as debate, play performance, journalism, in-depth research, and journal writing. Use substantive discussion and discussion assessment (Dixon, 2000).

ﻬ Compact the curriculum to make time for in-depth language arts study.

ﻬ Use classic and exceptional contemporary literature as reading and discussion materials. Read these aloud to students of all ages, as well.

At School

ﻬ Provide an environment in which students feel free to be engaged in learning and share their thoughts in writing and discussion.

ﻬ Provide role models, first by ensuring that language arts teachers are enthusiastic readers and writers themselves (Kolloff, 2002), and then by including professional writers in many fields as guest speakers and as mentors.

REFERENCES

Aldrich, P. W. (1996). Evaluating language arts materials. In J. VanTassel-Baska, D. T. Johnson, & L. N. Boyce (Eds.), *Developing verbal talent: Ideas and strategies for teachers of elementary and middle school students* (pp. 218–239). Needham Heights, MA: Allyn & Bacon.

Aldrich, P., & McKim, G. (1992). *The consumer's guide to English-language arts curriculum.* Saratoga Springs, NY: Saratoga-Warren Board of Cooperative Educational Services.

Alvino, J. (1991). An investigation into the needs of gifted boys. *Roeper Review, 13,* 174–180.

Barron, F. (1972). *Artists in the making.* New York: Seminar Press.

Black, S. (2005). Adventures with words: Storytelling as language experience for gifted learners. In S. K. Johnsen & J. Kendrick (Eds.), *Language arts for gifted students* (pp. 107–121). Waco, TX: Prufrock Press.

Bloom, B. (Ed.). (1985). *The development of talent in young people.* New York: Ballantine.

College of William and Mary Center for Gifted Education. (1998a). *Journeys and destinations: A language arts unit for high-ability learners in grades 2 and 3.* Dubuque, IA: Kendall and Hunt.

College of William and Mary Center for Gifted Education. (1998b). *Literary reflections: A language arts unit for high-ability learners in grades 4 and 5.* Dubuque, IA: Kendall and Hunt.

College of William and Mary Center for Gifted Education. (1998c). *The 1940s: A decade of change: A language arts unit for high-ability learners in grades 6 to 10.* Dubuque, IA: Kendall and Hunt.

Dixon, F. A. (2000). The discussion examination: Making assessment match instructional strategy. *Roeper Review, 23,* 104–108.

Edmunds, A. L., & Noel, K. A. (2003). Literary precocity: An exceptional case among exceptional cases. *Roeper Review, 25,* 185–195.

Fehrenbach, C. R. (1991). Gifted/average readers: Do they use the same reading strategies? *Gifted Child Quarterly, 35,* 125–127.

Feldhusen, J. F. (1985). The teacher of gifted students. *Gifted Educational International, 3,* 87–93.

Feldman, D. (1986). *Nature's gambit: Child prodigies and the development of human potential.* New York: Basic.

Feng, A. X., VanTassel-Baska, J., Quek, C., Bai, W., & O'Neill, B. (2005). A longitudinal assessment of gifted students' learning using the Integrated Curriculum Model (ICM): Impacts and perceptions of the William and Mary language arts and science curriculum. *Roeper Review, 27,* 78–83.

Gardner, H. (1983). *Frames of mind: The theory of multiple intelligences.* New York: BasicBooks.

Goertzel, V., & Goertzel, M. G. (1962). *Cradles of eminence.* Boston: Little, Brown.

Graves, D. (1983). *Writing: Teachers and children at work.* Exeter, NH: Heinemann.

Halsted, J. W. (2002). *Some of my best friends are books: Guiding gifted readers from preschool to high school* (2nd ed.). Scottsdale, AZ: Great Potential Press.

Kennedy, D. M. (1993/1994). Finding and nurturing verbal talent. *Journal of Secondary Gifted Education, 5,* 19–22.

Kitano, M. K., & Espinosa, R. (1995). Language diversity and giftedness: Working with gifted English language learners. *Journal for the Education of the Gifted, 18,* 234–254.

Kolloff, P. B. (2002). Why teachers need to be readers. *Gifted Child Today, 25*(2), 50–55.

Lockwood, A. (1992). The de facto curriculum? *Focus in Change, 6,* 8–11.

MacKinnon, D. (1978). *In search of human effectiveness: Identifying and developing creativity.* Buffalo, NY: Bearly.

Malave, L. M. (Ed.). (1994). *Annual conference journal: Proceedings of the annual conference of the National Association for Bilingual Education.* Washington, DC: National Association for Bilingual Education.

Matthews, P. H., & Matthews, M. S. (2004). Heritage language instruction and giftedness in language minority students: Pathways toward success. *Journal of Secondary Gifted Education, 15,* 50–56.

National Assessment of Educational Progress. (1990). *Learning to read in our nation's schools: Instruction and achievement in 1988 at grades 4, 8, and 12.* Princeton, NJ: Educational Testing Service.

Ochse, R. (1990). *Before the gates of excellence.* New York: Cambridge University Press.

Piirto, J. (1992). *Understanding those who create.* Dayton, OH: Ohio Psychology Press.

Radford, J. (1990). *Child prodigies and exceptional early achievers.* New York: Macmillan.

Ravitch, D. (1991). *The American reader: Words that moved a nation.* New York: Harper Perennial.

Renzulli, J. S. (1981). Identifying key features in programs for the gifted. In W. B. Barbe & J. S. Renzulli (Eds.), *Psychology and education of the gifted* (3rd ed., pp. 214–219). New York: Irvington.

Robinson, A. (1986). Elementary language arts for the gifted: Assimilation and accommodation in the curriculum. *Gifted Child Quarterly, 30,* 178–181.

Sasser, E., & Zorena, N. (1991). Storytelling as an adjunct to writing: Experiences with gifted students. *Teaching Exceptional Children, 23,* 44–45.

Seeley, K. (1985). Facilitators for gifted learners. In J. F. Feldhusen (Ed.), *Toward excellence in gifted education* (pp. 106–133). Denver, CO: Love.

Silverman, L. K. (1995). To be gifted or feminine: The forced choice of adolescence. *Journal of Secondary Gifted Education, 6,* 141–156.

Silverman, L. K. (1997). Family counseling with the gifted. In N. Colangelo & G. A. Davis (Eds.), *Handbook of gifted education* (2nd ed., pp. 382–397). Boston: Allyn & Bacon.

Silverman, L. K. (1998). The highly gifted. In J. VanTassel-Baska (Ed.), *Excellence in educating gifted and talented learners* (3rd ed., pp. 117–128). Denver, CO: Love.

Smutny, J. F., & von Fremd, S. E. (2004). *Differentiating for the young child: Teaching strategies across the content areas (K–3).* Thousand Oaks, CA: Corwin Press.

Tchudi, S. (1991). *Planning and assessing the curriculum in English language arts.* Alexandria, VA: Association for Supervision and Curriculum Development.

VanTassel-Baska, J. (1986). Effective curriculum and instructional models for talented students. *Gifted Child Quarterly, 30,* 164–169.

VanTassel-Baska, J. (1995). The development of talent through curriculum. *Roeper Review, 18,* 98–102.

VanTassel-Baska, J., Johnson, D. T., & Boyce, L. N. (Eds.). (1996). *Developing verbal talent: Ideas and strategies for teachers of elementary and middle school students.* Boston: Allyn & Bacon.

VanTassel-Baska, J., Johnson, D. T., Hughes, C., & Boyce, L. N. (1996). A study of language arts curriculum effectiveness with gifted learners. *Journal for the Education of the Gifted, 19,* 461–480.

VanTassel-Baska, J., Zuo, L., Avery, L. D., & Little, C. A. (2002). A curriculum study of gifted-student learning in the language arts. *Gifted Child Quarterly, 46,* 30–44.

Westberg, K. L., & Archambault, F. X., Jr. (1997). A multi-side case study of successful classroom practices for high ability students. *Gifted Child Quarterly, 41,* 42–51.

CHAPTER 18

READING INSTRUCTION

M any gifted students come to school already reading. Others come with the potential to develop their reading skills quickly. Traditional practices and materials do not promote the development of deep and enthusiastic reading among capable readers. To support and broaden their reading, talented readers need early individualized assessment, skill instruction based on that assessment, and many opportunities to read a variety of literary genres.

WHAT WE KNOW

Research on reading for able learners was prolific in the 1980s and 1990s. A picture of gifted readers, from precocious young children, to gifted elementary and middle school students, to advanced readers of adolescent age, was established. How to choose appropriate books, how to teach using classic and contemporary literature, and how to develop reading skills and an eagerness to read were studied. More recent research has built upon these understandings to place reading in the models and cur-ricula of today's schools.

Many talented students are gifted readers. Studies show that up to half of gifted students entering the first grade are exceptional readers, reading from one to three grade levels ahead of their age-mates (Bonds & Bonds, 1983; VanTassel-Baska, Johnson, Hughes, & Boyce, 1996; Witty, 1971). Bonds and Bonds sug-gested that primary gifted readers are those children who, "upon entering first grade, are reading substantially above grade level or who possess the ability to make rapid progress in reading when given proper instruction" (p. 4). Moreover, such students further demonstrate a strong interest in and motivation for reading. According to Brown and Rogan (1983), "intellectually gifted children almost by definition are good readers" (p. 6). Other gifted students may not be early readers, but have the potential for high performance given appropriate instruction.

Interest in Reading

There is evidence that capable readers lose interest and enthusiasm for read-ing as they progress in school. Martin (1984) investigated the reading attitudes of 124 sixth, seventh, and eighth graders, 41 of whom were classified as gifted. One in five of the gifted students expressed negative attitudes about reading. Students cited uninteresting and unchallenging assignments associated with reading instruction and lack of choice in selecting what they read as reasons for their dislike of reading. Further evidence of the decline in reading attitudes as talented learners progress through school was reported by Anderson, Tollefson, and Gilbert (1985), who evaluated the questionnaire responses of 276 gifted students in grades 1–12. They investigated attitudes toward reading assign-ments, reading workload, and preferences for recreational reading. They found that younger students read more for pleasure than older students and that their interests in reading were not significantly different from average ability readers: They held a preference for fantasy, mystery, and adventure. Anderson and her colleagues also reported that girls indicated more interest in leisure reading than did boys, and that older gifted students found their reading assignments easy and tediously long. In a later study, Henderson, Jackson, & Makumal (1993) noted that although reading lessons are often labeled by gifted students as being easy, some of the readers had gaps in their skills and were not able to make the neces-sary analysis connections and interpretations in what they read. Teachers have often reported that very able students do not always mentally attend to instruc-tion that seems "easy," and thus, miss vital instruction that they do, in fact, need.

The Needs of Talented Readers

The literature has focused on the importance of the initial primary expe-riences of gifted readers for setting the tone for their future approaches and attitudes toward reading. Students who enter school reading at considerably higher and more sophisticated levels than the rest of their classmates require special, advanced instruction to meet their needs (Gross, 2004; Jackson & Roller, 1993). Brown and Rogan (1983) and VanTassel-Baska (1998) strongly advocated that differentiated instruction must begin in the primary years and be continued throughout the school years. "Keeping gifted children plugged into the regular reading program frustrates and often destroys their belief that their schools and all the wonderful books found there were going to be exciting and joyful" (Brown & Rogan, p. 6). Differentiated reading instruction includes expanded vocabulary study, exposure to quality materials of fiction and non-fiction at the appropriate level of difficulty, and activities that capitalize on students' problem-solving and creative abilities. Opportunities for developing and applying higher level thinking skills through content that engages the reader on many levels, questioning strategies, discussion, written assignments, and sharing ideas with students of similar skills and interests are important components of appropriate instruction (Bailey, 1996). In essence, the requirement for reading instruction to be enriching, challenging, paced appropriately for the gifted student, and built on books that serve as a means for achieving these instructional goals has not diminished (Bonds & Bonds, 1983; Brown & Rogan; Coleman & Cross, 2005; Feldhusen & Van Tassel-Baska, 1989).

Basal Reading Programs

Despite the growth of alternatives, the traditional means of reading instruction in grades 1–8 in most schools continues to be a basal reading series. Advocates of basal reading programs have always viewed the complete package of books and supplementary materials as the heart of any reading program and the best way to ensure the mastery of skills required for independent reading (Aukerman, 1981; Carnine & Silbert, 1979). However, basal programs provide a structured system of instruction that is aimed at the average student in the grade level, and these systems do not provide modifications radical enough for precocious readers (Ellsworth, 1992). In Thompson's (1996) work using classics for reading instruction, he recalls and confirms Ganopole's (1988) belief that controlled-vocabulary basals and other sequenced skill programs actually fragment learning and are thus detrimental instead of helpful.

Caldwell (1985) reported that 80–90% of the reading programs in elementary schools used basal readers; in 2005, Education Market Research (EMR) reported the number to be 75%. In 1984, Mangieri and Madigan investigated 150 school districts and found that the same basal series was used for talented, as well as grade-level, readers; in 2005, the information from EMR showed that the five most-used basal programs had no text for advanced readers. The amount of attention given to gifted readers has been minimal. Aldrich (1996) searched commercially published textbooks for language arts resources of high quality for gifted readers, and described what she found as a "scanty collection of worthy materials" (p. 218).

Unfortunately, a cross-case analysis of 12 different classroom teachers in 11 different schools indicates that few opportunities for differentiated reading instruction exist (Reis et al., 2003). Researchers conducted a year-long field study of grade 3 and grade 7 classrooms and found some evidence of differentiated instruction in three classrooms, but little in the other nine. Talented readers were characteristically engaged in using the same basal program as grade-level readers and reading low-level trade books with little guidance from their teacher. In terms of performance on imaginative oral or written explanations, gifted elementary students failed to produce their best work unless they were actively prompted (Robinson & Feldhusen, 1984).

Reading for the Talented Learner

As VanTassel-Baska (1998) says, "The gifted child's major contact with the world of ideas is through literature. . . . Intellectual growth in gifted children depends on their access to and regular involvement in the reading process" (p. 451). At the instructional level, Reis and her colleagues (2005) applied the Schoolwide Enrichment Model to reading and found that students in grades 3–6 increased reading fluency, reading achievement test scores, number of hours spent reading, number of books read, and enjoyment of reading when compared with learners engaged in other forms of reading instruction, including Success For All. The Schoolwide Enrichment Reading Model (SEM-R) was used to enrich the reading experiences of students in four schools including children with special needs, those from diverse backgrounds, and those of low-socioeconomic income families. While other students continued with remedial reading instruction, the students in the randomly assigned treatment group were encouraged with high-interest books and self-selected reading and activities. Those who received the enriched reading time scored significantly higher in reading comprehension, fluency, and attitude toward reading. The researchers believe the results are applicable to all readers, including talented readers (Reis et al., 2005).

Grigorenko, Jarvin, and Sternberg (2002) conducted three large-scale studies (1,303 students in middle and high school, mostly from lower socioeconomic backgrounds) that examined the infusion of the triarchic theory of intelligence (Sternberg, 1985, 1999) into already existing curricula, including the language arts. Teachers of the experimental groups were given materials and instruction on how to make the tasks of this theory—analytical, creative, and practical—integral to their reading instruction and assessment. The content already in the curriculum remained the same, but the methods of teaching were enriched. Teachers of the control groups were given instruction in how to improve memory aids useful to students. Pre- and posttests in vocabulary and comprehension showed that the students in the triarchic groups advanced more than their peers in the control groups. The students and their teachers also rated the "interestingness" of the triarchic program higher. A very important aspect of this in-depth study showed long-lasting changes in teachers' behaviors and a growth in their ability to choose methods that improve learning.

At the organizational level, the issues of grouping, enrichment, and acceleration impact reading curriculum. How the curriculum will be delivered, the pacing and materials utilized, and the configurations of students who receive it are all aspects of the philosophy under which a school operates. These are addressed in more depth elsewhere in this volume. Yet, it must be acknowledged that reading ability pervades every corner of the curriculum, and therefore is central to these organizational discussions.

At the curricular level, VanTassel-Baska and her colleagues (1996) developed thematic, literature-based units to address literary analysis and interpretation, persuasive writing skills, and linguistic competency to align with International Reading Association/National Council of Teachers of English (IRA/NCTE) Standards. The units, an application of the Integrated Curriculum Model (ICM), were investigated through a field study of 100 gifted students in experimental classes and 54 gifted students in comparison classes (VanTassel-Baska et al.). No basal series was used for either group. Students in the experimental classes showed significant gains in all targeted areas of instruction.

The Junior Great Books Program continues to be considered a strong choice for teaching students how to work with complex and rigorous texts that invite a number of interpretations. The program's foci on questioning, meaning, formulating opinions, and supporting ideas with evidence from the reading selection are hallmarks of a high-level thinking approach (Aldrich, 1996; Killion, 2002a, 2002b; National Diffusion Network, 1994–1995).

Thompson (1996) set forth an argument for the use of classics as the basis of a strong literature-based reading program for the gifted. *Classics* are defined as "the rich body of authentic past and contemporary international literature (poetry, fiction, and nonfiction) that is, for various reasons, timeless, and that forms for all of us our sometimes tacit and sometimes explicit sense of good reading" (p. 59). He argued that through classical literature, students can have intelligent experiences, develop educated vocabularies, develop critical and creative thinking skills, develop values and a sense of humanity, and acquire knowledge of intellectual and cultural heritage.

Mallea (1992) pointed out that high-quality adult literature, classic and contemporary, can be key in re-igniting enthusiasm for reading in teens. A curriculum that is based on popular, culturally relevant literature and that allows teen readers to confront and wrestle with important personal and societal issues is highly motivating. Dixon (1993) found that the seminar approach to reading instruction, with open discussions about this same kind of provocative, relevant high-quality literature, is an effective mode of instruction for gifted teens. Students who have been taught from their early years how to interact intelligently and personally with the written word can grow in ways that benefit them for life.

What We Can Do

At Home

❧ Parents should be encouraged to read to and with their children beginning when the children are very young and continuing as long as possible. A family reading time gives children the message that reading is valued. There should be time to discuss what individuals are reading and opportunities for whole-family discussions about what is read in the group. Family stories that are compared and contrasted to what is read are especially good to engage children.

In the Classroom

❧ Advanced readers should be assessed individually in the primary grades. If a student is already reading when he or she enters school, further assessment by the teacher is needed to determine the extent of specific skill instruction necessary for the student.

❧ The reading curriculum should provide opportunities to read a variety of genres. Students tend to read in the area of greatest interest, and self-selection is important to maintain student interest. However, students should also be encouraged to do exploratory reading and research over an extended period of time.

❧ Reading skills and the use of literature should be integrated into the curriculum in ways that build knowledge, analysis, and appreciation for ideas and people. Opportunities for interaction, free and guided discussion, and engaging activities around literature should be provided.

❧ It is highly recommended that high-quality, culturally relevant trade books, rather than a basal series, be the primary reading material. There should be plenty of independent reading time in a curriculum for advanced readers of all ages.

At School

❧ Administrators need to recognize that talented readers do not need to jump the hurdles of the grade-level reading curriculum. School leaders can set a climate that accepts the talented reader in the elementary grades by encouraging access to advanced material and providing grouping opportunities that are appropriately challenging for the students.

REFERENCES

Aldrich, P. W. (1996). Evaluating language arts materials. In J. VanTassel-Baska, D. Johnson, & L. Boyce (Eds.), *Developing verbal talent* (pp. 218–239). Boston: Allyn & Bacon.

Anderson, M., Tollefson, N., & Gilbert, E. (1985). Giftedness and reading: A cross-sectional view of differences in reading attitudes and behaviors. *Gifted Child Quarterly, 29,* 186–189.

Aukerman, R. (1981). *The basal reader approach to reading.* New York: Wiley.

Bailey, J. M. (1996). Literacy development in verbally talented children. In J. VanTassel-Baska, D. Johnson, & L. Boyce (Eds.), *Developing verbal talent* (pp. 97–114). Boston: Allyn & Bacon.

Bonds, C., & Bonds, L. (1983). Reading and the gifted student. *Roeper Review, 5,* 4–6.

Brown, W., & Rogan, J. (1983). Reading and young gifted children. *Roeper Review, 5,* 6–9.

Caldwell, S. (1985). Highly gifted preschool readers. *Journal for the Education of the Gifted, 8,* 165–172.

Carnine, D., & Silbert, J. (1979). *Direct instruction reading.* Columbus, OH: Merrill.

Coleman, L. J., & Cross, T. L. (2005). *Being gifted in school: An introduction to development, guidance, and teaching* (2nd ed.). Waco, TX: Prufrock Press.

Dixon, F. A. (1993). Literature seminars for gifted and talented students. *Gifted Child Today, 16*(4), 15–19.

Education Market Research. (2005, January). *The complete k–12 newsletter.* Rockaway Park, NY: Open Book.

Ellsworth, J. (1992). Evaluation of realistic fiction in selected basal reading series: Assessment of messages of empowerment or reproduction for marginalized groups. *Dissertation Abstracts International, 50,* 07A. (University Microfilms No. AAG-92-35775)

Feldhusen, J., & VanTassel-Baska, J. (1989). Social studies and language arts for the gifted. In J. Feldhusen, J. VanTassel-Baska, & K. Seeley (Eds.), *Excellence in educating the gifted* (pp. 213–227). Denver, CO: Love.

Ganopole, S. J. (1988). Reading and writing for the gifted: A whole language approach. *Roeper Review, 11,* 88–94.

Grigorenko, E. L., Jarvin, L., & Sternberg, R. J. (2002). School-based tests of the Triarchic Theory of Intelligence: Three settings, three samples, three syllabi. *Contemporary Educational Psychology, 27,* 167–208.

Gross, M. U. M. (2004). *Exceptionally gifted children* (2nd ed.). New York: Routledge-Falmer.

Henderson, S. J., Jackson, N. E., & Makumal, R. A. (1993). Early development of language and literacy skills of an extremely precocious reader. *Gifted Child Quarterly, 37,* 78–83.

Jackson, N., & Roller, C. (1993). *Reading with young children.* Storrs: National Research Center on the Gifted and Talented, University of Connecticut.

Killion, J. (2002a). *What works in elementary grades: Results-based staff development.* Oxford, OH: Staff Development Council.

Killion, J. (2002b). *What works in high schools: Results-based staff development.* Oxford, OH: Staff Development Council.

Mallea, K. (1992). A novel approach for the gifted reader. *Middle School Journal, 24*(1), 37–38.

Mangieri, J., & Madigan, F. (1984). Issues in reading instruction for the gifted: What schools are doing. *Roeper Review, 7,* 68–70.

Martin, C. (1984). Why some gifted children do not like to read. *Roeper Review,* 73–75.

National Diffusion Network. (1994–1995). *Educational programs that work: The catalogue of the National Diffusion Network.* Longmont, CO: Sopris West.

Reis, S. M., Eckert, R. C., Schreiber, F. J., Jacobs, J., Briggs, C., Gubbins, E. J., et al. (2005). *The Schoolwide Enrichment Model reading study* (Research Monograph No. 05214). Storrs: National Research Center on the Gifted and Talented, University of Connecticut.

Reis, S. M., Gubbins, E. J., Briggs, C., Schreiber, F. J., Richards, S., Jacobs, J., et al. (2003). *Reading instruction for talented readers: Case studies documenting few opportunities for continuous progress* (Research Monograph No. 03184). Storrs: National Research Center on the Gifted and Talented, University of Connecticut.

Robinson, A., & Feldhusen, J. F. (1984). Don't leave them alone: Effects of probing on gifted children's imaginative explanations. *Journal for the Education of the Gifted, 7,* 156–163.

Sternberg, R. J. (1985). *Beyond IQ: A triarchic theory of human intelligence.* New York: Cambridge University Press.

Sternberg, R. J. (1999). The theory of successful intelligence. *Review of General Psychology, 3,* 292–316.

Thompson, M. (1996). Mentors on paper: How classics develop verbal ability. In J. VanTassel-Baska, D. Johnson, & L. Boyce (Eds.), *Developing verbal talent* (pp. 56–74). Boston: Allyn & Bacon.

VanTassel-Baska, J. (1998). Social studies and language arts for talented learners. In J. VanTassel-Baska (Ed.), *Excellence in educating gifted and talented learners* (p. 441–459). Denver, CO: Love.

VanTassel-Baska, J., Johnson, D., Hughes, C., & Boyce, L. (1996). A study of language arts curriculum effectiveness with gifted learners. *Journal for the Education of the Gifted, 19,* 461–480.

Witty, P. (1971). *Reading for the gifted and creative student.* Newark, NJ: International Reading Association.

CHAPTER 19

SCIENCE IN THE CLASSROOM

Research in science education suggests that a curriculum based on in-depth understanding of science concepts and "new science" standards that focus on an investigatory rather than the more traditional approach best develops the talents, interests, and motivation to do science in the real world for talented learners.

WHAT WE KNOW

As early as 1981, Brandwein urged the importance of providing a science curriculum for students of high ability in order to foster interest and to encourage careers in science. He called for a "dynamic program in science, with the fullest opportunities for laboratory work in science, [which] is obligatory in a modern society where science has such increasing impact on life and living" (p. 23). He further suggested that these programs should be available to students at the precollege level and begin as early as elementary school. In support of his position, Brandwein stated that

> the number of scientists in supply for future scientific operations is significantly related to the number involved in school science. Youngsters who like school science, and are successful in it on the school level, tend to make science a life work. (p. 25)

It cannot be assumed that talented students will develop their interest in science on their own. Sternberg (1982) also carried the same message, indicating that today's talented students may be some of our gifted researchers in the future. Therefore, school science programs need to provide them with the experiences of thinking as scientists with time to explore. To enhance the meaningfulness of science curricula for talented learners, there must be a real-world connection in the science curriculum (VanTassel-Baska, Bass, Ries, Poland, & Avery, 1998).

Although there have been changes and advancements in science education, achievement in science among students in the United States has not reached desired goals. The latest report from the Third International Mathematics and Science Study (TIMSS), which tests students of 41 nations at grades 4, 8, and end of high school in math and science, found that U.S. students in grade 4 performed comparably to other students (U.S. Department of Education, 1996). In comparison with other countries, however, 8th-grade students did less well, and 12th-grade students' scores fell significantly below the international average. The TIMSS results also reveal that American students have more instructional time than students in many countries that outranked the U.S. Furthermore, as American students progressed through school, their interest and liking of science diminished (U.S. Department of Education).

New Science Curriculum vs. Traditional Science

Traditional science curriculum emphasizes knowledge of facts, laws, theories, and application and uses laboratory activities as verification exercises or as secondary applications of concepts previously covered in class (Shymansky, Kyle, & Alport, 1983). These lab exercises are often referred to as "canned," due to the expected outcomes of very structured investigation. Critics of traditional science methods, especially those based on basal textbooks with accompanying canned labs, suggest the curriculum contributes little to the development of thinking like a scientist or to developing problem-solving skills (Roth, 1991; Shymansky et al.; Sternberg, 1982; VanTassel-Baska, 1997). Traditional science instruction tends to be teacher-centered with lecture and demonstration rather than congruent with actual practices in science. The labs lack natural problem-solving situations; there is little in the way of in-depth learning of scientific concepts. As Bleicher (1993) suggested, the lab experience is essential in the study of science methods and habits of mind. Unfortunately, the curriculum remains unfocused, skims areas, and rarely delves deeply into any single topic (Freedman, 1998).

In contrast, new science standards and curriculum have been established to promote the nature, structure, and processes of science. Project 2061 and the Benchmarks for Science Literacy (Freedman, 1998) and the National Science Curriculum Project for High-Ability Learners (VanTassel-Baska, 1997) have contributed to current thinking about science curricula. These programs have established specific goals for what students should know about scientific concepts at various grade levels. They focus on how one arrives at scientific conclusions and provide for hands-on, in-depth study. New science curricula stress the structure, process, and appreciation of science. Labs are considered an integral part of the curriculum and do not rely exclusively on set problems. Ideally, instruction is guided in small-group and independent activities. Further emphasis is on multidisciplinary in-depth study that meets the needs and interests of the high-ability student (Bass & Ries, 1995; VanTassel-Baska et al., 1998).

In attempting to increase the realism of science classes, Sternberg (1982) outlined what scientists do and what experiences students, especially high-ability students, need. Sternberg suggested four components for science curricula: problem finding, problem solving, problem reevaluation, and reporting. Problem finding involves learning to find problems worthy of study rather than assigning set problems to students. Problem solving includes problem identification, selection of the process for solving, solution monitoring, responding to feedback, and implementing an action plan. Problem reevaluation requires analyzing the outcomes that may be expected or unintended. Reporting, or writing up research reports, Sternberg suggested, is extremely important, because it clarifies thinking and is an integral part of the scientific process.

Research on problem-based learning has investigated similar outcomes. Gallagher, Stepien, and Rosenthal (1992) investigated the effects of problem-based learning with gifted high school students. The experimental group enrolled in an interdisciplinary problem-based course called Science, Society, and the Future (SSF). They were compared with an equally talented group of students who took a more traditional science course on the use of problem-solving steps in ill-structured problems. Students in the experimental condition scored significantly higher than those in the comparison group on a measure of problem finding. The importance of problem finding was emphasized by Gallagher and her colleagues: "The comparison students actually became more fixed in the pattern of jumping from gathering information to implementing solutions without systematic analysis of the problem or possible solutions" (p. 199).

A number of empirical studies have demonstrated academic and motivational benefits as a result of involvement by gifted secondary students in inquiry-driven, realistic science programs. Tyler-Wood, Mortenson, Putney, and Cass (2000) engaged gifted secondary students in a 2-year integrated mathematics and science program with realistic laboratories. Sustained superior science and mathematics achievement was recorded until the completion of high school. Etkina, Matilsky, and Lawrence (2003) involved students in a year-long astrophysics program. Scientific concepts were enhanced, and the students' performance on Advanced Placement (AP) tests was superior without having taken the AP course. Stake and Mares (2001) did not find an overall attitudinal benefit from a science enrichment program, but girls with supportive teachers and parents did benefit directly. Melber (2003), examining a museum-based program, found an interesting switch from a career interest in medicine to science itself.

Curriculum in Science for High–Ability Students

What makes an effective science program for high-ability students? At issue is the need for exemplary materials, a curriculum that is tied to the materials, and teacher effectiveness (Johnson, Boyce, & VanTassel-Baska, 1995). According to VanTassel-Baska (1997), the curriculum, including materials and instruction, should focus on active learning; problem solving; in-depth study in units; and independent, as well as small-group, learning. Reading should be advanced appropriately for high-ability learners. The materials, activities, and methods of instruction should develop curiosity, objectivity, and skepticism. As a part of the National Science Curriculum Project for High-Ability Learners, Johnson et al. reviewed 27 sets of science materials available for grades K–8. Their purpose was to "specify appropriate science standards for high-ability learners and to apply those standards to the review of existing science materials and to the development of new science curriculum" (p. 36). Based on criteria established for this project, the results indicated that the least desirable materials for this student population were basal science texts. Basal science texts do not provide for in-depth study; they attempt to "cover" a wide range of topics, are generally written for the average student, and do not provide for the problem-solving activities in science that high-ability students need to promote their interest in science. What the review did indicate was that modular and other supplementary materials do provide curricula that meet the needs of high-ability students through their depth and complexity by being inquiry-based and by engaging students in higher level thinking skills. Neu, Baum, and Cooper (2004), based on a case study of an exceptional science fair laureate, suggested that traditional teaching methods might be appropriate for non-science majors who need the content as a means rather than end, but nurturing focused science talent requires experiential pedagogy that includes scientific inquiry.

Examples of modular units for high-ability students were developed through funding from the Jacob K. Javits Gifted and Talented Students Act (VanTassel-Baska, 1997). Units focus on the concept of systems and connect science systems to social, political, and economic systems. Each unit encourages students to do scientific research of their own design and provides in-depth study of issues related to the central theme of the unit. To assess student achievement in science skills, a national study of one unit called Acid, Acid Everywhere was conducted in 17 school districts. Forty-five experimental and 17 comparison classrooms in grades 4–6 included more than 1,000 high-ability and gifted learners in the field test (VanTassel-Baska et al., 1998). Teacher reports indicated that the problem-based, hands-on, student-centered units lead to significantly more student enthusiasm, interaction, and involvement. Students involved in the curriculum increased their ability to integrate science process skills when compared to students in classrooms not using this unit approach. Further, experimental students demonstrated increased ability to plan experiments, as well as data-gathering procedures. Both teachers and researchers recognized the importance of time and training in science and in dealing with high-ability learners to implement the curriculum effectively.

At the secondary level, community apprenticeship programs through universities and companies present alternatives for doing science and connecting science to real-world problems (Bleicher, 1993). Apprenticeship programs provide models for students to develop research strategies for ill-defined problems. The context of a working laboratory provides opportunity to practice technical skills and to develop conceptual tools (Roth, 1991).

Student Preferences in Science

Cross and Coleman (1992) investigated the science interests and preferences of high school students attending the Tennessee Governor's School for the Sciences. Students indicated frustrations with their high school science classes. Many students said they were "held back" by the pace and content of their courses. They wanted more hands-on learning experiences rather than lecture and memorization of terminology, more problem solving, more in-depth study of selected topics, and more application to the real world of science. In a secondary school AP program, Ngoi and Vondracek (2004) also have found that opportunities for original research and academic contests outside the curriculum were motivating for the students.

WHAT WE CAN DO

At Home

❧ Ensure the presence of real research activities over an extended period of time both inside and beyond the curriculum.

In the Classroom

ᵃ᷍ Reevaluate science curricula for grades K–12 in terms of methods of instruction and materials used with high-ability learners. Students with early interest in science should be introduced to experiential, hands-on, and problem-solving aspects of science.

ᵃ᷍ Prepare teachers to use materials that are different from the science basal series.

ᵃ᷍ Develop alternative methods of assessing student achievement be it through observation, use of problem-solving techniques, or product assessments.

At School

ᵃ᷍ Provide students with teachers who have strong content knowledge, as well as skills, in accommodating the needs of talented students.

ᵃ᷍ Provide teachers with the appropriate support materials for teaching science in an exploratory context.

REFERENCES

Bass, G., & Ries, R. (1995, April). *Scientific understanding in high ability high school students: Concepts and process skills.* San Francisco, CA: American Educational Research Association. (ERIC Document Reproduction Service No. ED387319)

Bleicher, R. (1993, April). *Learning science in the workplace: Ethnographic accounts of high school students as apprentices in university research laboratories.* Atlanta, GA: National Association for Research in Science Teaching Annual Meeting. (ERIC Document Reproduction Service No. ED360173)

Brandwein, P. (1981). *The gifted student as future scientist.* Ventura, CA: Ventura County Superintendent of Schools Office.

Cross, T. L., & Coleman, L. J. (1992). Gifted high school students' advice to science teachers. *Gifted Child Today, 15*(5), 25–27.

Etkina, E., Matilsky, T., & Lawrence, M. (2003). Pushing to the edge: Rutgers Astrophysics Institute motivates talented high school students. *Journal of Research in Science Teaching, 40,* 958–985.

Freedman, D. (1998, Fall). Science education: How curriculum and instruction are evolving. *Curriculum Update,* 1–3, 6, 8.

Gallagher, S., Stepien, W., & Rosenthal, H. (1992). The effects of problem-based learning on problem solving. *Gifted Child Quarterly, 36,* 195–200.

Johnson, D., Boyce, L., & VanTassel-Baska, J. (1995). Science curriculum review: Evaluating materials for high-ability learners. *Gifted Child Quarterly, 39,* 36–44.

Melber, L. M. (2003). Partnerships in science learning: Museum outreach and elementary gifted education. *Gifted Child Quarterly, 47,* 251–258.

Neu, T. W., Baum, S. M., & Cooper, C. R. (2004). Talent development in science: A unique tale of one student's journey. *Journal of Secondary Gifted Education, 16*, 30–36.

Ngoi, M., & Vondracek, M. (2004). Working with gifted science students in a public high school environment: One school's approach. *Journal of Secondary Gifted Education, 15*, 141–147.

Roth, W. (1991). *Aspects of cognitive apprenticeship in science teaching.* Lake Geneva, WI: National Association for Research in Science Teaching. (Eric Document Reproduction Service No. ED337350)

Shymansky, J., Kyle, W., & Alport, J. (1983). The effects of new science curricula on student performance. *Journal of Research in Science Teaching, 20*, 387–404.

Stake, J. E., & Mares, K. R. (2001). Science enrichment programs for gifted high school girls and boys: Predictors of program impact on science confidence and motivation. *Journal of Research in Science Teaching, 38*, 1065–1088.

Sternberg, R. J. (1982). Science and math education for the gifted: Teaching scientific thinking to gifted children. *Roeper Review 4*, 4–6.

Tyler-Wood, T. L., Mortenson, M., Putney, D., & Cass, M. A. (2000). An effective mathematics and science curriculum option for secondary gifted education. *Roeper Review, 22*, 266–269.

U.S. Department of Education National Center for Educational Statistics. (1996). *Pursuing excellence: A study of U.S. fourth-grade mathematics and science achievement in international context* (NCES Publication No. 97–255) Washington, DC: U.S. Government Printing Office.

VanTassel-Baska, J. (1997). What matters in the curriculum for gifted learners: Reflections on theory, research, and practice. In N. Colangelo & G. Davis (Eds.), *Handbook of gifted education* (2nd ed., pp.126–135). Boston: Allyn & Bacon.

VanTassel-Baska, J., Bass, G., Ries, R., Poland, D., & Avery, L. (1998). A national study of science curriculum effectiveness with high ability students. *Gifted Child Quarterly, 42*, 200–211.

PART III
SCHOOL

CHAPTER 20

MATHEMATICS CURRICULUM

Traditionally, mathematically gifted and talented students were identified as those who could compute more quickly and accurately than their classmates. Now we recognize other avenues for the exhibition of mathematical abilities: students who are talented problem solvers (even if they cannot compute very well), students who invent representations for mathematical ideas, and students who make use of technology to induce conjectures and later prove those conjectures. The evidence is growing, however, from analyses of performance within the U.S., as well as international comparisons of mathematical knowledge and performance, that deep understanding versus broad coverage, experiential learning versus drill and practice, elegance in addition to utility, and mathematics as a frame of mind for understanding the world versus an organized set of algorithms are among the underpinnings of success in the discipline and also generate defensible mathematical curricula. In addition to the opportunity to rapidly cover the subject matter, mathematics for able learners becomes a vehicle for inquiry, for esthetic expression, for satisfaction, and for making sophisticated learning connections. Seen in these ways, mathematics increases its attractiveness and importance as a core subject in general and gifted education.

WHAT WE KNOW

What Is Mathematics?
Where Is the Cutting Edge of Rich Mathematics Curriculum?

One potential obstacle to consensus about mathematics education and gifted students is that the term *mathematics* is sometimes not well understood. Mathematics includes, but is also much more than, numbers and calculating. Mathematics is also "a science of patterns . . . Investigations are always accompanied by opportunities for students to analyze and bring to the surface underlying mathematical structures that can be applied to other contexts and that can themselves be the subjects of further examination" (Schoen, Fey, Hirsch, & Coxford, 1999, p. 447). One example of this extrapolation is to be able to form generalizations from the results of problems or studies (Sriraman, 2003). This is a domain for inquiry, not merely rote memorization. Silver, Smith, and Nelson (1995) proposed that,

> Curriculum reform efforts based on a vision of school mathematics that emphasizes thinking, reasoning, problem solving, and communication rather than memorization and repetition . . . will be insufficient for students to take more mathematics courses, if those courses teach content that is too limited, if they fail to connect mathematics to students' life experiences, and if they fail to empower students to use mathematics in a wide variety of settings. (p. 22)

It is necessary to "conceive of mathematics education less as an instructional process . . . than as a socialization process" (Schoenfeld, 1992, p. 340). Students need to acquire "habits and dispositions of interpretation and sense-making" (p. 340) more than any particular set of skills to be mathematically educated. When exposed to such reconceptualized curricula, highly able pupils in grades 2–7 have been shown to achieve at high levels and to be very content with the curriculum (Robinson & Stanley, 1989).

This reconceptualization of mathematics emphasizes the depth of mathematics even as an elementary or secondary school subject and suggests two critical issues for policymakers: the possibility that not all students may have the necessary cognitive abilities to do more abstract mathematics (Stanley, Lupkowski, & Assouline, 1990), and that even the fundamentals go well beyond simple computation. The latter may be more defensible. For example, the average Japanese or Singapore student demonstrates a level of abstraction identified with a small percentage of U.S. students, but average students in the best performing U.S. public schools also attain this level of understanding (Kimmelman at al., 1999). Contemporary rich mathematics curricula may not necessarily be an elite topic under suitable circumstances.

The level of training of teachers who teach mathematics at all levels appears to be relevant (Ma, 2003). U.S. Department of Education (n.d.) statistics compiled in the wake of the 1993–1994 TIMSS grade 12 report showed that 28% of U.S. secondary school mathematics teachers did not have either a major or minor in mathematics and that the problem was more serious in minority and low-SES schools. In an innovative study, Leinhardt (1989) compared the lessons of expert teachers versus novices. Experts were four teachers whose students experienced the highest 15% of growth and whose pupils' final performance was in the top 20% for the district. The teachers were each observed for 3 months. In contrast to the novice teachers, the expert group "tended to use well-known representations and also to use the same representation for multiple explanations" (p. 66). They wove together series of lessons, explicitly helped the students make shifts across topics, gave logical and rule-bound explanations of new material and linked it to previous topics, made differentiated judgments about how much repetition and practice were needed, and generally provided "rich agendas" (p. 52). They were also intentional in deciding for each topic "whether the explanations should be discovered, guided, or directly given . . ." (p. 74).

Looking at what outstanding teachers do, in combination with a contemporary definition of mathematics, leads to the question of what should be a modern mathematics curriculum in general, and specifically for gifted students. The National Council of Teachers of Mathematics' (1991) *Professional Teaching Standards,* which have guided curricula in the 1990s, promote the kind of teaching style observed in Leinhardt's (1989) expert teachers noted above, but some states, notably California, have adopted standards that veer in exactly the opposite direction (Cossey, 1999). Most textbook curricula in the United States favor broad coverage of topics rather than deep understanding, problem finding, and problem solving. Computational skills are often, but not always, developed in isolation; some do have strong problem-solving emphases. Cossey noted that higher TIMSS results were correlated with focused curricula, covering fewer topics in greater depth—a key element in contemporary rich mathematics curricula. Battista (1999) lamented that there are no commercially available mathematics curricula that are "systematically and completely based on scientific constructivism" (p. 432) and went so far as to describe most existing curricula as "mere caricatures of genuine reform curricula" (p. 433), but there are in fact an increasing number of curricula and texts that include some or most of the desirable qualities of good mathematics curricula, and perhaps none can ultimately do it all. Canadian TIMSS scores were above those of the U.S. (531 versus 502, overall average 487) in 1999 even though similar curricular materials were used in both countries. The highest

Canadian province was Quebec where, as in most of Canada, mathematics is compulsory through the end of high school and the curriculum (*Défi* in French, or *Challenge* in English) is designed around the newer conceptualizations in mathematics, but it remains a broad curriculum; however, high school ends at grade 11 in Quebec. Together, these potentially conflicting views suggest that strong performance in challenging mathematical curriculum is attainable for more U.S. students than those that now benefit, and it is perhaps attainable at a younger age—a point further explored below (cf. Usiskin, 1987). A corollary is that creatively challenging mathematics curriculum that includes, but also goes beyond, traditional expectations may not be the exclusive prerogative of the gifted. One of the richest sources of examples of promising mathematics curricula is Sheffield's (1999) *Developing Mathematically Promising Students*, whose 32 chapters are too numerous to describe in detail here, but from which examples have been drawn for the concluding section of this chapter. There is considerable reason to be optimistic about the potential to enhance mathematical abilities in U.S. youth.

What Does it Mean to Be Mathematically Gifted? Is the Mathematical Thinking of Gifted Students Unique?

As shown in two reviews of the literature (Sowell, 1993; Sowell, Bergwall, Zeigler, & Cartwright, 1990), there is no single definition of mathematical giftedness, but the direction of thinking is toward successful performance in the kinds of curricula being advocated in reform efforts since those reviews were written. The Russian psychologist Krutetskii (1976) provided some of the richest descriptions of such thinking. Able pupils see even single problems as part of a class or category of problems. They identify the hidden generality as what may seem to others to be disparate elements. They generalize quickly and broadly both knowledge of the subject matter (declarative knowledge to a cognitive scientist) and of the processes by which problems are solved (procedural knowledge). In a large series of detailed case studies, he showed that gifted pupils seek the clearest, shortest, and simplest solutions to problems, consistent with what mathematicians call elegance. He referred to mathematically gifted pupils as having a "mathematical cast of mind" (p. 302) and noted that this appears by age 7 or 8. This is consistent with recent research that shows that what parents identify as mathematical ability at kindergarten age is highly correlated with IQ (.92) and a differentiated mathematical ability might only appear later (Pletan, Robinson, Berninger, & Abbot, 1995). Calculating ability does not appear early, but there is typically an early interest in numbers (Radford, 1990).

Even in the 1960s, Krutetskii noted that able students' problem solving is characterized by insight and seeing general phenomena through a mathematical lens. They report much less fatigue in mathematics classes, and they made fewer errors. The characteristics reported by Krutetskii are highly consistent with the evolving view of mathematics as a domain centered on recognizing patterns in events as they occur, on reframing familiar events into mathematical terms, tackling problems in depth for extended periods of time, and in relation to other knowledge. It is also explicit that mathematical performance is both a cognitive and an affective event, so mathematical curricula need to address both content and motivation. In effect, able mathematics students think mathematically in ways that are comparable to the ways expert or professional mathematicians think about mathematical problems (Pelletier & Shore, 2003; Sriraman, 2004).

The directions of contemporary thinking within the discipline reveal many similarities to curricular advice in gifted education. Schoen et al. (1999) pondered: "Can a curriculum that works well for average and below average students be challenging enough for the most talented students?" (p. 449). Whatever curriculum one selects or designs is likely to need some adaptation for highly able students. There are many mathematics curricula and there are many kinds of giftedness, so the needed adaptations will depend on choices regarding both. Mathematics is unquestionably a domain relevant to gifted education. Knowing how gifted children think mathematically and how this thinking differs from other students can help design both regular and differentiated mathematics curricula. These curricula may not be entirely the same, but they are likely to be more similar in terms of thinking process and to differ more in terms of the specific mathematical content, especially with regard to level of abstraction. Earlier research has focused almost exclusively on speed and breadth of mathematics learning; these differences persist and need to be acknowledged, while new ones are added.

The Study of Mathematically Precocious Youth (SMPY) experience has shown that high achieving seventh- and eighth-grade students can learn the high school mathematics curriculum in a quarter to a third of the usual time (Bartovitch & Mezynski, 1981). Students found fast-paced summer courses challenging and that such accelerated courses did prepare them for the next level of studies (Mills, Ablard, & Lynch, 1992). Cossey's (1999) reference to the TIMSS advantage in focused curricula covering fewer topics in greater depth may not be contradictory: For young teenagers who have already demonstrated the capacity to independently learn large portions of mathematics curriculum available in texts and other materials, the Saturday and summer experiences provided by SMPY (cf. Fox, 1974, for the original description) may well have provided greater depth in selected topics.

Even at the elementary level, cognitive gaps in abstract reasoning can span four grade levels (Ablard & Tissot, 1998). These observations typically led to advice to accelerate the progress of such students through the mathematics or total curriculum. Similarly, Mason (1997) found that more than a third of gifted students in grades 6–8 skipped steps in four-level hierarchy of geometric thinking. Even though they did not know all the definitions in geometry, they attempted to deduce the definition from context and then reasoned consistently with that definition, correct or not. Although reasoning was their strength, this did not mean they could, a priori, construct a formal geometric proof. Mason and Moore (1997) concluded that compacting, acceleration, and advanced placement under certain conditions were compatible with these differences in mathematical thinking.

Acceleration at the very least achieves efficient content coverage. It also benefits social and emotional adjustment (Benbow, 1991), and there are no signs of ill effects in important domains such as friendships or work (Brody & Benbow, 1987). However, it is not clear to what extent these positive outcomes are the result of any suitable attention at all rather than the best possible outcomes. Acceleration on its own does not address the critical question of what characterizes the mathematical thinking processes of highly able young mathematicians. Stanley et al. (1990) viewed it as a means to a good educational fit for a small percentage of children, not as a universal solution. Even from that narrow perspective, the follow-up studies of accelerated students support the absence of disadvantages, but also report small conceptual gains years later (Swiatek & Benbow, 1991). The advantage of a year or more gained to do other things is not a mathematical question; whether or not this advantage might be gained at a possible price in mathematical sophistication has not been reported. There are also many different kinds of acceleration. Accelerated students, whether this is achieved by summer courses, curriculum compacting, fast-paced courses, grade skipping, or other means, obtain two further advantages that have two distinct benefits for bright students: They are congregated at least part-time with other children who are able and interested in mathematics, and a space is created in the curriculum to extend the exploration of mathematics or other subjects.

Before leaving the acceleration issue that has played such a prominent role in the gifted education literature, two other points are relevant. First, as just suggested, acceleration comes in many forms. These vary in two main dimensions: first, the time of introduction of a topic, and second, the pace of teaching an idea. The U.S. standard curriculum teaches many subjects considerably later than in other countries, so teaching these subjects earlier is not acceleration in international terms. Algebra and geometry are most often taught at grades 9 and 10 in the U.S., 2 years later than for students in Japan, Singapore, Ireland, and Canada. Some of the best U.S. schools already teach these subjects in grades 8 and 9; this may be acceleration to some U.S. educators, but it is still a year behind the point of introduction of these subjects elsewhere. Only 1–2% of U.S. students take algebra in grade 7 or 8; perhaps these are the only U.S. students getting the equivalent of the standard mathematics education in the highest performing countries. Stanley may be right that fast-paced mathematics around grades 7 or 8 is only suitable for a few, but earlier introduction of mathematical topics seems appropriate for most U.S. students under good environmental conditions. That seems to offer the greatest promise of raising national performance. Even earlier introduction may also meet the needs of some gifted children.

Wieczerkowski and Prado (1993) reviewed two important issues: Is mathematical giftedness an expression of specific cognitive abilities or is it largely due to general intellectual abilities, and is it a uniform construct, or are there many different profiles of mathematical giftedness? Their conclusion was that it is not uniquely the expression of some mathematical ability, because it includes a number of cognitive abilities that function in many domains, for example, the ability to easily shift between different mental representations, being able to readily create new mental representations, and metacognitive abilities (also see Benito, 2000). This is consistent with Krutetskii's (1976) conceptualizations, the idea of domain-general versus domain-specific abilities (Keating, 1990), and the relationship between giftedness and expertise (Pelletier & Shore, 2003; Shore, 2000). For example, most successful mathematics students, when faced with a challenge, switched to another appropriate strategy rather than trial-and-error (Kaizer & Shore, 1995)—this division occurred at a relatively high level of overall performance, consistent with the suggestion by Stanley et al. (1990) that only a minority of students may be able to cope with the most abstract topics. While domain-general abilities are involved in the process of, for example, linking new learning to old, domain-specific knowledge is essential to being able to recognize a mathematical problem as part of a larger class of problems, or as a member of several categories of problems depending on the content or perspective. Wieczerkowski and Prado further concluded that learners themselves report that in their experience mathematical thinking is different, a position consistent with nearly a century of factor-analytic studies in which spatial-mathematical thinking shows some different subtest intercorrelations than vocabulary and general knowledge. Consider that up to 76% of students who are enrolled in high-ability mathematics classes are also in high-ability English courses (U.S. Department of Education, 1994; also see references to Friedman [1994, 1995] in the next section). "Interest in mathematical problems is almost always related to a higher level of achievement and conception of oneself as a bright achiever" (Wieczerkowski & Prado, p. 448). Mathematical ability may be only a partly unique ability. Although perhaps not at the most extreme high levels, but perhaps so at the level of what we might refer to as high-ability or gifted classes in which children variously identified are congregated part- or full-time, it might be appropriate to question the existence of mathematical ability as a special gift, therefore offering a challenge to models of intelligence that stress the distinctness of mathematical ability (e.g., multiple intelligences).

There is not yet clear evidence that mathematical ability is a different kind of ability, nor does there have to be. The differences that are found could be the results of selective attention steered by opportunity and interest. This, if confirmed, would be the ideal outcome and opportunity for educators, because it would mean that students' success in mathematics is the result of learning.

Gender Differences in Mathematics Learning

Gender differences are addressed elsewhere in this volume, and partly in terms of mathematics. The key question here is whether there are any gender differences in mathematical thinking that matter. Some apparently relevant differences have been found. Becker (1990) looked at the kinds of mathematics problems and test items on which boys and girls differed in performance. Boys' performance tended to be higher in algebra (relatively abstract), and girls were better in problems involving data sufficiency (analytical skills were needed to detect the need to reframe the problem) and on mathematical reasoning unrelated to the specific curriculum (both tasks possibly aided by verbal abilities). Within mathematics, Sprigler and Alsup (2003) found no significant differences in reasoning ability. It is also interesting that girls found the algebra word problems to be harder, and this suggests that they may not have had as much instruction or experience in making transformations from one representation to another. Halpern (1986) concluded that there are not substantial structural differences in the mathematical abilities of boys and girls, except for visual-spatial differences that may be related to different characteristics for each sex. She noted that verbal differences are small, quantitative or computational abilities intermediate, and visual-spatial abilities large, but that even small differences can be important with extreme giftedness. In a series of meta-analyses of studies on gender differences in mathematical thinking among gifted and college-bound adolescents, Friedman (1994, 1995) found that verbal and mathematical skills are more highly correlated than spatial and mathematical skills, and mathematical-spatial correlations are higher among girls than boys. However, the decrease observed in recent decades in gender differences in both mathematical and spatial skills that she summarizes supports the notion that the quality of instruction, experience, or opportunity are important variables. This absence of gender difference was also reported, for example, in geometric proof writing (Senk & Usiskin, 1983).

The idea that boys and girls in the same class might not just learn but also be taught different things may sound preposterous, but Fox and Soller (1999) sat girls and boys in a grade 7 accelerated mathematics class on opposite sides of the classroom and then observed that the teacher taught to the boys' side only. To add to the irony, the gifted boys were more likely than the girls to have noticed this biased behavior. The success of single-sex schooling may be the result of not ignoring the girls rather than teaching them differently, and it may affect motivation; this success is also related to SES.

Lubinski and Humphreys (1990), reviewing SMPY data going back to the 1960s, concluded that gifted students display less sex-stereotyped behavior and are more likely to diverge in the direction of the opposite sex in interests: Females reject male stereotypic career paths and were less stereotypic on verbal-spatial ability. Ravaglia, Suppes, Stillinger, and Alper (1995) also noted that among highly successful computer-instructed Advanced Placement (AP) calculus and physics students, male and female performance was virtually equal. These are two situations in which the teaching may have been more equal in attention and opportunity. Stumpf and Stanley (1996) reviewed 625 articles on gender differences and mathematics published between 1980 and 1995. They concluded that most gender differences are in achievement, not the ability to master the content. Consider that almost half the students taking AP calculus courses in 1994 were female. Nearly half (46%) of all bachelor's degrees in the mathematical sciences to U.S. citizens and permanent residents go to females (in 1997, these degrees were awarded to 5,931 women and 6,938 men). The percentage of doctorates in mathematics given to women has risen from about 10% of the cohort to about 25% in the past generation (in 1997, 172 female and 447 male students received these degrees; Hill, 2000; also see National Science Board, 1999, for earlier data). This strongly suggests that the gender gap is an educational gap (perhaps social, perhaps cognitive—but all educational) that can be reduced.

Despite reported marginalization in the classroom that includes being asked lower level questions, reinforced for cautious rather than intellectually risk-taking replies, reminded that mathematics is not a female domain, and dissuaded from emotional involvement in a topic seen as cut-and-dried by too many teachers and administrators, gifted girls do know that mathematics is important to their lives and careers. The "gender gap" that possibly remains in mathematics needs to be reconceptualized as gender differences in performance on complex mathematics problems (Gallagher, 1996), and likely only under certain conditions. For example, cooperative (versus competitive) learning, although rarely described for mathematics classes, has been shown to be potentially relevant (Neber, Finsterwald, & Urban, 2001), and especially on challenging tasks (Diezmann & Watters, 2001).

Gender differences are relevant in the sense that girls and boys may not receive equal treatment in mathematics classrooms (Tiedemann, 2002), but there is no evidence that any difference in their mathematical thinking is important enough to require differentiated curriculum. Even the persistent difference in visual-spatial thinking is relevant to boys and girls, because the critical function in mathematics is not one or another representation, but the ability to shift among mental representations, including visual-spatial and verbal. For this very reason, one should not fall into the 1970s tendency to make explanations based on aptitude-treatment interactions to address any lingering gender differences in mathematics learning. Under this quite reasonable view, if a teaching treatment could be allied with a particular student learning style, aptitude, or preferred type of mathematical thinking, then the student would learn more. The problem was and is that good teaching helped everyone, and it was not possible to identify really important learning-style differences early enough or precisely enough to connect them to particular teaching approaches. Aptitude-treatment interactions slipped into oblivion. So might gender differences.

WHAT WE CAN DO

At Home

Parental involvement should start before school age:

ᣔ Talk to your children using good grammar and assume they can reason even when they are very young, but do not expect them to reason as adults do.

๖ Read numbers, as well as words, to your child. Look at the weather page of the newspaper every day or at the weather charts on television or the Web, or look at the sides of food packages and comment on the ingredients therein.

๖ Have calculators and rulers around and take advantage of opportunities to use them in making purchases of furniture, food, light bulbs, or in calculating costs (speaking aloud) even before your child has a full understanding.

๖ Have a computer available for a child to use without adult help, and software that they can play with or explore on their own (5 or more years old computers are almost given away these days, and they can serve a young child's needs very well with lower risk of going somewhere undesirable on the Internet).

๖ Encourage participation in games of strategy such as Monopoly, Clue, chess, checkers, or Othello on game boards or a computer.

๖ Buy puzzle books (new or used) or obtain the puzzles in newspapers or downloaded from Web sites and work with your children on them until the children tell you they would rather do it themselves.

๖ Make sure your children have ample time to play and supply them with all kinds of assorted materials (white glue, toilet paper rolls, scrap blocks of wood, blunt-tipped scissors, and colored paper) to explore shapes, patterns, and relationships.

    With older children:

๖ Parental support is especially important for students' decisions to select high-level mathematics courses, and this is especially so for girls (Gallagher, 1996).

๖ Through career-exploration books, seminars, and Web sites, look for and discuss potential career goals that are good matches for high interest, hard work, and success in mathematical studies (Keynes, 1995), such as management and accounting, research in most quantitative fields, aircraft piloting, weather fore-casting, investments, sports statistics, pharmacy, banking, insurance, and furniture making. Encouragement is generally best done through positive responses to mathematics-oriented initiatives or by information, rather than by pushing for such career decisions (Lupkowski-Shoplik & Assouline, 1993).

๖ Offering to go together to job and career fairs, or encouraging children's schools to have such events are two examples of useful parental interventions. It is extremely important to avoid openly or subtly giving clues of disapproval or ridicule of choices of mathematically related careers by either boys or girls.

๖ Most parents' mathematical education is rather outdated and often limited. It is often impossible to personally help children with more advanced homework problems. Parents can help by showing that they value good effort in mathematics by offering to drive children or friends so that they can study together. Making mathematics a pleasurable social activity and expressing gentle admiration at home that the subject has become more demanding since we were in school can help students feel positive about their mathematics studies.

❧ Do not say "Math was tough for Dad, too." (Or for Mom!)

In the Classroom

❧ On a day-to-day basis, teachers can pay attention to all students and hold high expectations for each of them, avoid stereotypes and ban all racist or sexist humor, and have students express how they work their way through problems, not only solutions.

❧ A key classroom activity that requires thoughtful advanced planning is helping all students to master the transformation at the heart of mathematical thinking (Ablard & Tissot, 1998), such as changing words into formulae, expressing visual patterns in words, making written musical notation into variations of rhythm and pitch, and solving a problem using different techniques. These exercises can be made into games, art projects, dramatic performances, or whatever is needed to make them second nature. For students to be able to read and speak the language of mathematics, it cannot remain a foreign language.

❧ Lupkowski-Shoplik and Assouline (1993) proposed, perhaps controversially, that teachers should not race through the curriculum, but leave time for complex thinking and ignore the prescribed sequence of topics if it helps students to understand better. They say there is not a need to intensively study mathematics every day. At the elementary level that can mean leaving a break between mathematics classes, and at the elementary and secondary levels, interspersing mathematical recreations such as puzzles. This advice, contradictory to support for acceleration in one form or another, should probably be seen as suitable for some of the students some of the time. The contradiction is that time for complex thinking and mathematical recreations can sometimes be achieved by curriculum compacting or in-class acceleration elsewhere in the curriculum. Some suitable combination of these approaches may be defensible, depending on the class, teacher, and topics.

❧ Gallagher (1996) recommended introducing young women to the modern and ancient history of mathematics, including day-to-day applications and examples that are experienced by women as well as men, avoiding stereotypical representations. This is primarily a reference to the teacher's own choices of words and examples. Mathematical texts in North America now are rarely problematic in this regard, and the level of female participation has risen dramatically, so this is probably not the primary issue, although it remains a concern in the general gifted literature.

❧ Remain vigilant to possible inequitable practices and keep in mind that cooperative learning is not inherently equitable (depending on the cooperative model chosen), and neither is a single sex-classroom—the group dynamics need to be monitored carefully (Fox & Soller, 1999). This does not argue against cooperative learning models or single-sex classes, but merely points out that the reasons to choose or not to choose such alternatives lie elsewhere than in the mathematics curriculum.

æ Mathematics achievement on the TIMSS appears to be unrelated to the use of instructional aids or manipulatives in measurement; they were somewhat related in geometry and highly related in ratio, proportion, and percentage (Raphael & Wahlstrom, 1989). Perhaps these topics are increasingly abstract and less directly experienced in children's daily lives. Their relevance may have less to do with their being hands-on classroom aids than their reflection of time taken to develop links between mathematical concepts and children's experiences in other domains. A meta-analysis of 60 studies supports the selective long-term use of manipulatives other than pictures and diagrams (Sowell, 1989), perhaps because they too are abstract objects that may not relate to the learners' prior experiences.

æ The secondary mathematics Core-Plus curriculum (National Science Foundation, 2003) is one example of several that now include a capstone project for every course or project ideas in or at the end of each chapter. Students learn a lot from the in-depth examination of questions that interest them. Such activities, balanced by other pedagogical approaches, foster students' deep understanding and motivation. Niemi (1996) demonstrated that having students learn to explain topics to each other, even after just 7 days of instruction on explaining, drastically improved deep understanding, much more than direct teaching. Therefore, asking students to explain concepts and procedures to each other and the teacher, and to visitors through displays and knowledge fairs, should be part of classroom activity.

æ Niemi (1997) summarized the teacher's role in a curriculum not limited to mathematics:

> The teacher's task is to conceptualize pathways to guide students toward greater competence. In order to formulate such pathways, the teacher must have a model of both the student's conceptual understandings and the goal, that is, the expert conceptualizations toward which the student can be guided. Without doubt, this is a tall order, but it still does not cover everything teachers need to know. Teachers must achieve not only deep understanding of the subjects they teach but also broad knowledge about how that understanding typically develops over time and how it may be assessed. (p. 245)

To which we add to the last sentence: "...And how that understanding might atypically develop in highly able pupils."

At School

• There are many kinds of mathematics curricula that can engage gifted students. The difference that matters lies in teachers' and parents' expectations, and in the extra things teachers do with their students. To the extent possible, elements of rich mathematics curricula should be included, including in-depth understanding, active student participation in learning, and the encouragement of students' independence as mathematical thinkers, but there is also much to enjoy and learn in the worlds of computations, measurement, and number recreations.

• Due to the considerable challenge presented by advanced and abstract topics, it is very important to create intellectual peer groups by some acceptable means (Lupkowski-Shoplik & Assouline, 1993). Consider a pilot project with one or more of the promising curricular projects presented in the February 1999 issue of *Phi Delta Kappan* (cf. Reys, Robinson, Sconiers, & Mark, 1999; Schoen et al., 1999) and now commercially available, wherein many of these concepts are articulated in straightforward language.

• Introduce mathematics as early as possible for some students, and offer acceleration in some form for students. For the most advanced students, AP courses achieve this end with resources focused outside the school, or within.

• Start a mathematics club.

• Offer high-achieving mathematics students (and anyone else who would like to try) opportunities to participate in local, national, and international mathematical competitions, and treat the preparation for these as social, as well as learning, events.

• Make available to all students information about summer, weekend, and afterschool programs. Put somebody in charge of gathering and circulating this information. Try to secure some scholarships from local service groups.

REFERENCES

Ablard, K. E., & Tissot, S. L. (1998). Young students' readiness for advanced math: Precocious abstract reasoning. *Journal for the Education of the Gifted, 21,* 206–223.

Bartovitch, K. G., & Mezynski, K. (1981). Fast-paced precalculus mathematics for talented junior high students: Two recent SMPY programs. *Gifted Child Quarterly, 25,* 73–80.

Battista, M. T. (1999). The mathematical miseducation of America's youth: Ignoring research and scientific study in education. *Phi Delta Kappan, 80,* 424–433.

Becker, B. J. (1990). Item characteristics and gender differences on the SAT-M for mathematically able youths. *American Educational Research Journal, 27,* 65–87.

Benbow, C. P. (1991). Meeting the needs of gifted students through use of acceleration. In M. C. Wang, M. C. Reynolds, & H. J. Walberg (Eds.), *Handbook of special education: Research and practice* (Vol. 4, pp. 23–36). Oxford, England: Pergamon Press.

Benito, Y. (2000). Metacognitive ability and cognitive strategies to solve maths and transformation problems. *Gifted Education International, 14,* 151–159.

Brody, L. E., & Benbow, C. P. (1987). Accelerative strategies: How effective are they for the gifted? *Journal of Educational Psychology, 82,* 886–875.

Cossey, R. (1999). Are California's math standards up to the challenge? *Phi Delta Kappan, 80,* 441–443.

Diezmann, C. M., & Watters, J. J. (2001). The collaboration of mathematically gifted students on challenging tasks. *Journal for the Education of the Gifted, 25,* 7–31.

Fox, L. H. (1974). A mathematics program for fostering precocious achievement. In J. C. Stanley, D. P. Keating, & L. H. Fox (Eds.). *Mathematical talent: Discovery, description, and development* (pp. 101–125). Baltimore: Johns Hopkins University Press.

Fox, L. H., & Soller, J. F. (1999). The mathematically gifted: Bridging the gender gap. *Gifted Child Quarterly, 13,* 2–7.

Friedman, L. (1994). Meta-analytic contributions to the study of gender differences in mathematics: The relationship of spatial and mathematical skills. *International Journal of Educational Research, 21,* 361–371.

Friedman, L. (1995). The space factor in mathematics: Gender differences. *Review of Educational Research, 65,* 22–50.

Gallagher, S. A. (1996). A new look (again) at gifted girls and mathematics achievement. *Journal of Secondary Gifted Education, 7,* 459–475.

Halpern, D. F. (1986). *Sex differences in cognitive abilities.* Hillsdale, NY: Erlbaum.

Hill, S. T. (2000). *Science and engineering degrees, by race/ethnicity of recipients 1989–97* (NSF 00-311). Arlington, VA: National Science Foundation, Division of Science Resource Studies.

Kaizer, C., & Shore, B. M. (1995). Strategy flexibility in more and less competent students on mathematical word problems. *Creativity Research Journal, 8,* 113–118.

Keating, D. P. (1990). Charting pathways to the development of expertise. *Educational Psychologist, 25,* 243–267.

Keynes, H. B. (1995). Can equity thrive in a culture of mathematical excellence? In W. G. Secada, E. Fennema, & L. B. Adajian (Eds.), *New directions for equity in mathematics education* (pp. 57–92). Cambridge, England: Cambridge University Press.

Kimmelman, P., Kroese, D., Schmidt, W., van der Ploeg, A., McNeely, M., & Tan, A. (1999). *A first look at what we can learn from high performing school districts: An analysis of TIMSS data from the First in the World Consortium.* Washington, DC: National Institute on Student Achievement, Curriculum, and Assessment, Office of Educational Research and Improvement.

Krutetskii, V. A. (1976). *The psychology of mathematical abilities in schoolchildren.* Chicago: University of Chicago Press.

Leinhardt, G. (1989). Math lessons: A contrast of novice and expert competence. *Journal of Research in Mathematics Education, 20,* 52–75.

Lubinski, D., & Humphreys, L. G. (1990). A broadly based analysis of mathematical giftedness. *Intelligence, 14,* 327–355.

Lupkowski-Shoplik, A. E., & Assouline, S. G. (1993). Evidence of extreme mathematical precocity: Case studies of talented youths. *Roeper Review, 16,* 144–151.

Ma, X. (2003). Effects of early acceleration of students in mathematics on attitudes toward mathematics and mathematics anxiety. *Teachers College Record, 105,* 438–464.

Mason, M. M. (1997). The van Hiele model of geometric understanding and mathematically talented students. *Journal for the Education of the Gifted, 21,* 38–53.

Mason, M. M., & Moore, S. D. (1997). Assessing readiness for geometry in mathematically talented middle school students. *Journal of Secondary Gifted Education, 8,* 105–110.

Mills, C. J., Ablard, K. E., & Lynch, S. J. (1992). Academically talented students' preparation for advanced-level course work after individually-paced precalculus class. *Journal for the Education of the Gifted, 16,* 3–17.

National Council of Teachers of Mathematics. (1991). *Professional standards for teaching mathematics.* Reston, VA: Author.

National Science Board. (1999). *Science and engineering indicators—1998* (NSB 98-1). Arlington, VA: National Science Foundation.

National Science Foundation. (2003). *Contemporary mathematics in context: A unified approach.* Columbus, OH: Glencoe/McGraw-Hill.

Neber, H., Finsterwald, M., & Urban, N. (2001). Cooperative learning with gifted and high-achieving students: A review and meta-analysis of 12 studies. *High Ability Studies, 12,* 199–214.

Niemi, D. (1996). A fraction is not a piece of a pie: Assessing exceptional performance and deep understanding in elementary school mathematics. *Gifted Child Quarterly, 40,* 70–80.

Niemi, D. (1997). Cognitive science, expert-novice research, and performance assessment. *Theory and Practice, 36,* 239–246.

Pelletier, S., & Shore, B. M. (2003). The gifted learner, the novice, and the expert: Shaping emerging views of giftedness. In D. C. Ambrose, L. Cohen, & A. J. Tannenbaum (Eds.), *Creative intelligence: Toward theoretic integration* (pp. 237–281). New York: Hampton Press.

Pletan, M. D., Robinson, N. M., Berninger, V. W., & Abbot, R. D. (1995). Parents' observations of kindergartners who are advanced in mathematical reasoning. *Journal for the Education of the Gifted, 19,* 30–44.

Radford, J. (1990). *Child prodigies and exceptional early achievers.* London: Harvester Wheatsheaf.

Raphael, D., & Wahlstrom, M. (1989). The influence of instructional aids on mathematics achievement. *Journal for Research in Mathematics Education, 20,* 173–190.

Ravaglia, R., Suppes, P., Stillinger, C., & Alper, T. M. (1995). Computer-based mathematics and physics for gifted students. *Gifted Child Quarterly, 39,* 7–13.

Reys, B., Robinson, E., Sconiers, S., & Mark, J. (1999). Mathematics curricula based on rigorous national standards: What, why, and how? *Phi Delta Kappan, 80,* 454–456.

Robinson, A., & Stanley, T. D. (1989). Teaching to talent: Evaluating an enriched accelerated mathematics program. *Journal for the Education of the Gifted, 12,* 253–267.

Schoen, H. L., Fey, J. T., Hirsch, C. R., & Coxford, A. F. (1999). Issues and options in the math wars. *Phi Delta Kappan, 80,* 444–453.

Schoenfeld, A. H. (1992). Learning to think mathematically: Problem solving, metacognition, and sense making in mathematics. In D. A. Grouws (Ed.), *Handbook of research on mathematics teaching and learning* (pp. 334–370). New York: Macmillan.

Senk, S. L., & Usiskin, Z. (1983). Geometry proof writing: A new view of sex differences in mathematics ability. *American Journal of Education, 91,* 187–201.

Sheffield, L. J. (Ed.). (1999). *Developing mathematically promising students.* Reston, VA:
National Council of Teachers of Mathematics.

Shore, B. M. (2000). Metacognition and flexibility: Qualitative differences in how
gifted children think. In R. C. Friedman & B. M. Shore (Eds.), *Talents unfolding: Cognition and development* (pp. 167–187). Washington, DC: American
Psychological Association.

Silver, E. A., Smith, M. S., & Nelson, B. S. (1995). The QUASAR Project: Equity concerns meet mathematics education reform in the middle school. In W. G. Secada,
E. Fennema, & L. B. Adajian (Eds.), *New directions for equity in mathematics education* (pp. 9–56). Cambridge, England: Cambridge University Press.

Sowell, E. J. (1989). Effects of manipulative materials in mathematics instruction.
Journal of Research in Mathematics Education, 20, 498–505.

Sowell, E. J. (1993). Programs for mathematically gifted students: A review of empirical research. *Gifted Child Quarterly, 37,* 124–129.

Sowell, E. J., Bergwall, L., Zeigler, A. J., & Cartwright, R. M. (1990). Identification
and description of mathematically gifted students: A review of empirical research.
Gifted Child Quarterly, 34, 147–154.

Sprigler, D. M., & Alsup, J. K. (2003). An analysis of gender and the mathematical
reasoning ability sub-skill of analysis-synthesis. *Education, 123,* 763–769.

Sriraman, B. (2003). Mathematical giftedness, problem solving, and the ability to for-
mulate generalizations: The problem-solving experiences of four gifted students.
Journal of Secondary Gifted Education, 14, 151–165.

Sriraman, B. (2004). Gifted ninth graders' notions of proof: Investigating parallels in
approaches of mathematically gifted students and professional mathematicians.
Journal for the Education of the Gifted, 27, 267–292.

Stanley, J. C., Lupkowski, A. E., & Assouline, S. G. (1990). Eight considerations for
mathematically gifted youth. *Gifted Child Today, 13,* 2–4.

Stumpf, H., & Stanley, J. C. (1996). Gender-related differences on the College Board's
Advanced Placement and Achievement Tests, 1982–1992. *Journal of Educational
Psychology, 88,* 353–364.

Swiatek, M. A., & Benbow, C. P. (1991). A 10-year longitudinal follow-up of participants in a fast-paced mathematics course. *Journal of Research in Mathematics
Education, 22,* 138–150.

Tiedemann, J. (2002). Teachers' gender stereotypes as determinants of teacher perceptions in elementary school mathematics. *Educational Studies in Mathematics, 50,*
49–62.

U.S. Department of Education. (1994). *Curricular differentiation in public high schools.*
Washington, DC: Office of Educational Research and Improvement, National
Center for Educational Statistics.

U.S. Department of Education. (n.d.). *TIMSS 12th grade report: Questions and answers.*
Washington, DC: Office of Educational Research and Improvement.

Usiskin, Z. (1987). Why elementary algebra can, should, and must be an eighth-grade
course for average students. *Mathematics Teacher, 80,* 428–438.

Wieczerkowski, W., & Prado, T. M. (1993). Programs and strategies for nurturing
talents/gifts in mathematics. In K. A. Heller, F. J. Mönks, & A. H. Passow (Eds.),
International handbook of research and development of giftedness and talent (pp. 443–
451). Oxford, England: Pergamon.

AUTHOR NOTE

A note of special gratitude is due to Dr. Zalman Usiskin, University of Chicago, for copious detailed reviewer's notes and suggestions on the first draft of this chapter. The final version is certain not to do full justice to this and other feedback received, and the errors that remain are ours, not his.

CHAPTER 21

ARTS IN THE CURRICULUM

Education in the arts has the potential for developing problem-solving and critical thinking skills, self-confidence in one's expressive abilities, communication, work ethic, an appreciation for cultural uniqueness and contributions to society, a specific literacy, and perhaps a lifelong vocation or avocation.

WHAT WE KNOW

Despite the inclusion of the arts in the U.S. Department of Education's definition of gifted and talented (Marland, 1972) and as a core subject in the No Child Left Behind Act (U.S. Department of Education, 2001), few schools, districts, or states require artistic abilities to be assessed along with other aspects of intelligence or academic performance. (Oreck, Owen, & Baum, 2003, p. 63)

Perhaps because of this lack of assessment, there is a trend in many school districts to eye the visual and performing arts as a frill to be cut when budgets become tight (Fuller, 1994). However, others—mostly larger districts—recognize the presence of talented students by providing schools that focus on specialized training. Arts-focused schools are having success through strong emphasis on student-master faculty interaction, supportive environments for students who are often viewed as different from their age peers, active arts-community ties that provide venues for students, and parental involvement (Daniel, 2000). Recent studies, using qualitative, quantitative, and mixed methods of investigation, show the importance of these components for students who exhibit advanced abilities in music, dance, drama, and the visual arts. Interviews with master teachers and individuals who are now in performing and visual arts careers and studies that track students through their school years bear witness to the impact of opportunities provided by schools and special lessons (Clark & Zimmerman, 2002; Oreck, Baum, & McCartney, 2000; Stollery & McPhee, 2002). There is an emphasis placed on the necessity of excellent teaching by those who not only are very good at what they do, but also have teaching skills, project interest in their students, and motivate them (Burland & Davidson, 2002; Golomb, 2004; Haroutounian, 2000a, 2000b; Subotnik, 2002). Studies that confirm that a supportive school environment where parents are involved and where the students can be themselves and develop self-esteem and confidence is vital, although often elusive as artistically talented students may not be part of the mainstream culture of the school (Burland & Davidson; Dai & Schader, 2002; Haroutounian, 2000a, 2000b, 2000c).

Clark and Zimmerman (1994) and Eisner (1998) acknowledged the limited and isolated research in art education and called for the investigation of practices from preschool to adulthood. Eisner, in particular, commented that the research found in journals tends to claim the value of the arts as contributors to other areas of academic study. For example, music instruction improves mathematics achievement, and drama improves writing skills. Eisner considered basic skills to be auxiliary outcomes, and instead encouraged research that stressed what the arts can do in and of themselves. For Eisner, important outcomes are enrichment, development of discipline, appreciation and development of creativity, and honest critique of artists' endeavors.

The Importance of the Arts

In mainstream school classrooms, proponents of arts education link the contribution of all art forms to basic curricular goals such as problem solving, literacy, mathematics, cultural sensitivity, leadership, and neuromuscular development. According to Krause (1987), arts education develops creative leaders by encouraging creative approaches to problem solving. Eisner (1998) added that it enriches flexible thinking by transferring ideas, images, and feelings into an art form; by developing awareness of the qualities of the art form; and by building understanding of the time and culture in which the art form was created. "Arts contribute to intellectual capacities that may complement, but are different from traditional subjects" (Rasmussen, 1998, p. 1). Each discipline is unique, and so brings with it a specific strength, set of skills, vocabulary, and history; hence, the arts broaden intellectual learning and appreciation (Lehman & Sinatra, 1988).

Adams (1992) noted that the arts provide opportunities for creative thinking, foster imagination, and are a rigorous and substantive study of human culture and history that lead to aesthetic literacy. The arts build descriptive language and personal expression in many forms and provide emotional outlets and validate students' ideas and work. Webster (2000) gave an explanation for the problem-solving power of music. In case study examples of his musical improvisation/composition and active listening projects, he shows how students learn to make judgments about musical content, exercise their creative and critical thinking, and work with others to construct their collective understanding of the work under consideration. Webster incorporated the technology of multimedia software that asks students to demonstrate their understanding of this music both historically and musically.

Opportunities in the Arts

Lehman and Sinatra (1988) reported that during the early 1980s, music was offered in some fashion in 93% of U.S. public high schools, and art in 90%. They projected that by the end of the decade, 22 states would require a course in some area of the arts as a graduation requirement. They suggested that high school students preparing for college should have participated in intensive work in at least one of the arts. The value of such experiences can "provide students with the unique concepts and modes of thinking that are available through that art form" (p. 67). However, their prediction was not to become a reality. Many states lost their arts programs to budget cuts. In one startling statistic, although the Music Educator National Conference (MENC) recommended that schools have one qualified music teacher for every 450 students at the elementary level, Los Angeles, like other large cities, had one for every 4,700 students (Mann, 1988).

Few public schools have a differentiated curriculum for artistically gifted and talented students (Clark & Zimmerman, 1994). In secondary schools, the options are the traditional art class, band, orchestra, and choir. In many cases, smaller districts do not have even this range of options. In fact, most small school districts have no provision for a differentiated curriculum for talented students (Leonhard, 1991). According to Clark and Zimmerman (1994), program opportunities can consist of everything from heterogeneously grouped instruction and in-class enrichment to ability-grouped instruction, with most programs based on a predetermined curriculum for all students. Greenburg (1996) laments that the curriculum in art classes has been forced to fit into

Discipline Based Art Education (DBAE), eliminating spontaneous activity that art educators believe to be essential to creative activities. The secondary level is likewise fitted with a set curriculum that does not have room for extension for talented students and that focuses on products rather than on exploration and development. Greenberg criticized the emphasis on paper-and-pencil testing and assignments rather than the creative endeavors that should be part of the arts experience. She believes accountability procedures have curtailed creativity.

The Value of a Differentiated Arts Curriculum

According to Seeley (1989) and Fuller (1994), arts education designed properly for the talented learner has many values. Others agree. It promotes individuality, has cognitive, affective, and psychomotor benefits (Buchanan, 1989), and leads to development of other intelligences (Colwell & Davidson, 1996). This belief is supported by an analysis of the SAT scores from 2001–2005 as reported by MENC (2006). Students taking the SAT who had coursework and experience in music scored 51 points higher on the verbal part of the test and 39 points higher on the mathematics portion than students who had no coursework or experience in the arts. These achievements also held true for students in other areas of the arts. Moreover, the longer a student studied the arts, the higher the scores in both areas. These intriguing studies should be replicated with attention to population variables to extend understanding of this impact of the arts.

Despite the funding crisis for the arts, there are several programs appearing in schools, backed by private sponsors. A model program known as CREST (Creative Resources Enriching Student Talents) provides a differentiated curriculum for students talented in the arts (Krause, 1987). This model, which serves students from kindergarten through the sixth grade, includes a curriculum of activities not available in regular arts programs or easily provided by parents. CREST is based on student interests and includes problem solving and self-expression. Arts activities are taught by specialists and include creative writing, calligraphy, dance, drawing, drama, folk singing, organ and piano, pottery, music composition, storytelling, design, and puppetry. Structured as a pull-out program, CREST ultimately incorporates student achievements into classroom activities and leads to production of original individual and group projects. Evaluation has documented increased creative ability, more openness to new experiences, and increased reading levels for participants.

Another model program featuring dance, music, and theater called the Arts Connection–New Horizons program for elementary schools of New York City, has developed a talent identification process to assess potential abilities of students in grades 4–6 (Baum, Owen, & Oreck, 1996). The process has been used over a period of years and is found to be "valid, reliable, and equitable" (p. 17). Identified students who wish to participate receive an initial core arts curriculum, and when ready, may go on to more advanced experiences. The evaluators reported that "over 75% of the core group students received good to excellent end-of-year evaluations from the arts faculty" (p. 17). Other benefits of the Arts Connection were increased self-regulation in the other areas of school performance and improved scores on standardized reading and math tests. Classroom teachers in the students' home schools receive training to integrate curriculum with the Art Connection experiences of their students. Finally, parents and families are involved with the educational and artistic opportunities available not only in school, but throughout the city.

One area of research that gained interest in recent years is that of particular populations' responses to arts education. This necessitated a concerted effort in identification processes and program development that met the specific needs of groups such as disadvantaged urban and rural children and individuals with disabilities. A model program specific to music is called MUSICLINK (Haroutounian, 2000a). Begun in 1992, this University of Virginia program was adopted by the Music Teachers National Association (MTNA), an organization of college music faculty and independent music teachers, and national implementation was underway by 1998. Through their decision to voluntarily provide private music instruction to school students of any age who show evidence of potential talent in music and who cannot afford private lessons, talented students who would have had no opportunity to explore the possibilities are identified and served. Students are recommended by the school music specialist by use of a rating scale that gives a profile of the student's abilities. The program targets at-risk students and offers resources such as instruments, teachers who come to the home or school, an ongoing relationship with a caring adult through lessons, frequent evaluation reports, a structured activity for afterschool hours, recognition of progress, a path into higher education, and a marketable skill for the future. Independent studies completed by the students show remarkable skill and intellect. The students design their curriculum to meet their interests and strengths. For example, one sophomore combined her piano and flute skills with her interest in Spanish.

> She gathered together solo repertoire in flute and piano suitable for a recital of Spanish music, researching the Spanish musical style and writing suitable program notes in Spanish. . . . Her work will be assessed by her private music teacher, school music teacher, Spanish teacher, and guidance counselor. (pp. 18-19)

Students in rural areas often have limited or no opportunities for differentiated curriculum in the arts. Clark and Zimmerman (2001) developed a scheme of local and standardized measures to identify students who have potential in the visual arts. Their Project ARTS administered the Torrance Tests of Creativity (1990), Clark's Drawing Abilities Test (1989), and state achievement tests to all third-grade students. These measures correlated well to locate artistically able children, particularly economically disadvantaged and ethnically diverse students who would normally be omitted from art-talent programs. These students had little exposure to galleries, museums, concert halls, and other venues—the usual experiences needed to do well on typical identification measures (Torrance, 1997). Clark and Zimmerman (2001) noted that they brought rich cultural heritages that were tapped by this identification process. They called for multiple-criteria "with an emphasis on measures of various aspects of students' backgrounds, behaviors, skills, abilities, achievement, personalities, and values" (p. 105). They said that leaders need training in developing local identification measures that assess the unique social, support, motivation, ethnic, and economic characteristics of any site.

Reis, Schader, Milne, and Stephens (2003) extended the identification process to individuals with disabilities, specifically Williams syndrome, a disabling condition with attendant ability in music. The success of using a talent development approach instead of focusing on remediation was found to enhance participants' understanding of mathematics and build self-confidence and life enjoyment. This study opens possibilities for similar success for individuals with other conditions through a change in the way the person is viewed through talent development.

Oreck et al. (2003) and Morrissey (2001) addressed the identification of the creatively gifted person in contrast to the academically gifted person. Oreck et al. (2003) offer a Performing Arts Talent Assessment that is structured to give as many students as possible the opportunity to participate in an arts program. They posited that "[w]hen talent is defined and assessed too narrowly, many students will be missed, many more discouraged, and the conception of artistic talent will remain isolated from other abilities and intelligences" (p. 67). Through the use of multisession, multiobserver "authentic arts experiences" (p. 67) in dance, music, and theater, students who would be overlooked during traditional auditions are given the opportunity to show their potential. Morrissey examined the artistic life of guitarist Jimi Hendrix to provide clues to personal and environmental characteristics associated with gifted potential that are outside mainstream identification. Attributes such as extraordinary sensitivity to sound and powerful intrinsic motivation come to light, even though Hendrix's only early instruments were a straw broom and a cigar box with an elastic band (p. 7). The importance of background and personality strength, rather than only academic prowess, or even opportunity, must be considered if arts education is to be equitable.

Selby, Shaw, and Houtz (2005) reminded us that creativity has countless expressions and that all students have creative potential. They cautioned us not to ask, "How creative is this student?" but instead to ask, "How is this student creative?" (p. 300) They describe creative-performance levels as: "not yet evident," "emerging," "expressing," and "excelling" (p. 310). Students who are gifted in the areas of creativity have particular thinking and learning styles and personality characteristics that translate into instructional needs and real-world application of their talents. They benefit from programs and venues that offer support, opportunity, challenge, and recognition for their effort and growth.

WHAT WE CAN DO

At Home

ஐ Become advocates for arts education. Support balanced programs of K–12 instruction with qualified teachers. Encourage high school and university requirements for participation in the arts.

ஐ Examine state department guidelines. If they limit or do not include arts requirements, work to change the guidelines.

In the Classroom

ஐ Individualize arts experiences when appropriate.

ஐ Allow students to explore and solve problems in the arts. Provide time and tools for complex thinking and expression.

At School

ஐ Begin exposure to the arts early and keep the arts an integral part of the curricula. Infuse the arts curriculum into the content of the traditional classroom.

ஐ Provide talented students with experiences with working artists. Connect to programs that bring professionals and private teachers to students who show potential, especially those who are at risk because of social or economic disadvantage.

REFERENCES

Adams, R. (1992). *Improving characterization in scene study in a magnet middle school through learning directing skills.* New York: National Arts Education Research Center. (ERIC Document Reproduction Service No. ED367006)

Baum, S., Owen, S., & Oreck, B. (1996). Talent beyond words: Identification of potential in dance and music in elementary schools. *Gifted Child Quarterly, 40*, 93–101.

Buchanan, J. (1989, March). *Music education and the educationally disadvantaged gifted child.* Paper presented at the meeting of the Suncoast Music Forum on Creativity, Tampa, FL.

Burland, K., & Davidson, J. W. (2002). Training the talented. *Music Education Research, 4*(1), 121–140.

Clark, G. (1989). Screening and identifying students talented in the visual arts: Clark's Drawing Abilities Test. *Gifted Child Quarterly, 33*, 98–105.

Clark, G., & Zimmerman, E. (1994). *Programming opportunities for gifted and talented in the visual arts.* Storrs: National Research Center on the Gifted and Talented, University of Connecticut.

Clark, G., & Zimmerman, E. (2001). Identifying artistically talented students in four rural communities in the United States. *Gifted Child Quarterly, 45*, 104–114.

Clark, G., & Zimmerman, E. (2002). Tending the special spark: Accelerated and enriched curricula for highly talented art students. *Roeper Review, 24*, 161–168.

Colwell, R., & Davidson, L. N. (1996). Musical intelligence and the benefits of music education. *National Association of Secondary School Principals Bulletin, 80*(583), 55–64.

Dai, D. Y., & Schader, R. (2002). Decisions regarding music training: Parental beliefs and values. *Gifted Child Quarterly, 46*, 135–144.

Daniel, R. (2000). Performing and visual arts schools: A guide to characteristics, options, and successes. *Journal of Secondary Gifted Education, 12*, 43–48

Eisner, E. (1998). Does experience in the arts boost academic achievement? *Art Education, 51*(4), 7–16.

Fuller, F. (1994). The arts for whose children? A challenge to educators. *NASSP Bulletin, 78*(561), 1–6.

Golomb, C. (2004). Individual differences and cultural diversity in the art forms of children talented in the visual arts. In D. Boothe & J. C. Stanley (Eds.), *In the eyes of the beholder: Critical issues for diversity in gifted education* (pp. 33–47). Waco, TX: Prufrock Press.

Greenberg, P. (1996). Time, money, and the new art education versus art and irrelevance. *Studies in Art Education, 37*(21), 155–116.

Haroutounian, J. (2000a). MUSICLINK: Nurturing talent and recognizing achievement. *Arts Education Policy Review, 101*(6), 12–20.

Haroutounian, J. (2000b). Teaching talented teenagers at the Interlochen Academy: An interview with three master teachers: Crispin Campbell, Hal Grossman, and T. J. Lymenstull. *Journal of Secondary Gifted Education, 12*, 39–42.

Haroutounian, J. (2000c). The delights and dilemmas of the musically talented teenager. *Journal of Secondary Gifted Education, 12*, 3–16.

Krause, C. (1987). A creative arts model for gifted and talented students using community resources and people. *Roeper Review, 9*, 149–151.

Lehman, P., & Sinatra, R. (1988). Assessing arts curricula in the schools: Their role, content, and purpose. In J. T. McLaughin (Ed.), *Toward a new era in arts education* (pp. 53–79). New York: American Council for the Arts.

Leonhard, C. (1991). *The status of arts education in American public schools: Report on a survey conducted by the National Arts Education Research Center at the University of Illinois.* Champaign-Urbana: University of Illinois, Council for Research on Music Education.

Mann, L. (1998, Spring). Music education's forte. *Association for Supervision and Curriculum Development Curriculum Update*, 4–5, 8.

Marland, S. P., Jr. (1972). Education of the gifted and talented: Report to the Congress of the United States by the U.S. Commissioner of Education and background papers submitted to the U.S. Office of Education, 2 vols. Washington, DC: U.S. Government Printing Office. (Government Documents, Y4.L 11/2: G36)

Morrissey, A. (2001). Beyond the image: The giftedness of Jimi Hendrix. *Roeper Review, 24*, 5–10.

MENC: The National Association for Music Education. (2006). *Scores of students in the arts.* Retrieved on June 19, 2006, from http://www.menc.org/information/advocate/sat/html

No Child Left Behind Act, 20 U.S.C. §6301 (2001).

Oreck, B., Baum, S., & McCartney, H. (2000). *Artistic talent development for urban youth: The promise and the challenge.* Storrs: National Research Center on the Gifted and Talented, University of Connecticut.

Oreck, B., Owen, S. V., & Baum, S. (2003). Validity, reliability, and equity issues in an observational talent assessment process in the performing arts. *Journal for the Education of the Gifted, 27*, 62–94.

Rasmussen, K. (1998). Arts education: A cornerstone of basic education. *Curriculum Update, 1–3*, 6.

Reis, S. M., Schader, R., Milne, H., & Stephens, R. (2003). Music & minds: Using a talent development approach for young adults with Williams syndrome. *Journal for Exceptional Children, 69*, 293–313.

Selby, E. C., Shaw, E. J., & Houtz, J. C. (2005). The creative personality. *Gifted Child Quarterly, 49*, 300–314.

Seeley, K. (1989). Arts curriculum for the gifted. In J. VanTassel-Baska, J. F. Feldhusen, K. Seeley, G. Wheatley, L. Silverman, & W. Foster (Eds.), *Comprehensive curriculum for gifted learners* (pp. 300–313). Boston: Allyn & Bacon.

Stollery, P., & McPhee, A. D. (2002). Some perspectives on musical gift and musical intelligence. *British Journal of Music Education, 19*, 89–102.

Subotnik, R. F. (2002). Talent developed: Conversations with masters in the arts and sciences. Eliot Feld: Innovator in choreography and dance company development. *Journal for the Education of the Gifted, 25*, 290–302.

Torrance, E. P. (1990). *Torrance tests of creative thinking.* Bensenville, IL: Scholastic Testing Service.

Torrance, E. P. (1997). Talent among children who are economically disabled or culturally different. In J. F. Smutny (Ed.), *The young gifted child* (pp. 95–118). Cresskill, NJ: Hampton.

Webster, P. (2000). Reforming secondary music teaching in the new century. *Journal of Secondary Gifted Education, 12*, 17–24.

CHAPTER 22

LEARNING MULTIPLE LANGUAGES

For the verbally talented student, an in-depth, coordinated language curriculum should introduce the study of a second language early. Facility in more than one language enriches leadership opportunities in careers that rely on cross-cultural understanding and communication. For students who arrive at the school door as adept bilinguals, recognition of their linguistic talents and opportunities to develop both languages have benefits.

WHAT WE KNOW

Opportunities for learning more than one language should be provided to all students in an increasingly smaller world with the concomitant need for communication across languages and cultures. Unfortunately, opportunities for the in-depth study of foreign languages to proficiency level is not a priority in most U.S. school districts. According to Draper and Hicks (2002) about 5% of students in U.S. elementary schools study a language; approximately one third of the students in grades 7–12 do so. Only about 9% of college students take language courses, and those are concentrated at the beginning levels. What is more discouraging is that only 3% of U.S. high school and college graduates achieve proficiency in a second language. For high-ability learners, three issues related to languages in the curriculum are particularly relevant: Latin instruction, opportunity for proficiency in more than one language, and appreciation for bilingual learners who display linguistic talents. The issues differ, as does the research that informs them, but all point to a sound educational practice—students in largely monolingual cultures should pursue facility in more than one language.

Learning Latin

As VanTassel-Baska (2004) pointed out, Latin may be questioned as irrelevant to a modern society, but numbers of capable high school students take the Advanced Placement (AP) Latin examination for college credit. In fact, the study of Latin provides achievement benefits in addition to the obvious achievement of learning a classical language. Taking Latin increases English vocabulary learning for high-ability learners when compared with taking a Greek and Latin roots course in English (VanTassel-Baska, 1987). In addition, one year of Latin enhances the understanding of English grammar (VanTassel-Baska, 1987). Learning the origins of words and examining the differences in a second language that cannot be easily translated into one's own language are important outcomes of language study. VanTassel-Baska concluded that if vocabulary development and linguistic competence in English are desirable program objectives for talented students, then Latin would be a logical second language choice, preferably introduced by the fourth grade (p. 160).

Language Study in the Elementary and Middle School

Some states provide opportunities for exposure to multiple languages at the elementary level, but they are the exception. For example, North Carolina mandated that all public school children study a foreign language in elementary school, and Louisiana has a foreign language program in grades 4–6 as a requirement for academically able students (Met & Rhodes, 1990). However, these are isolated examples. One reason for limited language opportunities before the high school years may be the lack of administrative support among elementary principals for foreign language in the curriculum. A study of Maryland public school elementary principals showed that more than half had a positive attitude toward such instruction, but that it was not high on their list of priorities. Most considered foreign language something that might be offered before or after school. Many introduced such programs as a response to parental demands (Baranick, 1986). Lack of interest by school leaders at the elementary level is unfortunate because greater facility with a language and increased academic achievements are associated with earlier onset of language instruction (Dominiguez & Pessoa, 2005). For example, Shults and Willard-Holt (2004) found higher achievement among learners who began language study in middle school rather than high school. In comparing three groups of students, those who studied no second language, those who began language in high school, and those who began in middle school, differences on grade 11 state achievement tests were found favoring students with middle school onset.

According to the proponents of foreign language study for the talented learner, the advantages are many (Thompson & Thompson, 1996). Because these students represent future leaders, they need to be proficient in one or more languages. They will be a part of the global market; as such, they will be limited by being monolingual. Being bilingual opens career opportunities. The study of one or more languages can lead to a multicultural perspective and an understanding of cultural differences and similarities. Language studies can contribute to the elimination of cultural provincialism for students, especially those for whom English is their only language or for students who do not live in a multicultural community. The study of multiple languages can be interdisciplinary and include the history, arts, geography, and the customs of a culture.

Program Models in Language Instruction

At the elementary level, there are basically two kinds of models employed for teaching a language: those that focus on exposure to the culture and varying amounts of language, Foreign Language Exploratory (FLEX) and Foreign Language in the Elementary Schools (FLES), and total or partial immersion programs that target language proficiency. In the 1990s, most elementary programs were FLES or FLEX oriented; proficiency was not a focus (Griffin, 1993.) Programs vary in the amount of weekly instruction and in the length for the course. Total or partial immersion programs appear to have the strongest effects on proficiency if language instruction continues beyond the elementary level (Met & Rhodes, 1990).

Bilingualism as a Talent

Although concerns continue to be expressed about the underrepresentation of second language learners in programs for high-ability learners, bilingualism can be viewed as a talent (Valdés, 2002). There is evidence that bilingualism provides selected cognitive benefits to young children on different types of tasks (Bialystok & Senman, 2004; Bialystok & Shapero, 2005), that talented learners become proficient in both languages (Kogan, 2001), and that bilingual high-school-aged learners who are identified by their families as young interpreters display a range of complex linguistic and social skills as they move rapidly back and forth between two languages and two worlds.

WHAT WE CAN DO

In the Classroom

ஃ Encourage language instruction at an early age. Kindergarten or first grade is not too soon. There is evidence to suggest that later entrance (i.e., fifth or sixth grade) does not detract from language learning (Griffin, 1993); however, younger students are more flexible, less self-conscious, and more open to new ideas. Early programs provide more opportunity to develop proficiency and to later add a third or fourth language.

ஃ At the elementary level, emphasis should be on listening and speaking and thus on the development of vocabulary. Middle or junior high and high school should include more grammar, reading, writing, and literary analysis, as well as conversation.

ஃ To foster proficiency, create normal situations in which students must communicate in the language. Use lunch breaks, as well as class times, for communication.

ஃ Arrange for experiences with native speakers as students develop proficiency. Take advantage of exchange students at local colleges and universities who would be willing to work with students. Parents need to be active in requesting language opportunities for their verbally talented child.

At School

ஃ Ensure that the language curriculum reflects a long-range plan that moves students through their full academic trajectory. There should be continued opportunities to advance to high school programs when in middle or junior high school or to advance to college programs when in high school.

ஃ Develop program options for high-ability learners in which language proficiency is a goal.

ஃ Nontraditional critical languages such as Chinese, Japanese, Russian, and Arabic are increasingly important, as well as the more prevalent Spanish. Therefore, offer opportunities for learning more than one language during the K–12 years. Sophisticated resources are available for doing so (Leaver, Ehrman, & Lekic, 2004).

The learning of multiple languages can enhance the sense of language, the importance of communication, and the acceptance and understanding of other cultures.

REFERENCES

Bialystok, E., & Senman, L. (2004). Executive processes in appearance-reality tasks: The role of inhibition of attention and symbolic representation. *Child Development, 75*, 562–579.

Bialystok, E., & Shapero, D. (2005). Ambiguous benefits: The effects of bilingualism on reversing ambiguous figures. *Developmental Science, 8*, 595–604.

Baranick, W. (1986). Attitudes of elementary school principals toward foreign language instruction. *Foreign Language Annals, 19*, 481–489.

Dominiguez, R., & Pessoa, S. (2005). Early versus late start in foreign language education: Documenting achievements. *Foreign Language Annals, 38*, 473–483.

Draper, J. B., & Hicks, J. H. (2002). *Foreign language enrollments in public secondary schools, Fall 2000*. Alexandra, VA: American Council of the Teaching of Foreign Languages.

Griffin, G. (1993). *The relationship between starting age and second language learning*. Unpublished master's thesis, Dominican College of San Raphael, CA. (ERIC Document Reproduction Service No. ED375613)

Kogan, A. (2001). *Gifted bilingual students: A paradox?* New York: Peter Lang.

Leaver, B. L., Ehrman, M., & Lekic, J. (2004). Distinguished-level learning online: Support materials from LangNet and RussNet. *Foreign Language Annals, 37*, 556–566.

Met, M., & Rhodes, N. (1990). Priority: Instruction. Elementary school foreign language instruction: Priorities for the 1990s. *Foreign Language Annals, 23*, 433–443.

Shults, D. L., & Willard-Holt, C. (2004). Promoting world languages in middle school: The achievement connection. *Foreign Language Annals, 37*, 623–629.

Thompson, M., & Thompson, M. (1996). Reflections on foreign language study for highly able learners. In J. VanTassel-Baska, D. Johnson, & L. Boyce (Eds.), *Developing verbal talent* (pp. 149–173). Needham Heights, MA: Allyn & Bacon.

Valdés, G. (2002). *Understanding the special giftedness of young interpreters* (Research Monograph No. 02158). Storrs: National Research Center on the Gifted and Talented, University of Connecticut.

VanTassel-Baska, J. (1987). The case for teaching Latin to the verbally talented. *Roeper Review, 9*, 159–161.

VanTassel-Baska, J. (2004). Quo Vadis? Laboring in the classical vineyards: An optimal challenge for gifted secondary students. *Journal of Secondary Gifted Education, 15*, 56–60.

CHAPTER 23

CAREER EDUCATION

areer education is a potentially valuable part of the curriculum for gifted children, and in many ways it is uniquely so. It is highly valued by the students, and it may help them navigate adolescence burdened by inadequate knowledge about the world of work or their own needs, multipotentiality, or of interesting occupations not normally encountered by teenagers at home or in school. Career education can facilitate later life decisions, and it offers opportunities for interesting and challenging curricular activities that can address a number of academic and social-emotional needs of gifted children. Career education is different from career choice. The literature on career education documents the problems it can ameliorate, but so far it says little about the particular contribution or effectiveness of specific curricular program models, content, or outcomes. This support for career education in gifted education is, like so much else, given on the basis of an incomplete knowledge base, but the research that exists on this topic points in very similar directions toward readily definable and defensible curriculum practices.

WHAT WE KNOW

Career education is on nearly every list of program advice in gifted education. Highly able young people have a wide range of potential occupational opportunities, and some parts of the gifted population, including girls (Grant, 2000; Greene, 2003; Nepper Fiebig, 2003) and some minorities (Kerr, 2003), are widely acknowledged to have been constrained by social circumstances in their access to the full range of these alternatives and in the formation of personal expectations. These circumstances range, for example, from parental and community relationships to biases and stereotyping. The wide range exists both within the gifted individual and in the context in which she or he studies or works. Gifted youth are often interested in and capable of doing several occupations. The internal condition is typically addressed under the heading of *multipotentiality* (Greene; Rysiew, Shore, & Leeb, 1999; Sajjadi, Rejskind, & Shore, 2001). The external reality of multiple career opportunity is both a burden and an opportunity, demanding considerable investment in making a reasonable choice at the end of the process.

Career education must not, however, be confused with career choice (Howley, 1989). Its goal is career- and self-awareness, enabling and facilitating the process of making later career-related decisions. Making career decisions too early can close doors to alternatives that might be more satisfying, but have not yet been considered (Buescher, 1985). Howley also cautioned that confusing career education and career choice could aggravate problems that young people, especially gifted young people, have with separating their concerns for higher pay and prestige from a search for personal satisfaction and fulfillment. Career choices are also lifestyle choices and are value-driven (Rysiew et al., 1999). Frederickson (1979) warned that some gifted persons take a chance rather than make an informed choice about careers. In addition to an association with multipotentiality, career satisfaction or dissatisfaction in gifted persons might also be linked to perfectionism.

The research literature supports these concerns. Accepting as a given that a greater variety of especially high-level occupations is available to highly able people and that able people are often multipotentialed, research on gender differences in careers highlights the accuracy of the general portrait just outlined. Reis (1995) surveyed 61 female education graduate students and interviewed 25 of them. They recalled being unsure of their impending career choices, yet seeing male siblings favored in the pursuit of high-status occupations through parental encouragement or willingness to support educational choices. They felt steered toward female-stereotyped occupations and had little time devoted to pursuing their areas of talent. Peterson (1982a, 1982b) interviewed 31 gifted adolescents about their career thinking. Both males and females had high career expectations at that time of their lives, and the girls did not favor gender-stereotyped careers. On the other hand, the girls scored lower on all the subscales of a career-planning interview except with regard to the accuracy of self-appraisal. The girls expressed more varied interests than the boys, but they were less able to connect them with specific occupational preferences. Girls expressed values toward work as a form of self-expression, but the boys expressed values that were more materialistic. The Reis and Peterson women experienced adolescence in different decades, albeit only one decade or so apart. Taken together, these studies suggest that gifted young women may be anticipating the positive side of the opportunity, but they and the boys appear not to be ready for the barriers that they might encounter. Learning to explore these links and personal values would be valuable contributions of career education for both girls and boys.

Willings (1980, 1983), over many years of clinical experience and observation, reported that creatively gifted young people experience difficulty in the employee role. This conflict typically arises from having unconventional career aspirations or seeking unconventional combinations of multiple careers. He noted that creatively gifted young people might be stubborn, sensitive to criticism, and vulnerable to peer rejection. They may also be easily bored. Frequent job changes might therefore be the result of them learning as much that could be learned from any one job in just a few years whereas others less able might take in a lifetime. They could conceivably contribute as much. Career becomes a part of personal identification for many highly able people, and this can be associated with strong external expectations. Although most studies define giftedness in terms of intelligence or academic performance, young people need to contemplate their needs with regard to work satisfaction, as well. Exploring these needs would also be a defensible component of career education for the gifted, as well as the exploration of alternative outlets for talent and interests, because total or overinvestment in the career component alone could be devastating if it should fail in any way.

Where it exists, research clearly shows that career education is perceived as important and is well-received by highly able youth. Delisle (1982) conducted a longitudinal survey that linked the absence of career education with handicaps in making good career decisions, and Clark (1988) noted that career education was the most highly rated part of adolescents' high school experience.

Research informs our knowledge base on career education to the extent that there are problematic areas of gifted children's career thinking and decision making that could be informed by specific topics, and the experience is well received by students. The research literature stops short of validating specific practices or career curricular models. Career education curricular advice is abundant, but untested. Future research into its effectiveness must take care to dig below the surface of expressed satisfaction in light of Clark's (1988) report: If career education is such a highly regarded curricular component, then, even if it is not of the highest quality, it might still evoke high ratings of satisfaction at the time it is experienced.

WHAT WE CAN DO

Although action could be considered at all three levels of home, school, and classroom, career education generally extends the horizons created by home and classroom experiences. It is therefore best thought of as a school-level responsibility, and it probably needs to be taught by a specialist teacher or counselor who is familiar with the specific topics of gifted children and career counseling. Research suggests five topics worthy of inclusion in a career education curriculum for gifted adolescents:

- personal values and needs, and barriers to their realization in the world of work;
- the challenges and benefits of multiple career interests and opportunities;
- convention and risk-taking in career choice;
- intrinsic and extrinsic reward in work; and
- connecting values, needs, motivation, and talents to career and lifestyle options.

Pyryt (1993) identified six recurring themes or issues in the career development literature for gifted students: (a) multipotentiality, (b) expectations, (c) lifestyle, (d) investment, (e) mobility, and (f) innovativeness. He then cross-referenced seven strategies that could address at least some of these themes and that suggest testable hypotheses in career education. The six themes are consistent with the five research-supported curricular topics and can be represented in relation to several of the seven specific strategies:

- content acceleration (addresses investment, especially of time);
- self awareness training (expectations and lifestyle);
- self-concept development (expectations, investment, and mobility);
- interpersonal effectiveness training;
- creative problem solving (investment and mobility);
- sex-role awareness; and
- stress and time management (investment, mobility, and expectation).

Each of these strategies could be examined in relation to a variety of outcomes for career education, but content acceleration is probably more complementary than central to the need for career education. The impact of concomitant content acceleration on a career education program would, nonetheless, be interesting to know.

In an exercise that began with a career education curriculum for general education that was then compared to widely accepted curricular needs of the gifted, Macdonald, Shore, and Thomas (1987) distilled 11 specific activities to include in a career education curriculum for gifted pupils. References in parentheses identify the original sources of core parts of these ideas to which some elaboration has been added. Some of these specific activities could be undertaken at home or within the classroom outside a formal career education program.

At Home

❧ Discuss the portrayal of job roles in television programs, the characteristics of the holders of the positions, and the realism of portrayal; distinguish the glamour from the essence of the work; and identify the limited range of careers presented on television (Clark, 1983);

In the Classroom

❧ Have small groups examine classified advertisements to discern trends, gender biases, skills, and education requirements (Clark, 1983);

❧ Create lists of people students know, the jobs they hold, and characteristics and backgrounds of the people (Clark, 1983);

❧ Use newspapers and news magazines to identify major local, national, or international problems that need solutions and analyze the problems in terms of new job opportunities that could be created to address them and how one might best train for such opportunities; small groups could share their results in class conferences (Clark, 1983);

❧ Conduct simulations of or role-play real-life situations to see how different job roles can collaboratively or separately solve problems (Willings, 1983);

❧ Have students' reflect on themselves in imagined future roles or lifestyles, keeping logs of their feelings or opinions (Betts & Neihart, 1985);

❧ Sort cards on which areas of college and university study have been named and briefly described into piles of prime, intermediate, and low interest, and then discuss the reasons for accepting and discarding the choices in terms of where they could lead in career, values, needs, or interests (Culbertson, 1985);

❧ Read biographies of eminent people in different career paths, analyzing how their eminence arose and the different ways they coped with their uniqueness (VanTassel-Baska, 1983); and

❧ Create a learning center on occupations, education, and interesting people with multiple career experiences.

At School

℣ Invite guest speakers who can share career path experiences and also role-play job interviews and give advice in writing personal résumés (Culbertson, 1985; Martin, 1984);

℣ Invite teachers or counselors who can sponsor extracurricular clubs to discuss careers outside the formal curriculum, a context that may help female, minority, or other students for whom the classroom itself may present barriers to full expression of career aspiration or potential (Grau, 1985);

Recent writing about giftedness and careers has focused more on career thinking rather than career education. Macdonald et al.'s (1987) advice remains relevant. To that counsel we might add making career assessment available to students (Greene, 2003; Kerr, 2003).

References

Betts, G. I., & Neihart, M. F. (1985). Eight effective activities to enhance the emotional and social development of the gifted and talented. *Roeper Review, 8,* 18–23.

Buescher, T. M. (1985). A framework for understanding the social and emotional development of gifted and talented adolescents. *Roeper Review, 8,* 10–15.

Clark, B. (1983). *Growing up gifted: Developing the potential for children at home and at school* (2nd ed.). Columbus, OH: Merrill.

Clark, B. (1988). *Growing up gifted: Developing the potential of children at home and at school* (3rd ed.). Columbus, OH: Merrill.

Culbertson, S. (1985, May/June). Career guidance for the gifted. *G/C/T, 32,* 16–17.

Delisle, J. R. (1982). Reaching towards tomorrow: Career education and guidance for the gifted and talented. *Roeper Review, 5,* 8–11.

Frederickson, R. H. (1979). Career development and the gifted. In N. Colangelo & R. Zaffrann (Eds.), *New voices in counseling the gifted* (pp. 264–276). Des Moines, IA: Kendall/Hunt.

Grant, D. F. (2000). The journey through college of seven gifted females: Influences on their career related decisions. *Roeper Review, 22,* 251–260.

Grau, P. N. (1985, May/June). Counseling the gifted girl. *G/C/T, 32,* 8–11.

Greene, M. J. (2003). Gifted adrift? Career counseling of the gifted and talented. *Roeper Review, 25,* 66–72.

Howley, C. B. (1989). Career education for the gifted. *Journal for the Education of the Gifted, 12,* 205–217.

Kerr, B. (2003). Career assessment with intellectually gifted students. *Journal of Career Assessment, 11,* 168–186.

Macdonald, K., Shore, B. M., & Thomas, M. (1987). *Gifted students and career education.* Unpublished manuscript, Protestant School Board of Greater Montreal and the Ministère de l'éducation du Québec (Ministry of Education of Quebec).

Martin, G. (1984, January/February). Finding the right slot. *G/C/T, 31,* 10–12.

Nepper Fiebig, J. (2003). Gifted American and German early adolescent girls: Influences on career orientation and aspirations. *High Ability Studies, 14*, 165–183.

Peterson, K. (1982a). *Gifted children and career decision making.* Unpublished master's thesis, McGill University, Montreal, QC, Canada.

Peterson, K. (1982b). Gifted girls and career decision-making [Jeunes filles sourdouées et prise de décision professionnelle]. *Cognica, 14*(2), 1–3.

Pyryt, M. C. (1993). Career development for the gifted and talented: Helping adolescents chart their futures. *Journal of Secondary Gifted Education, 5*, 18–22.

Reis, S. M. (1995). Talent ignored, talent deviated: The cultural context underlying giftedness in females. *Gifted Child Quarterly, 39*, 162–170.

Rysiew, K. J., Shore, B. M., & Leeb, R. T. (1999). Multipotentiality, giftedness, and career choice: A review. *Journal of Counseling and Development, 77*, 423–430.

Sajjadi, S. H., Rejskind, F. G., & Shore, B. M. (2001). Is multipotentiality a problem or not? A new look at the data. *High Ability Studies, 12*, 27–43.

VanTassel-Baska, J. (1983). The teacher as counselor for the gifted. *Teaching Exceptional Children, 15*, 144–150.

Willings, D. (1980). *The creatively gifted: Recognizing and developing the creative personality.* Cambridge, England: Wookhead–Faulkner.

Willings, D. (1983). Issues in career choice for gifted students. *Teaching Exceptional Children, 15*, 226–233.

CHAPTER 24

SCHOOL PROGRAMS

Providing appropriate programs in school for gifted and talented students is more complex than introducing an administrative model and purchasing materials to use with the children. Issues of philosophical position, identification, grouping, teacher preparation, parental support, evaluation, and logistics of space and schedules are all parts of planning for defensible programs. These programs often "feel budgetary scissors first when funds get cut" (Peine, 1998), so having a program in place does not mean it will always be there. Although some researchers who work in higher education report a new wave of academic interest in gifted programming, those on the local front lines find a decline in options and support actually available for the students (Purcell, 1994).

WHAT WE KNOW

Feldhusen (1998a) defined a program model as a deliberately planned "system that facilitates interaction of gifted youth with curriculum to produce learning" (p. 211). He pointed out that programs are designed with a particular purpose in mind: to deliver content more quickly, more extensively, or more complexly to fit the learners' precocity and interests. The preferred way of choosing a program is to find out what needs the students have and design the program (or programs) to meet those needs. However, more often a program is designed that is administratively convenient and students are sought to participate. Feldhusen (1998b) continued to emphasize that the identification process must find the students who match the program that is available (p. 194).

Program decisions that involve placing students in particular class settings include: clustering several gifted children together in one classroom; assembling groups of children to participate in pull-out programs of a general nature or more specific subject area instruction during certain times of a day or week—by grade level or in cross-grade groupings; assigning students to full-time gifted programs within a regular school; or drawing students from a larger area to attend magnet schools that usually have a focus such as math, technology, or the arts. Programs that occur within regular classrooms are those that change the nature of the curriculum and add enrichment opportunities. Programs that are in addition to the school schedule are those led by parent volunteers such as mentoring and Junior Great Books discussion groups; special classes offered by universities and local museums, theaters, or libraries; and clubs or service organizations. It is interesting that even with this wide array of services, Rogers' (1999) research pointed to the substantial academic gains made by students who take part in any of them. It may be the curriculum, the leadership of a teacher who is prepared to work with gifted students, the pacing, the motivating elements—or a combination of all of these that might be unique for each student. In a national study of the effects of programs on student outcomes, Delcourt and her colleagues (Delcourt, Lloyd, Cornell, & Goldberg, 1994) investigated more than 1,000 students in grades 2 and 3 over a 2-year period. Students in programs performed better than those not served. Those who were served by special schools, separate class programs, and pull-out programs achieved better than students served by within-class programs. However, according to the researchers, no model met all the needs of the talented learners. They cautioned that choices about program models are highly dependent upon context. To illustrate their points, exemplary programs of each model are described.

Many of the programs that have the strongest base for best practices are discussed in other parts of this volume. The essential and controversial decisions about if and how to group the students to receive the services, the merits of acceleration, classroom techniques of compacting and using higher level thinking skills and inquiry, and the place university programs and mentoring hold in meeting the needs of gifted students are investigated in their own sections of this book. The program options that are offered here generally fall under the following categories: enrichment, differentiated curriculum, individualization, special classes, competitions, and extraschool experiences. It must be noted that there is a great deal of overlap among the programs, because they are all built on basic principles of what is appropriate for gifted students. Some of the programs have been utilized for as many as 20 years or more and others are more recent approaches to providing a smorgasbord of choices for students' varied needs.

Enrichment

The Purdue Three Stage Enrichment Model (Feldhusen & Kolloff, 1981) and the Enrichment Triad Model (Renzulli, 1977) are two well-researched programs that are used in part or whole around the world (George, 1993). Each has three levels of activities that lead to independent investigations and substantial products. Students who are able and motivated move to the highest level, while others can participate to the extent of their abilities. In 1994, Renzulli expanded the Triad to become a schoolwide model aimed at improving the quality of learning for all students.

Rogers (1999) reported that in-depth concept development is the most effective type of enrichment. Extension of the regular curriculum and opportunities for exposure to new ideas and interests are less productive, but may be first steps to concept development. As with all learning, the enrichment should be a well-articulated program and not a provisional extra (Tannenbaum, 1998).

Differentiated Curriculum

Models used extensively in gifted programming are based on changing the curriculum to reflect accelerated, complex, and in-depth content; the teaching and integration of creative and cognitive processes; and the synthesis and communication of learning through significant products. Generally these programs are based on literature with activities using the higher level thinking strategies of Bloom's taxonomy (1956) or on the classics (Thompson, 1996); studies of cultures, scientific topics, or current issues; the use of Creative Problem Solving (Osborn, 1963); development of original works of art and creative drama; specific personal growth interests; and service learning. For example, Benbow and Stanley (1983) and VanTassel-Baska (1982) effectively reorganized the content areas of mathematics and Latin (respectively) according to higher level skills and concepts, creating an efficient and holistic way for students to learn.

Some attempts at differentiating curriculum have reputations of being excellent; others are mediocre, or too flimsy to be defensible. Tannenbaum (1998) warned that unless a modified curriculum is created with purpose and used conscientiously, nothing much will happen for gifted students, even in special classes. Archambault et al. (1993) and Shore and Delcourt (1996) pointed out that in a national look at 3,400 classrooms only minor curriculum modifications were made for the gifted students, even in those schools where a within-class gifted program existed.

Perhaps one of the most extensively differentiated precollege programs is the International Baccalaureate program in selected high schools (see http://www. ibo.org). This is a challenging, university freshman/sophomore level, multinational curriculum of in-depth and comprehensive studies that includes courses in theory of knowledge; two languages; high-level math, sciences, and social sciences; creative, aesthetic endeavors; and global citizenship and service.

Many programs at all grade levels are using problem-based learning, which integrates conceptual understanding; differentiated content, processes, and products; and self-directed learning into complex units of study (Center for Gifted Education, 1997; Gallagher, 1997).

Individualization

Tomlinson (1999) wrote that differentiation is "a teacher's response to a learner's needs guided by general principles of differentiation such as respectful tasks, flexible grouping, and ongoing assessment and adjustment" (p. 15). Administrators and teachers who respond to the individual needs of learners use a wide range of strategies in selecting appropriate programming for students: choosing materials that engage a student's interest and move his or her thinking to higher levels, independent studies, compacting the curriculum, and others (Belcastro, 1987; Feldhusen, 1991; Goldstein & Wagner, 1993; Hoover, Sayler, & Feldhusen, 1993; Renzulli, Smith, & Reis, 1982; Treffinger, 1986). There was a time when individualized instruction meant each child was working alone on an individual program; it is now understood that it is more important that each child be seen and planned for as an individual and that sometimes the best plan involves being with others needing the same intervention.

Special Classes

Students who have a particular interest and talent may not be able to develop their abilities within the time or expertise limits of the regular classroom. Most often, parents provide lessons, tutors, and practice in the arts, sports, languages, and the like. Teachers may be able to help parents find teachers and mentors. Secondary school programming options such as Advanced Placement (AP) courses that earn college credit and honors classes in subjects ranging from art to zoology are program options that offer students challenging study. Younger children can benefit from programs such as the Junior Great Books discussion groups for verbally talented students (Nichols, 1992). Many universities now offer correspondence courses. This individualized method of acceleration is available for those students who meet the grade and prerequisite requirements of the university to receive credit for the course, or they may choose to take a correspondence course in an area of interest without school credit.

Academic Competitions

School-based competitions are good opportunities for students to develop talent and confidence in their abilities. Among the best-known programs are Odyssey of the Mind, Destination Imagination, Math Olympics, Invention Convention, Future Problem Solving, spelling bees, forensics and debates, and contests sponsored by foundations and local clubs and universities. Parents arc often instrumental in bringing these programs to a school and serving as coaches and leaders.

Extraschool Experiences

Parents and teachers can work together to keep students informed of opportunities for advancement of talent that occur outside of school. University-based summer and Saturday programs, call-outs for civic theater productions, and organizations such as 4-H, Future Teachers of America, and Junior Achievement are all worthy settings for gifted students to look for a match for their interests and talents. Most of these types of opportunities are advertised through schools, and many of them require a teacher's recommendation and/or grade records. As students and their families make decisions about how to spend their afterschool time, teachers can facilitate admission, help find financial assistance if needed, and generally encourage the best choices.

Special Schools

In a radical effort to meet the needs of gifted students who have not been successful in mainstream schools, some very unique high schools have been established. Buchanan and Woerner (2002) report on 6 of 15 such schools across the U.S. The innovative programs feature small learning communities, a holistic education plan built around "big ideas" and world problems instead of discrete content disciplines, and program goals that include the enjoyment of learning and development of meaningful lives. Their research was limited in that they did not get a good picture of academic achievement for various reasons (some schools are very new, and others are in the implementation, not the evaluation stage); however, the students' qualitative data pointed to substantial personal satisfaction and perceived academic growth.

Programs That Target Specific Populations

Recent research addresses educators' concerns that many of the existing gifted programs in schools are not reaching students of color and students whose experiences have been limited by poverty. Equitable identification of these students and their retention in programs are important foci for all school districts. Underrepresented population studies include Montgomery's (2001) investigation of Native American Indian involvement in school programs, which also put the spotlight on the challenges of rural districts, and Grantham's (2003) study of the advocacy effort to increase Black student participation in school programs.

Borland, Schnur, & Wright (2000) offered a promising, albeit complex identification and follow-up process for providing programming to economically disadvantaged minority students. Their Project Synergy (Borland & Wright, 1994, gives the details of the processes) begins with kindergartners identified as potentially gifted through a case-study approach that uses psychometric and sociometric data along with recurring interviews with teachers and parents and observations of the children over several years. Their findings validate the identification processes and provide hope for finding and providing appropriate programming for nurturing a population of children who have been left out of programs.

WHAT WE CAN DO

At Home

❧ Parents have a responsibility to know about the programs available to their children, to understand the goals and purposes of the options, and to be part of the team that makes decisions about their children's participation.

❧ Schools do not have the personnel to offer many of the programs to students. Parents and other adults in the community must step forward to lead and provide the programs needed by the students. Some businesses are finding that allowing their workers time off to volunteer in the schools is paying benefits in public respect and better-educated students.

At School

❧ Teachers and other school personnel have responsibility for creating programs that meet the needs of their students, providing teachers with professional development and supervision to ensure the program's tenets are being followed, and evaluating the program's effectiveness for individual children on a regular basis.

❧ Counselors, teachers, and parents must work together to instill in students the desire to work hard and make the most of the opportunities available to them to develop their talents.

❧ With the multitude of programs, kits, and packaged lessons on the market, and extracurricular options competing for students' time, adults must be wise in their counsel to students and in their choices of innovations brought into the school. Changes must be made, and the best choices are those made by teams of teachers, parents, students, and administrators with the help of best-practice-based research.

❧ Gifted students must have programs that are defensible and appropriate for their talents. This means students must be assessed and planned for on an individual basis.

REFERENCES

Archambault, F. X., Jr., Westberg, K. L., Brown, S. W., Hallmark, B. W., Emmons, C. L., & Zhang, W. (1993). *Regular classroom practices with gifted students: Results of a national survey of classroom teachers* (Research Report No. 93101). Storrs: National Research Center on the Gifted and Talented, University of Connecticut.

Belcastro, F. P. (1987). Elementary pullout program for the intellectually gifted—boon or bane? *Roeper Review, 9,* 4–11.

Benbow, C., & Stanley, J. (1983). *Academic precocity.* Baltimore: Johns Hopkins University Press.

Bloom, B. (Ed.). (1956). *Taxonomy of educational objectives: The classification of educational goals. Handbook I: Cognitive domain.* New York: Longmans Green.

Borland, J. H., Schnur, R., & Wright, L. (2000). Economically disadvantaged students in a school for the academically gifted: A postpositivist inquiry into individual and family adjustment. *Gifted Child Quarterly, 44,* 13–32.

Borland, J. H., & Wright, L. (1994). Identifying young, potentially gifted, economically disadvantaged students. *Gifted Child Quarterly, 38,* 164–171.

Buchanan, N., & Woerner, B. (2002). Meeting the needs of gifted learners through innovative high school programs. *Roeper Review, 24,* 213–219.

Center for Gifted Education. (1997). *What a find! A problem based unit.* Dubuque, IA: Kendall/Hunt.

Delcourt, M. A. B., Lloyd, B. H., Cornell, D. G., & Goldberg, M. D. (1994). *Evaluation of the effects of programming arrangements on student learning outcomes* (Research Monograph 94108). Storrs: National Research Center on the Gifted and Talented, University of Connecticut.

Feldhusen, J. F. (1998a). Programs and services at the elementary level. In J. VanTassel-Baska (Ed.), *Excellence in educating gifted and talented learners* (pp. 211–223). Denver, CO: Love.

Feldhusen, J. F. (1998b). Identification and assessment of talented learners. In J. VanTassel-Baska (Ed.), *Excellence in educating gifted and talented learners* (pp. 193–210). Denver, CO: Love.

Feldhusen, J. F. (1991). Gifted students must have time together in learning activities at their level and pace. *Images, 5*(2), 2–3, 12–13.

Feldhusen, J. F., & Kolloff, M. B. (1981). A three stage model for gifted children. In R. E. Classen, B. Robinson, D. R. Classen, & G. Libster (Eds.), *Programming for the gifted, talented, and creative: Models and methods book of readings* (2nd ed., pp. 111–117). Madison: University of Wisconsin-Extension.

Gallagher, S. A. (1997). Problem-based learning: Where did it come from, what does it do, and where is it going? *Journal for the Education of the Gifted, 20,* 332–362.

George, D. R. (1993). Instructional strategies and models for gifted education. In K. A. Heller, F. J. Mönks, & A. H. Passow (Eds.), *International handbook of research and development of giftedness and talent* (pp. 411–425). Oxford, England: Pergamon Press.

Goldstein, D. R., & Wagner, H. (1993). Afterschool programs, competitions, school olympics, and summer programs. In K. A. Heller, F. J. Mönks, & A. H. Passow (Eds.), *International handbook of research and development of giftedness and talent* (pp. 593–604). Oxford, England: Pergamon Press.

Grantham, T. C. (2003). Increasing Black student enrollment in gifted programs: An exploration of the Pulaski County Special School District's advocacy efforts. *Gifted Child Quarterly, 47*, 46–65.

Hoover, S. M., Sayler, M. F., & Feldhusen, J. F. (1993). Cluster grouping of gifted students at the elementary level. *Roeper Review, 16*, 13–15.

Montgomery, D. (2001). Increasing Native American Indian involvement in gifted programs in rural schools. *Psychology in the Schools, 38*, 467–475.

Nichols, T. M. (1992). A program for students and teachers: The Junior Great Books Program. *Gifted Child Today, 15*(5), 50–51.

Osborn, A. (1963). *Applied imagination.* New York: Scribner's.

Peine, M. (1998). Practical matters. *Journal for the Education of the Gifted, 22*, 37–55.

Purcell, J. H. (1994). *The status of programs for high ability students* (Collaborative Research Study CRS94305). Storrs: National Research Center on the Gifted and Talented, University of Connecticut.

Renzulli, J. S. (1977). *The enrichment triad model: A guide for developing defensible programs for the gifted and talented.* Mansfield Center, CT: Creative Learning Press.

Renzulli, J. S. (1994). *Schools for talent development: A practical plan for total school improvement.* Mansfield Center, CT: Creative Leaning Press.

Renzulli, J. S., Smith, L. H., & Reis, S. M. (1982). Curriculum compacting: An essential strategy for working with gifted students. *Elementary School Journal, 82,* 185–194.

Rogers, K. (1999, March). *Research synthesis of best practices.* Paper presented at the National Curriculum Conference, College of William and Mary, Williamsburg, VA.

Shore, B. M., & Delcourt, M. A. B. (1996). Effective curricular and program practices in gifted education and the interface with general education. *Journal for the Education of the Gifted, 20*, 138–145.

Tannenbaum, A. J. (1998). Programs for the gifted: To be or not to be. *Journal for the Education for the Gifted, 22*, 3–36.

Tomlinson, C. A. (1999). *The differentiated classroom: Responding to the needs of all learners.* Alexandria, VA: Association for Supervision and Curriculum Development.

Thompson, M. C. (1996). Mentors on paper: How classics develop verbal ability. In J. VanTassel-Baska, D. T. Johnson, & L. N. Boyce (Eds.), *Developing verbal talent: Ideas and strategies for teachers of elementary and middle school students* (pp. 56–74). Needham Heights, MA: Allyn & Bacon.

Treffinger, D. J. (1986). Fostering effective, independent learning through individualized programming. In J. S. Renzulli (Ed.), *Systems and models for developing programs for the gifted and talented* (pp. 429–460). Mansfield Center, CT: Creative Learning Press.

VanTassel-Baska, J. (1982). Results of a Latin-based experimental study of the verbally precocious. *Roeper Review, 4*, 35–37.

ACCELERATION

Talented students who are accelerated achieve more than their equally talented age-mates who are not. In some cases, students can acquire mastery of school subjects in a fraction of the time generally allotted to them in the usual curricular sequence. Acceleration is often equated with grade skipping in the public mind, but there are numerous forms of acceleration. Achievement and educational attainment outcomes are positive. Educators and parents worry that acceleration places high-ability learners at risk for social and emotional difficulties. These effects are less thoroughly researched than academic outcomes, but recent analyses have uncovered questions that would benefit from additional investigation rather than problems that would prevent the use of accelerative strategies.

WHAT WE KNOW

Acceleration of academically talented students is one of the most commonly recommended practices (Shore, Cornell,

Robinson, & Ward, 1991). Favorable empirical studies appeared as early as the 1930s and consistently positive reviews appeared in the succeeding decades (Daurio, 1979; Passow, 1958; Pressey, 1949; Rogers, 2004). Most recently, a national report, *A Nation Deceived: How Schools Hold Back America's Brightest Students*, focused on the benefits of acceleration and communicated them to policymakers and the public (Colangelo, Assouline, & Gross, 2004). In general, *acceleration* is defined as the recognition of students' prior achievement (Southern, Jones, & Stanley, 1993). However, the practice also includes academic progress based on individual abilities without regard for age (Paulus, 1984) and implies adjustment of the curriculum, as well as administrative procedures, for student placement (Schiever & Maker, 2003).

Although educators tend to assume that acceleration means grade skipping (Southern, Jones, & Fiscus, 1989), there are several other kinds of acceleration: early entrance to kindergarten or first grade, subject acceleration in which a student attends part of a day at a more advanced grade level, telescoping curriculum to accomplish 3 years of instruction in 2, fast-paced extracurricular classes, and early college entrance (Southern & Jones, 2004).

Early Admission

Although studies on early admission to kindergarten or first grade exist, many of the studies are more concerned with school readiness and do not generally account for early admission cases based on precocious achievement (Southern et al., 1993). Rogers' (1992) meta-analysis included studies of early entrance, but noted that the information in the studies was often so sketchy that it was difficult to analyze. More recently, Gagné and Gagnier (2004) found few differences between early entrants and a comparison group of regular-aged children when evaluated by kindergarten and grade 2 teachers. Robinson and Weimer (1991) and Robinson (2004) reviewed the early entrance literature and concluded that while the studies of late birth date children obscured our understanding of early entrance on carefully selected precocious learners, the academic and social and emotional results are positive.

Grade Advancement for Talented Students

In 1984, Kulik and Kulik published an influential meta-analysis on acceleration. Nearly a decade later, Kulik (1992) revisited the analysis with much the same results. The 1984 review included 21 reports, and the 1992 review had 23 studies. To be included in the meta-analysis, the studies had to use control or comparison groups. All studies used standardized tests of achievement as the outcome measure (Kulik, 1992, p. 36).

Kulik and Kulik (1984) found two kinds of comparisons: Half of the studies used same-age equally able students who were not accelerated to assess the effects of acceleration; the other half compared accelerants with older academically able control students. Results for the two types of comparisons differ. When compared with same age talented nonaccelerants, accelerated students scored approximately one grade higher. When compared with older equally able students, accelerants held their own. Kulik (1992) noted that the comparison of accelerants with older students was particularly impressive because most accelerants were at least one year younger than their talented counterparts.

The studies included in the meta-analytic review tended to investigate telescoped curriculum in upper elementary or junior high grade levels (Kulik, 1992). Nine of the 23 studies focused on mathematics. For example, Ludeman (1969) investigated the compression of seventh- and eighth-grade mathematics in 1 year rather than 2; Klausmeier and Wiersma (1964) looked at the compression of six semesters of mathematics in grades 9 and 10. The other studies examined more comprehensive acceleration programs, which usually shortened 3-year curriculum programs to 2 years. Several of the studies reviewed by the Kuliks (1984) reported school district program evaluations, thus strengthening the real-world applicability of acceleration.

The studies of grade advancement tend to examine modest acceleration, perhaps 1 year. The cases of radical acceleration in which students skip more than 2 years, pass a school milestone like entrance into high school or college 2 to 3 years early, or complete coursework in very short time periods (Brody & Stanley, 1991) were not represented in the meta-analyses on acceleration (Kulik, 1992; Kulik & Kulik, 1984). Kulik (2004) commented that key studies on acceleration that use other designs are not generally included in meta-analyses. Taking them into account provides additional support for the practice.

For example, schools tend to accommodate radical acceleration on a case-by-case basis. Therefore, the research base tends to include case studies of individual children in heterogeneous settings (Kennedy, 1995) or as they attempt to accelerate through schools and university (Gross, 2003). To assess the effects of radical acceleration on extremely able children requires long-term follow-up of the individuals over several years. By necessity, reports are qualitative or anecdotal, but they consistently document advanced achievement, particularly in college trajectories (Gross; Stanley, 1985).

Fast-Paced Classes

For students with an intense and focused interest, fast-paced classes in content areas provide opportunities for students to master challenging material. The classes tend to be extracurricular offerings during 3-week summer sessions or Saturdays during the academic year. Sometimes, but not always, students receive credit or placement within the school program for these extracurricular classes (Lynch, 1990; Olszewski-Kubilius & Lee, 2005). The content areas most frequently reported in the literature are mathematics, science, and foreign language. Generally, the effects are demonstrated by the accomplishments of small groups of students taking specific classes in university-based or collaborative university-school programs.

Research on fast-paced classes is generally conducted in the context of talent searches, a model for identifying and developing high-level academic talents established by Julian Stanley at Johns Hopkins University. Students whose grade-level achievement test scores exceed the 95th percentile are given further out-of-level tests, usually the Scholastic Assessment Test (SAT I) or the American College Testing Program (ACT) at ages younger than usual. Thus, students who participate in talent searches that are voluntary and for whom the fast-paced classes are designed constitute a very academically able group of learners.

The short-term accomplishments of students in fast-paced classes are often described in terms of hours or weeks of instruction rather than months. For example, Stanley and Stanley (1986) reported that students learned high school biology, chemistry, or physics in 3 weeks. VanTassel-Baska (1987) found similar effects for students in a fast-paced Latin class. Their achievements can be impressive; Kolitch and Brody (1992) found that 43 math-accelerated students typically took their first calculus course by grade 9. With the use of technology, Ravaglia, Suppes, Stillinger, and Alper (1995) documented two groups of junior high age students who completed one or two calculus courses in a year through a combination of a summer course in precalculus and computer-based self-paced instruction with the aid of a teaching assistant during the academic year. A third group of students ranging from grades 8–12 who had completed calculus also took a physics course with a home-based laboratory component. To assess achievement, students took the Advanced Placement (AP) Calculus AB, Calculus BC, or Physics C: Mechanics Exam. Thirteen of the 15 students enrolled in the first calculus course completed it. Approximately half of them received a score of 5 on the Advanced Placement Calculus AB exam; none received a score lower than 3. All four students who took the second calculus course at the junior high level scored 5s on the AP Calculus BC exam. The 10 students who enrolled in the physics course completed the course; one student did not take the exam, one student received a score of 3, four students received a score of 4, and four students received a score of 5. Because the course was self-paced, it is difficult to estimate the hours spent by students on the course-work; however, the authors note that for every hour spent online, students typically did 45 minutes of homework.

The long-term contributions of fast-paced course taking are documented by Swiatek and Benbow (1991) who did a follow-up study on students in a mathematics course whose original achievements were investigated 10 years earlier (Benbow, Perkins, & Stanley, as cited in Swiatek & Benbow, 1991). The students participated in the first two fast-paced mathematics classes organized by the Study of Mathematically Precocious Youth (SMPY). Meeting on Saturday mornings for approximately a year, the goal was to accomplish algebra I, algebra II, plane geometry, trigonometry, and analytic geometry. Of the students enrolled in the first of the two classes, eight completed 4.5 years of mathematics, two completed 3.5 years of mathematics, and six students completed 2 years of mathematics. Ten years later, the students continued to thrive when compared with equally able students who had not participated in the fast-paced classes. Fast-paced course attendees were more likely to attend graduate school (particularly the girls) and to have entered college at an earlier age. Both groups of students expressed positive attitudes toward mathematics and science (Swiatek & Benbow). Other studies of participation in fast-paced classes confirm the long-term positive benefits (Lubinski, Webb, Morelock, & Benbow, 2001).

Early College Entrance

Grade advancement in the elementary, middle, or high school, and fast-paced extracurricular courses may contribute to a third type of accelerative option—early entrance to college. As is the case for the acceleration studies reported by Kulik (1992), early entrance to college may be modest in terms of time saved. Many early entrants are one year younger than their peers when they enter college.

A few studies investigate the effects of college entrance on much younger students. Janos, Robinson, and Lunneborg (1989) investigated the effects of early college entrance on 43 students who had entered college on or before the age of 14. The students participated in a specialized program that admitted students in cohorts of 12–15 youths, provided a transition program, and offered academic counseling and a location for social and recreational activities. The early entrants were compared with three other groups of students: students who had qualified for early entrance but chose to attend high school, typical undergraduate students at the institution who tended to be 4 years older than the early entrants, and undergraduate students who were National Merit finalists. Early entrants earned an average GPA comparable to the National Merit finalists and consistently higher than the typical undergraduate. They earned as many credits as their college-aged peers. Several measures of adjustment were included in the study with few differences between the early entrants and the college-age comparison groups. Of particular interest, measures of parent and peer attachment indicated that young early entrants trusted and communicated with their family and friends as much as their age peers who remained in high school and the college-age comparison students.

Janos, Sanfilippo, and Robinson (1986) also examined a group of early entrants whose GPAs were 2.9 or below on a 4.0 scale. The students were achieving less than other early entrants whose readiness scores were similar, and they expressed dissatisfaction with themselves for not doing better. Twelve students out of 56 met the criteria and were compared on measures of achievement, personality, and family environment. The less successful students had patterns of successful and poor semesters, but few personality and no family environment differences were found. There were gender patterns with males expressing conflict about their spotty achievement; girls with inconsistent achievement records, however, were more mature than their achieving counterparts and reported satisfaction in the extracurricular opportunities available to them. Gross and van Vliet (2005) reviewed the research on early entrance to college for highly able youth and concluded that it was a viable option. They also noted that certain programmatic features protected against problems, including counseling support, study skills sessions, and explicit social opportunities to build cohorts or friendships.

Advanced Placement as Acceleration

Students who participate in AP courses and take the examinations related to those courses acquire college-level learning in secondary school and are well prepared for further academic study when they arrive at college. In a case study of the AP program as a model for setting national content standards, Kelley (1994) noted that the College Board regularly conducts studies to assess program effectiveness. Adelman (1999) noted that participation in rigorous high school coursework such as AP is the best predictor of success in college.

Fears that students who receive credit and advanced course standing will "get in over their heads" during their first year in college are not warranted. For example, when compared with 229 college students enrolled in the equivalent course, a sample of 247 AP calculus students who took the BC Calculus examination did as well or better than the group of equally able counterparts (Dickey, 1986).

A decade later, the pattern is robust. In a survey of 21 colleges and universities, when AP students enrolled in a second calculus course were compared with students who had taken a traditional first college calculus course, the AP students had higher grade averages and greater percentages of A and B grades in the subject area (Morgan & Ramist, 1998). The full study involved 11,212 students and compared achievement across 25 different AP examination areas. Students scoring a 5 on the AP examination had higher course grade averages than non-AP students who took the prerequisite course. For about half of the subject matter areas, students who received AP examination scores of 4 outperformed their comparisons. Finally, for students who received examination scores of 3, course grades continued to be largely in their favor. In only two courses, Microeconomics and Studio Art-General, did students who took the prerequisite course outperform the students who were placed in the second sequence course on the basis of their AP examination (Morgan & Ramist).

In terms of continuing interest in the subject, longitudinal studies found that AP students continue to take university courses in the area in which they present AP examinations. Concerns that able students will rush through requirements and truncate their involvement in a subject matter area are not borne out in biology, calculus, or chemistry (Morgan & Crone, 1993). Students may take more than one AP examination; those applying to selective universities typically take at least three (Stumpf & Stanley, 1996). A longitudinal study of highly able students participating in AP classes indicated that they were more likely to earn an advanced degree and more frequently expressed satisfaction with their high school experience (Bleske-Rechek, Lubinski, & Benbow, 2004).

Although Advanced Placement has grown exponentially and is open to a wide range of learners, poorer districts are less likely than higher income districts to offer AP courses (Hiller, 1996). However, a policy study in a low average income state indicates that AP incentive legislation increases the numbers of districts that offer AP courses and that greater numbers of students take examinations (Robinson, Anthony, & Dickersen, 1999).

Advanced Placement participation by culturally diverse students also shows gains. In a review of its member states, the Southern Regional Education Board noted increases in the numbers of African American, Hispanic, and Asian students taking examinations (Creech, 1995). The general trend of increases in minority student participation continues; however, recent meteoric increases in participation across all cultural groups, including White students, show persistent gaps. Shipman-Campbell (1994) reports a program that encourages early participation and provides coaching to increase minority student examination completion patterns in AP English. When the program worked with 63 students of Latino and African American background during their junior year, the number of students who took the examination and who reported confidence in themselves as English students increased.

Frequency of Acceleration and Practitioner Objections

Despite the research evidence supporting the practice of acceleration, it is used very conservatively in schools. In an investigation of eighth-grade students in the National Educational Longitudinal Study (NELS), Sayler and Brookshire (1993) noted that only 1.4% of the students reported being accelerated. Surveys of school districts report the availability of accelerative options (Jones & Southern, 1992; Southern et al., 1989), but do not report numbers of students who take advantage of the option.

One reason for the infrequent use of acceleration in the schools can be traced back to the discomfort of school personnel with the practice. Many educators do not differentiate among types of acceleration and equate it with grade skipping (Southern et al., 1989).

Social and Emotional Adjustment of Accelerants

The most persistent concern voiced about acceleration is its effect on the social and emotional well-being of accelerants. The research on social and emotional outcomes is far more limited than that on academic outcomes, and as Robinson (2004) pointed out, more difficult to define. A study by Ma (2003) investigated acceleration on attitudes toward math and mathematics anxiety and found that anxiety did not increase among gifted learners, but did among accelerated regular students.

The early meta-analysis by Kulik and Kulik (1984) made little headway in answering the question of adjustment effects because few studies included affective variables. Later, Kulik (2004) examined the 14 studies with social and emotional outcomes and found results varied by the kind of outcome variable used. Acceleration had a positive effect on a student's educational plans, no effect on a student's participation in extracurricular activities, and inconsistent effects on a student's liking for a school subject. Kulik found only four studies that examined the effects on personal adjustment; these were characterized by slightly negative but statistically insignificant differences or no differences. The research based on acceleration through talent search programs has uncovered few adjustment problems, but the measures tend to be survey items on mailed or telephone questionnaires. In follow-up studies of accelerants at ages 18 and 23, Richardson and Benbow (1990) did not uncover negative effects on social interactions or self-acceptance; the authors noted that their data were self-reported. In a study drawn from the National Education Longitudinal Study: 1988 (NELS: 88), comparisons were made among accelerants who entered school early or who were grade skipped, students who were served in gifted programs, and the general cohort of eighth-grade students. Using the survey data, Sayler and Brookshire (1993) found that accelerants reported feelings of acceptance and peer approval more frequently than their general cohort peers and at about the same level as their nonaccelerated peers served through a gifted program. As in previous survey studies, the authors noted that the limited number of items for each of the social, emotional, and behavioral adjustment measures was a limitation.

Cornell and his colleagues investigated women participants in an accelerated residential college program and reported wide variation in the responses of the young women (Cornell, Callahan, & Lloyd, 1991). In a review of the affective development of accelerants, Cornell, Callahan, Bassin, and Ramsay (1991) cautioned that assessment of accelerants with standard psychological batteries was sorely missing from the literature. Thus, generalizations about the social and emotional effects of acceleration—either positive or negative—continue to be clouded. Adjustment has been less well investigated, few significant negative effects have been reported in the studies that do exist, and the means of addressing the question of social and emotional concerns in older accelerants has largely been through mailed questionnaires.

WHAT WE CAN DO

At Home

❧ Families considering early entrance to college should investigate the kinds of supports universities offer to early entrants. Parents should look for programs that admit students in cohorts, encourage transition, and provide specialized academic counseling and socialization opportunities with other early entrants.

At School

❧ Modest forms of acceleration such as subject matter acceleration for an individual child in a single content area and telescoping a 3-year curriculum into 2 years should be readily considered by schools when a student or a cohort of students are ready for curriculum beyond current grade placement. The content areas most likely to be considered for telescoping are mathematics and science.

❧ Schools should develop policies to address acceleration. Both educators and parents need guidance in choosing to accelerate a child and then in making the transition as smooth as possible. Schools should also develop policies and procedures to award credit based on demonstrated performance in fast-paced, extracurricular classes.

❧ Because educators tend to lump most forms of acceleration together, pre- and in-service professional development should be available to develop a clearer understanding of the kinds of acceleration possible and the indicators schools can use to determine if a child should be accelerated.

❧ Offer at least three AP courses in all high schools. According to Stumpf and Stanley (1996), students attending selective universities tend to take at least three AP examinations. To assist talented students who wish to attend selective universities, schools should provide at least this minimum level of opportunity.

❧ Provide support and encouragement to culturally diverse students. The increasing numbers of culturally diverse students taking AP examinations indicates that interest in these college preparatory opportunities exists across all cultural groups. The success of individual initiatives in schools indicates that persistent local efforts encourage academically gifted culturally diverse students to participate in AP classes and to complete examinations.

REFERENCES

Adelman, C. (1999). *Answers in the tool box: Academic intensity, attendance patterns, and bachelor's degree attainment.* Washington, DC: Office of Educational Research and Improvement, U.S. Department of Education.

Bleske-Rechek, A., Lubinski, D., & Benbow, C. P. (2004). Meeting the needs of special populations: Advanced Placement's role in developing exceptional human capital. *Psychological Science, 15,* 217–224.

Brody, L., & Stanley, J. (1991). Young college of students: Assessing factors that contribute to success. In W. T. Southern & E. D. Jones (Eds.), *The academic acceleration of gifted children* (pp. 102–132). New York: Teachers College Press.

Colangelo, N., Assouline, S. G., Gross, M. U. M. (Eds.). (2004). *A nation deceived: How schools hold back America's brightest students* (Vol. 2). Iowa City, IA: The Connie Belin & Jacqueline N. Blank International Center for Gifted Education and Talent Development.

Cornell, D. G., Callahan, C., & Lloyd, B. (1991). Socioemotional adjustment of adolescent girls enrolled in a residential acceleration program. *Gifted Child Quarterly, 35,* 58–66.

Cornell, D. G., Callahan, C., Bassin, L. E., & Ramsay, S. G. (1991). Affective development in accelerated students. In W. T. Southern & E. D. Jones (Eds.), *Academic acceleration of gifted children* (pp. 74–101). New York: Teachers College Press.

Creech, J. D. (1995). *Challenging students to higher standards through Advanced Placement.* Atlanta, GA: Southern Regional Education Board. (ERIC Document Reproduction Service No. ED387753)

Daurio, S. P. (1979). Educational enrichment versus acceleration: A review of the literature. In W. C. George, S. J. Cohn, & J. C. Stanley (Eds.), *Educating the gifted: Acceleration and enrichment* (pp. 13–63). Baltimore: Johns Hopkins University Press.

Dickey, E. (1986). A comparison of Advanced Placement and college students on a calculus achievement test. *Journal of Research in Mathematics Education, 17,* 140–144.

Gagné, F., & Gagnier, N. (2004). The socio-affective and academic impact of early entrance to school. *Roeper Review, 26,* 128–138.

Gross, M. U. M. (2003). *Exceptionally gifted children* (2nd ed.). London: Routledge Falmer.

Gross, M. U. M., & van Vliet, H. E. (2005). Radical acceleration and early entry to college: A review of the research. *Gifted Child Quarterly, 49,* 154–171.

Hiller, R. B. (1996). School district wealth and participation in college preparatory courses. *High School Journal, 80,* 49–59.

Janos, P. M., Robinson, N. M., & Lunneborg, C. E. (1989). Markedly early entrance to college: A multi-year comparative study of academic performance and psychological adjustment. *Journal of Higher Education, 60,* 495–518.

Janos, P. M., Sanfilippo, S. M., & Robinson, N. M. (1986). Underachievers among markedly accelerated college students. *Journal of Youth and Adolescence, 15,* 303–311.

Jones, E., & Southern, T. (1992). Programming, grouping, and acceleration in rural school districts: A survey of attitudes and practices. *Gifted Child Quarterly, 36,* 112–117.

Kelley, C. (1994). Determining curricula and exam content in the Advanced Placement program: Implications for national standards. *Education and Urban Society, 26,* 172–184.

Kennedy, D. (1995). Glimpses of a highly gifted child in a heterogeneous classroom. *Roeper Review, 17,* 164–168.

Klausmeier, H. J., & Wiersma, W. (1964). Effects of condensing content in mathematics and science in the junior and senior high school. *School Science and Mathematics, 64,* 4–11.

Kolitch, E. R., & Brody, L. (1992). Mathematics acceleration of highly talented students: An evaluation. *Gifted Child Quarterly, 36,* 78–86.

Kulik, J. A. (1992). *An analysis of the research on ability grouping: Historical and contemporary perspectives* (Research Monograph No. 9204). Storrs: National Research Center on the Gifted and Talented, University of Connecticut.

Kulik, J. A. (2004). Meta-analytic studies of acceleration. In N. Colangelo, S. G. Assouline, & M. U. M. Gross (Eds.), *A nation deceived: How schools hold back America's brightest students* (Vol. 2, pp. 13–22). Iowa City, IA: The Connie Belin & Jacqueline N. Blank International Center for Gifted Education and Talent Development.

Kulik, J. A., & Kulik, C. L. C. (1984). Effects of accelerated instruction on students. *Educational Research, 54,* 409–425.

Lubinski, D., Webb, R. M., Morelock, M. J., & Benbow, C. P. (2001). Top 1 in 10,000: A 10-year follow-up of the profoundly gifted. *Journal of Applied Psychology, 86,* 718–729.

Ludeman, C. J. (1969). A comparison of achievement in an accelerated program and a standard program of high school mathematics in Lincoln, Nebraska schools. *Dissertation Abstracts International, 31,* 299. (University Microfilms No. AAD70-12271)

Lynch, S. (1990). Credit and placement issues for the academically talented following summer studies in science and mathematics. *Gifted Child Quarterly, 34,* 27–30.

Ma, X. (2003). Effects of early acceleration of students in mathematics on attitudes toward mathematics and mathematics anxiety. *Teachers College Record, 105,* 438–464.

Morgan, R., & Crone, C. (1993). *Advanced Placement examinees at the University of California: An examination of the freshman year courses and grades of examinees in biology, calculus and chemistry* (Statistical report 98-13). Princeton, NJ: Educational Testing Service.

Morgan, R., & Ramist, L. (1998). *Advanced Placement students in college: An investigation of course grades at 21 colleges* (Statistical Report 98-13). Princeton, NJ: Educational Testing Service.

Olszewski-Kubilius, P., & Lee, S-Y. (2005). Investigation of high school credit and placement for summer coursework taken outside of local schools. *Gifted Child Quarterly, 49,* 37–50.

Passow, A. H. (1958). Enrichment of education for the gifted. In N. B. Henry (Ed.), *Education for the gifted: Fifty-seventh yearbook of the National Society for the Study of Education: Part I* (pp. 193–221). Chicago: University of Chicago Press.

Paulus, P. (1984). Acceleration: More than grade skipping. *Roeper Review, 7,* 98–100.

Pressey, S. L. (1949). *Educational acceleration: Appraisal of basic problems* (Bureau of Educational Research Monographs No. 31). Columbus: Ohio State University.

Ravaglia, R., Suppes, P., Stillinger, C., & Alper, T. (1995). Computer-based mathematics and physics for gifted students. *Gifted Child Quarterly, 39,* 7–13.

Richardson, T. M., & Benbow, C. P. (1990). Long-term effects of acceleration on the social-emotional adjustment of mathematically precocious youths. *Journal of Educational Psychology, 82,* 464–470.

Robinson, A., Anthony, T. S., & Dickersen, L. (1999). *A carrot is better than a stick: The effects of the Arkansas Advanced Placement legislation. Report to the Walton Foundation.* Little Rock: University of Arkansas at Little Rock, Center for Research on Teaching and Learning.

Robinson, N. M. (2004). Effects of academic acceleration on the social-emotional status of gifted students. In N. Colangelo, S. G. Assouline, & M. U. M. Gross (Eds.), *A nation deceived: How schools hold back America's brightest students* (Vol. 2, pp. 59–67). Iowa City, IA: The Connie Belin & Jacqueline N. Blank International Center for Gifted Education and Talent Development.

Robinson, N. M., & Weimer, L. J. (1991). Selection of candidates for early admission to kindergarten and first grade. In W. T. Southern & E. D. Jones (Eds.), *The academic acceleration of gifted children* (pp. 29–73). New York: Teachers College Press.

Rogers, K. B. (1992). A best-evidence synthesis of the research on acceleration options for gifted learners. In N. Colangelo, S. G. Assouline, and D. L. Ambroson (Eds.), *Talent development: Proceedings from the 1991 Henry B. and Jocelyn Wallace national research symposium on talent development* (pp. 406–409). Unionville, NY: Trillium Press.

Rogers, K. B. (2004). The academic effects of acceleration. In N. Colangelo, S. G. Assouline, & M. U. M. Gross (Eds.), *A nation deceived: How schools hold back America's brightest students* (Vol. 2, pp. 47–57). Iowa City, IA: The Connie Belin & Jacqueline N. Blank International Center for Gifted Education and Talent Development.

Sayler, M., & Brookshire, K. (1993). Social, emotional and behavioral adjustment of accelerated students, students in gifted classes, and regular students in eighth grade. *Gifted Child Quarterly, 37*, 150–154.

Schiever, S. W., & Maker, C. J. (2003). New directions in enrichment and acceleration. In N. Colangelo & G. A. Davis (Eds.), *Handbook of gifted education* (3rd ed., pp. 163–173). Needham Heights, MA: Allyn & Bacon.

Shore, B. M., Cornell, D. G., Robinson, A., & Ward, V. S. (1991). *Recommended practices in gifted education: A critical analysis.* New York: Teachers College Press.

Shipman-Campbell, A. (1994). *Increasing the number and success rate of junior honors English students in taking English Advanced Placement examinations.* (ERIC Document Reproduction Service No. ED376496)

Southern, W. T., & Jones, E. D. (2004). Types of acceleration: Dimensions and issues. In N. Colangelo, S. G. Assouline, & M. U. M. Gross (Eds.), *A nation deceived: How schools hold back America's brightest students* (Vol. 2, pp. 5–12). Iowa City, IA: The Connie Belin & Jacqueline N. Blank International Center for Gifted Education and Talent Development.

Southern, W. T., Jones, E. D., & Fiscus, E. D. (1989). Practitioner objections to the academic acceleration of young gifted children. *Gifted Child Quarterly, 33*, 29–35.

Southern, W. T., Jones, E. D., & Stanley, J. C. (1993). Acceleration and enrichment: The context and development of program options. In K. A. Heller, F. J. Mönks, & A. H. Passow (Eds.), *International handbook of research and development of giftedness and talent* (pp. 387–409). Oxford, England: Pergamon Press.

Stanley, J. (1985). How did six highly accelerated gifted students fare in graduate school? *Gifted Child Quarterly, 29*, 180.

Stanley, J. C., & Stanley, B. K. (1986). High school biology, chemistry, or physics learned well in three weeks. *Journal of Research in Science Teaching, 23*, 237–250.

Stumpf, H., & Stanley, J. C. (1996). Gender-related differences on the College Board's Advanced Placement and achievement tests, 1982–1992. *Journal of Educational Psychology, 88*, 252–364.

Swiatek, M. A., & Benbow, C. P. (1991). Ten-year longitudinal follow-up of ability-matched accelerated and unaccelerated gifted students. *Journal of Educational Psychology, 83*, 528–538.

VanTassel-Baska, J. (1987). The case for teaching Latin to the verbally talented. *Roeper Review, 9*, 159–161.

CHAPTER 26

MULTIPLE CRITERIA FOR IDENTIFICATION

The literature strongly advocates that using multiple criteria for identification is a desirable practice in general and is especially useful to overcome the underrepresentation of minority students in gifted and talented programs. The research literature does not fully support the accusation that standardized tests are inherently biased, but a shortage of referrals of minority students excessively narrows program options, and poor matches between programs and selection criteria underlie much of the underrepresentation. Multiple identification criteria based on multiple sources may help solve this problem if programs are appropriately diversified and matched to criteria chosen, if they are used to include rather than exclude, and if their design and implementation is undertaken in partnership with parents and teachers representative of the diversity in the community served.

WHAT WE KNOW

The primary focus in virtually all the relevant literature on multiple criteria is redressing the nearly universal observation that minority populations are underrepresented in academic programs for gifted and talented students. We shall take this as a given in this discussion, consistent with the experience of nearly all educators. This and related literature has been reviewed elsewhere to an extent that cannot be fully replicated here, for example, by Ford and Harris (1999); Bermúdez and Rakow (1993); Green (1992); Shore, Cornell, Robinson, and Ward (1991); and Frasier, Garcia, and Passow (1995). Many of the key references were also indicated in those sources. We should begin, however, with a selective overview of the wealth of material presented by Frasier et al. (1995), with some interwoven comments.

The NRC/GT Review

The National Research Center on the Gifted and Talented (NRC/GT) commissioned a thorough examination of the underrepresentation of minorities in gifted and talented programs (Frasier et al., 1995). It discussed three reasons usually given for this underrepresentation: (a) test bias—widely asserted to be the most critical, (b) selective referrals, and (c) the ongoing emphasis on redressing deficits in education for minorities (cf. Johnson, Starnes, Gregory, & Blaylock, 1985; also see Lidz & Macrine, 2001; Sarouphim, 2002, 2004). Bermúdez and Rakow (1993) added a fourth reason: (d) decisions based on a single test administration; this is not the same as a single criterion, but refers to the lack of ongoing assessment—once a child is in or out, that is final—a serious problem with special education in general for many years.

The prevalence and nature of use of multiple criteria is uncertain. Patton, Prillaman, and VanTassel-Baska (1990) found that more than 90% of states and territories used norm-referenced tests as their only or primary method of identification for gifted programs, and only 40% indicated a lesser use of anything else. Coleman and Gallagher (1994) found that all 49 states with gifted and talented education policies used one or another IQ or achievement test; 46 take note of activities outside the school, 43 include measures of creativity, and several permit teacher, parent, student, and other input. Data from multiple criteria appear to be widely available and collected, however, it is not at all clear what precise weight is given to them in screening or selection decisions. A suggestion of what regular education teachers and teachers of the gifted believe to be appropriate practice in this regard was found in a U.S. national survey (2,918 respondents, also including 2 from Canada). Among four other qualities, a factor analysis demonstrated moderately strong support for the use of multiple identification criteria and opposition to unique dependence on IQ or performance results (Brown et al., 2005). Teacher beliefs may now be ahead of and not in synchrony with common policy and practice.

Are standardized IQ and achievement tests the culprits they are made out to be? The hard data only partly support the charge. Reynolds and Kaiser (1990), Anastasi (1988), Kamphaus (1993), and others have concluded that IQ tests are not biased in their prediction of later academic success. Frasier et al. (1995) added:

> Any evidence of bias occurred infrequently, with little or no observable patterns, except when instruments of poor reliability and high specificity of test content were examined. When bias in predictive validity did occur, it most often favored low socioeconomic status, disadvantaged ethnic minority children, or other low scoring groups. (p. 4)

One should not, however, confuse predictive validity with group differences in scores. IQ tests, while apparently predictively valid, do not tap the full richness of intelligence or giftedness, and differences do occur between different ethnic and racial groups (Borland, 1986). These differences can fuel prejudices, especially if they are seen exclusively as causes of school performance rather than indicators of the same circumstances that can lead to underperformance.

At the individual level, the potential advantage of multiple criteria is in receiving students whose strengths are different from whatever IQ and achievement tests measure. At the group level, multiple criteria provide the promise of fair and democratic treatment. It is important to have current data on minority representation in programs as a preliminary step so that it is clear what problems we are trying to solve by the promotion of multiple criteria for identification, and to assess our progress toward the solutions. One study did just this. Heath (2002) examined the impact of the imposition of a multiple criteria approach in an Atlanta, GA, school district. The proportional representation of African American elementary pupils in the gifted program increased significantly and there were, overall, slight increases in minority representation.

In addition to being widely advocated but rarely invoked, alternative criteria are not without risk. Critics say their use waters down program standards, stigmatizes children so identified, and contributes to "reverse discrimination" (majority children being held to a higher standard for admission). These criticisms remain to be put to empirical test. Most seriously, however, the amended criteria are not necessarily accompanied by a revised program, so minority children could end up being admitted on the basis of criteria that are a bad fit to the curricular demands of the program (Richert, 1991), thereby further disadvantaging them. Heath's (2002) useful study addressed representation but we need to know the pedagogical outcomes, as well.

Treffinger (1991) has usefully suggested that identification should focus more on gifted children's needs and less on labeling or identification as such. Wiggins (1989) stated, "When an educational problem persists despite the well-intentioned efforts of many people to solve it, it's a safe bet that the problem hasn't been properly framed" (p. 703). The real need is to increase the selection pool of minority children, and this is not accomplished by the use of tests to filter out and label those who already demonstrate potential or accomplishment. Part of the problem is historically seeing gifted and talented education as something separate from quality general education, with services earmarked only for children who are formally admitted to a specific program, rather than as a complement to general curriculum planning that can serve more than a subgroup of children who are formally tagged. Frasier et al. (1995) suggested two ways of looking at the problem of identifying minority children: social inequity or assessment inequity. The latter contains the potential for reexamining the basic concepts of giftedness and the goals being addressed; it therefore offers greater potential as a useful path of resolution.

Giftedness needs to be defined beyond IQ or high standardized achievement results, beyond rigid cut-off scores and "hard-core labeling" (Renzulli & Delcourt, 1986). Progress is apparent at the conceptual (cf. Ambrose, Cohen, & Tannenbaum, 2003; Friedman & Shore, 2000; Horowitz & O'Brien, 1985; Sternberg & Davidson, 1986) and even at program levels, but identification is influenced much more by legislative practice. Identification practice is not keeping up with conceptual advances in gifted education, and there has been widespread discrepancy in practice (Hoge, 1988).

The identification process most often begins with referral or nomination of a child by a teacher or parent. Both are reputed to favor high-achieving, compliant students, but when teachers are instructed about traits of giftedness, they can provide more reliable referrals. Of course, this reliability must be assessed against some criterion, and this needs to be appropriate, including how these traits occur in underrepresented groups if that is part of the goal, or the extent of diversity in the identified group. Parents of minority children have been shown to be as knowledgeable as other parents about their children's characteristics that suggested giftedness, but minority parents were also much less likely to have requested formal identification for inclusion in a program (Scott, Perou, Urbano, Hogan, & Gold, 1992). Outreach regarding information and advocacy to both teachers and parents would seem to be an essential component of any effort to broaden identification criteria and, in particular, to give greater weight to nominations (Bermúdez & Rakow, 1993; Ford & Harris, 1999).

Renzulli and Delcourt (1986) suggested that the largest gain in additional identification would come from alternative criteria precisely because they correlate poorly with IQ. Criteria that are well correlated with IQ will identify the same children already identified by that means. A critical problem is the attractiveness of data like IQ scores or other quantitative data because they can averaged, summarized, and otherwise easily manipulated. This is not the case with most alternative identification criteria. Arithmetically combining most alternative criteria creates a virtually meaningless score. The result is another single hurdle over which every student must leap, and if the field of students is at all strong, then every successful student will have excelled at every one of the criteria in the battery. This is counterproductive. The critical goal is to create appropriate alternative paths to inclusion, not multiple hurdles. The onus then falls on the program to ensure that the different talents for which selection then occurs are addressed by the programming provided and, vice versa, each of the criteria must be relevant to some curricular offering. This means planning for individual or small groups of students with particular strengths or needs, not necessarily in unison for all students identified.

Other Studies

Bermúdez and Rakow (1993) reported an interesting case of a Texas school district whose student population is 98.6% Hispanic. Locally chosen standardized tests (language, creative thinking, and Raven's Progressive Matrices and Creativity), parent questionnaires, teacher ratings, and student portfolios are used in Spanish, English, or pantomime as needed. A committee reviews all files, the pool is regularly reexamined, and parents are involved in the nominations and as classroom volunteers. The three-tiered program is focused on creative thinking. They reported more than 500 active parent volunteers in the school. The example illustrates that multiple criteria can be implemented, but it is not just the multiple criteria that make it work. The inclusive and participative manner of implementation is also critical.

Unfortunately, the study does not report data on the proportions of children in the school who participate in the three levels of the program, labeled essential, enriched, and exceptional—such data would be useful indices of the success of multiple criteria in actually raising the participation rate of minority children. The large parental involvement suggests but does not confirm success in such terms. Another study did provide some data of this sort, and showed that some of the apparent limitations of multiple criteria may be overcome by in-service training. Kofsky (1992) found that four sessions focused on gifted characteristics and eligibility criteria with elementary teachers led to a 10% increase in Black and Hispanic students identified for a gifted program, increased referrals in 80% of the low-referring schools, and increased early screening referrals of minority students.

Green (1992, 1993) reinforced these same points in a rigorous examination of a very different program. The recurring search for the complementarity of excellence and equity (cf. Gardner, 1961) was illustrated in the conscious effort of the Indiana Academy for Science, Mathematics, and Humanities. Applicants supplied a large battery of formal assessments, a teacher's recommendation, and a personal statement. Three reviewers examined each file, including one from the region of the state where the applicant came from in an effort to ensure sensitivity to the ethnic and cultural differences that existed. This identification plan increased the diversity of the selected student group: Over the 2 years of the study, females were admitted to 49% and 59% of the places, and minorities to 13% and 17%, and in both years these figures were above the proportion of girls and minorities in the state population.

Benefits of multiple criteria were harder to evaluate in terms of student achievement because students' success in the program continued to be assessed in terms of traditional academic achievement. Teacher nominations were, not surprisingly, positively but weakly correlated with success defined by achievement, and better correlated with SAT scores and the Test of Standard Written English. Part of the low correlations could be explained by the fact that nearly all the students succeeded at a high level; it is the nature of correlations that, without variability on both measures, the correlation will be low (Sprinthal, 2003, p. 86, gives a gifted example). Teachers' recommendations were, on the other hand, well correlated with the admissions reviewers' ratings of applicants' overall accomplishments (based on personal and school statements), and these accomplishment ratings were the best single predictor ($r = .91$) of the total file rating at admission. So, teachers were rating something very relevant to student admission and success, but it was not IQ or marks. Students from areas of the state with lower group performance had their application GPAs recalculated to reflect their relative performance amongst their peers. Students with low recalculated GPAs but strong teacher recommendations also received high ratings of accomplishments. Past performance in a domain is often the best indicator of future performance when it is similarly assessed. Marks predict marks on similar kinds of tests, and teachers may be "on to" something different but important. The same may apply to parents. It would be interesting to revisit these students in a decade to ascertain their life accomplishments and to see if those are correlated with any of the identification criteria.

Green (1992) studied one residential high school for mathematically and scientifically able students. This might somewhat limit the generalizability of his results. On the other hand, Jarwan and Feldhusen (1993) studied seven schools. Consistent with Green's results, the adjusted GPA from the students' home schools was the best predictor of residential school GPAs, and in contrast with Green's data, minorities were underrepresented. Respondents in all seven schools saw the use of multiple criteria as a strength, and minority underrepresentation, as well as high rates of attrition, as weaknesses. Why did these weaknesses materialize? The lack of depth in typical survey data (e.g., not asking respondents to explain why they answered each question as they did) makes interpretation difficult, but some hypothesis that fit the data include (a) the seven schools did not use locally specified measures and selection panels that took local background into account, (b) multiple criteria in and of themselves are not a solution to the problem of underrepresentation of minorities whose day-to-day circumstances may not sufficiently provide incentive and opportunity to children in the domains to be assessed, (c) narrowly defined academic achievement goals are imperfect performance indicators of the success of a program for gifted students drawn from diverse backgrounds, and (d) GPAs predict GPAs (that being an example of the maxim in assessment that reliably measured prior performance of any type is the best predictor of future similar performance). As an example of what might be lacking, Wakefield (1992) added expert ratings of artistic work to predict artistic talent, because IQ does not tap creative skills such as problem finding.

The extent to which teacher, parent, or self-nominations could replace conventional criteria was examined by Shore and Tsiamis (1986). They conducted a direct test of an extreme alternative to formal testing, namely an open-door admissions policy. They compared the middle-grades students in two summer programs for gifted and talented students, one in which all students who apply are admitted, in effect by teacher and parent referral, and another in which students had to overcome the hurdle of high achievement and IQ scores. The students were compared on a wide range of measures including IQ subtests, creativity measures, school performance data, self-esteem, and teacher ratings. No significant differences were found between the two groups on any of the measures. Though this study would benefit from replication in a regular rather than summer school, it strongly suggests that the clientele we presently serve could be identified much more economically. On the other hand, they also found that the open door did not result in a higher level of participation by underrepresented groups. That observation is confounded by the fact that this particular open-door program charged a fee (though a few scholarships were available) and the other program that demanded high achievement and IQ scores was free and paid for by the school board. Nevertheless, while multiple criteria may not be essential from a purely measurement basis, they may be an important part of addressing underrepresentation.

In an earlier overview of practice regarding multiple criteria, Shore et al. (1991) concluded that, because multiple sources of data provide useful information that is not correlated well with data from grades and standardized tests,

> The use of multiple criteria reduces the chance that a gifted child with specific disabilities or a history of underachievement will be ignored. It serves social justice by increasing the possibility of recognition to poor, minority, and other systematically different groups of children. Multiple criteria also favor selection for specialized programs where traditional scholastic prowess is not a priority, such as in the arts. . . . (p. 49)

Conclusion

The practice of providing multiple windows to include, not multiple barriers designed to exclude, is defensible. Such a conclusion is slightly in contradiction with one statement in the otherwise compatible position paper from the National Association for Gifted Children (1997): "Given the limitations of all tests *no single measure* should be used to include a child in or exclude a child from gifted educational services" (p. 1). We have no argument with the proscription against exclusion based on one measure, but if multiple criteria are to provide multiple opportunities, then acceptance based on one criterion (not necessarily a measure or score) from among many should be acceptable. Having only one criterion that every individual needs to surpass is not appropriate, but it should be sufficient for an individual to excel on one relevant criterion. The ultimate impact is not created only by the measures chosen, however, but by how people responsible for judgments use the information available and the policy framework within which the program operates.

The identification discrimination problem is not exclusively or perhaps even primarily a problem of test bias. Rather, it is a more complex result of narrow program goals, intentionally or otherwise matched to narrow identification criteria that are applied insensitively. This includes the nearly universal hurdle of high IQ or achievement being used to exclude without alternative windows of opportunity. It is partly a result of insufficient referral of underrepresented students. Whether or not it is a direct result of a bias in educational practice to apply a deficit model to the education of minority groups was not addressed by empirical data revealed in our search of the literature. Finally, identification costs front-load the costs of the program and in a zero-sum budget are necessarily traded off against programming. The particular choice of instruments may not be as critical as the context in which the data are used, and consideration should be given to keeping the largest possible portion of resources for programming, especially for underrepresented students who may need additional support if they are admitted to programs on the basis of alternative criteria and a conscious effort to provide fair opportunity for all, those who have achieved by conventional criteria, and those whose potential is only visible through another lens by a responsive viewer.

WHAT WE CAN DO

At Home

The literature primarily addresses the interaction between parents and schools in the identification process. However, the first two points below apply equally to parents who make some of the provision for their children's high ability, or create an environment conducive to talent development and identification in activities of support they create at home or in settings other than school (e.g., afterschool programs, summer programs, private lessons).

• For multiple identification criteria to be able to respond to multiple forms of potential, opportunities are needed for interests and abilities to flourish. Parents can therefore assist the process by helping their children explore, persist with, and develop interests in at least a small number of different activities. These may include music, athletics, reading, arts, travel, leadership, community service, religion, or any number of personal hobbies (e.g., collecting stamps or coins), or other activities. A child who has experienced two or three organized activities from such a list will have experiences and opportunities to be identified by multiple criteria that reach beyond the traditional way of identifying students.

❧ Parents should tell the school about their children's strengths and insist that districts and schools report annually on their general demographic composition in special services of all types.

❧ Parents should be informed in a welcoming manner that exceptional abilities occur everywhere in society and the school district and school should welcome their nominations of their children as valuable program guidance and not regard these nominations as immodest or inappropriate.

In the Classroom

In the identification process, the teacher's greatest contribution is referral. This needs to be supported by regular in-service opportunities, and teachers' advice must be acted upon if it is to be offered freely. Teachers are also the best placed to interact with parents and to ask explicitly about children's strengths outside school, and to help parents make referrals. The teachers' role interacts with the need for schools to treat programs for the gifted as part of the central core of programming, not as add-on or elite enterprises, otherwise, some teachers might see referrals as detracting from the quality of their working environment and not enhancing it. Teachers should therefore:

❧ Inform parents about ways in which their children's school performance excels over time or on specific occasions.

❧ Seek from parents information about their children's interests and areas of achievement outside the school.

❧ Anticipate that there is no one way to be gifted and that program adjustments may need to vary for different children.

❧ Share information about student strengths and interests with other teachers so that superior and more available services, plus some efficiencies of effort, might be achieved by practices such as cluster grouping or enabling children to join activities that meet their interests and needs in other classes.

At School

School and district responsibilities apply to both parents and children, at the levels of both policy and practice. With regard to parents and children:

❧ Parents and teachers should be offered information sessions about the nature of high abilities, the needs of these children for some degree of differentiated services, and the importance of parent and teacher input in identifying children who can benefit most from these services. Parents and teachers should be asked for nominations at least every year.

Ș One of the most original ideas that allows any referrals to be received in a positive relationship and combined with other information is that of a talent pool (Renzulli & Reis, 1986). Whatever program model is developed, the talent pool can likely facilitate the process of using students identified by multiple criteria.

Ș Ensure multiple identification criteria from multiple sources are appropriately included in policies and practice for identifying highly able pupils for differentiated services. The data collected should be relevant to the program options available or anticipated.

Ș Passow and Frasier (1996) recommended that the identification of potential in underserved populations in particular should be varied and ongoing, draw on performance relevant to students' experiences, and integrate assessment with learning opportunities. Regional or cultural communities should be involved in the process.

Ș Be proactive and not wait for parental referrals, because differences in culture and personal comfort in dealing with bureaucracies and the school system may cause some parents to refrain from nominating their own children.

Ș Use locally adjusted norms on standardized tests, an inclusive approach to relevant multiple criteria, and include parents and teachers, representative of the diversity of their constituencies, in the design and implementation of identification processes.

There is no evidence to support the ban of the use of IQ or performance data, as long as they are not mandatory hurdles for selection at the individual level, they are used to identify students for program options for which they are appropriate, and they do not exclude students whose other achievements, motivation, or complementary talents, who may also succeed with a supportive, rather than sink-or-swim, philosophy.

Ș A selection process based partly on student needs could facilitate linking programs with counseling and other student-support services.

Ș Offer multifaceted services that respond to multiple criteria from diverse sources.

REFERENCES

Ambrose, D. C., Cohen, L., & Tannenbaum, A. J. (Eds.). (2003). *Creative intelligence: Toward a theoretical integration.* New York: Hampton Press.

Anastasi, A. (1988). *Psychological testing* (6th ed.). New York: Macmillan.

Bermúdez, A. B., & Rakow, S. J. (1993). Examining identification and instruction practices for gifted and talented limited English proficient students. In L. M.

Malave (Ed.), *Annual conference journal: Proceedings of the annual conference of the National Association for Bilingual Education* (pp. 99–114). Washington, DC: National Association for Bilingual Education. (ERIC Document Reproduction Service No. ED360871)

Borland, J. H. (1986). IQ tests: Throwing out the bathwater, saving the baby. *Roeper Review, 8,* 163–167.

Brown, S. W., Renzulli, J. S., Gubbins, E. J., Siegle, D., Zhang, W., & Chen, C.-H. (2005). Assumptions underlying the identification of gifted and talented students. *Gifted Child Quarterly, 49,* 68–79.

Coleman, M. R., & Gallagher, J. J. (1994). *Updated report on state policies related to the identification of gifted students.* Chapel Hill: University of North Carolina, Gifted Education Policy Studies Program.

Ford, D. Y., & Harris, J. J., III. (1999). *Multicultural gifted education.* New York: Teachers College Press.

Frasier, M. M., Garcia, J. H., & Passow, A. H. (1995). *A review of assessment issues in gifted education and their implications for identifying gifted minority students.* (Report No. RM95204). Storrs: National Research Center on the Gifted and Talented, University of Connecticut.

Friedman, R. C., & Shore, B. M. (Eds.). (2000). *Talents unfolding: Cognition and development.* Washington, DC: American Psychological Association.

Gardner, J. W. (1961). *Excellence: Can we be equal and excellent too?* New York: Harper and Row.

Green, J. E. (1992). *Evaluation of a holistic method for identifying pupils for state academies for the academically gifted.* Unpublished manuscript, Teachers College, Ball State University. (ERIC Document Reproduction Service No. ED358668)

Green, J. E. (1993). *State academies for the academically gifted* (Fastback Series No. 349). Bloomington, IN: Phi Delta Kappa.

Heath, W. M. (2002). Results of the implementation of Georgia's multiple-criteria rule on minority representation in programs for the gifted and talented. *Dissertation Abstracts International: Humanities and Social Sciences, 63*(3-A), 859–908. (Dissertation Abstracts No. 2002-95017-018)

Hoge, R. D. (1988). Issues in the definition and measurement of the giftedness construct. *Educational Researcher, 17*(7), 12–16, 22.

Horowitz, F. D., & O'Brien, M. (Eds.). (1985). *The gifted and talented: Developmental perspectives.* Washington, DC: American Psychological Association.

Jarwan, F. A., & Feldhusen, J. F. (1993). *Residential school of mathematics and science for academically talented youth: Analysis of admission programs* (Collaborative Research Series Document No. CRS93304). Storrs: National Research Center on the Gifted and Talented, University of Connecticut.

Johnson, S. T., Starnes, W. T., Gregory, D., & Blaylock, A. (1985). Program of assessment, diagnosis, and instruction (PADI): Identifying and nurturing potentially gifted and talented minority students. *Journal of Negro Education, 54,* 416–430.

Kamphaus, R. W. (1993). *Clinical assessment of children's intelligence: A clinical handbook for professional practice.* Boston: Allyn & Bacon.

Kofsky, G. E. (1992). *Increasing the number of minority elementary students found eligible for placement in a gifted program by enhancing the quality of screening instruments and inservice training provided to school staff.* Unpublished doctoral practicum report, Nova Southeastern University, Fort Lauderdale, FL. (ERIC Document Reproduction Service No. ED346697)

Lidz, C. S., & Macrine, S. L. (2001). An alternative approach to the identification of gifted culturally and linguistically diverse learners. *School Psychology International, 22,* 74–96.

National Association for Gifted Children (1997). *Position paper: The use of tests in the identification of gifted children.* Washington, DC: Author.

Passow, A. H., & Frasier, M. M. (1996). Toward improving identification of talent potential among minority and disadvantaged students. *Roeper Review, 18,* 198–202.

Patton, J. M., Prillaman, D., & VanTassel-Baska, J. (1990). The nature and extent of programs for the disadvantaged gifted in the United States and territories. *Gifted Child Quarterly, 34,* 94–96.

Renzulli, J. S., & Delcourt, M. A. B. (1986). The legacy and logic of research on the identification of gifted persons. *Gifted Child Quarterly, 30,* 20–23.

Renzulli, J. S., & Reis, S. M. (1986). The Enrichment Triad/Revolving Door Model: A schoolwide plan for the development of creative productivity. In J. S. Renzulli (Ed.), *Systems and models for developing programs for the gifted and talented* (pp. 215–266). Mansfield Center, CT: Creative Learning Press.

Reynolds, C. R., & Kaiser, S. M. (1990). Bias in assessment of aptitude. In C. R. Reynolds & R. W. Kamphaus (Eds.), *Handbook of psychological and educational assessment of children: Intelligence and achievement* (pp. 611–653). New York: Guilford.

Richert, E. S. (1991). Rampant problems and promising practices in identification. In N. Colangelo & G. A. Davis (Eds.), *Handbook of gifted education* (pp. 81–96). Boston: Allyn & Bacon.

Sarouphim, K. M. (2002). Discover in high school: Identifying gifted Hispanic and Native American students. *Journal of Secondary Gifted Education, 14,* 30–38.

Sarouphim, K. M. (2004). Discover in middle school: Identifying gifted minority students. *Journal of Secondary Gifted Education, 15,* 61–69.

Scott, M. S., Perou, R., Urbano, R., Hogan, A., & Gold, S. (1992). The identification of giftedness: A comparison of White, Hispanic, and Black families. *Gifted Child Quarterly, 36,* 175–184.

Shore, B. M., Cornell, D. C., Robinson, A., & Ward, V. S. (1991). *Recommended practices in gifted education: A critical analysis.* New York: Columbia University, Teachers College Press.

Shore, B. M., & Tsiamis, A. (1986). Identification by provision: Limited field test of a radical alternative for identifying gifted students. In K. A. Heller & J. F. Feldhusen (Eds.), *Identifying and nurturing the gifted: An international perspective* (pp. 93–102). Bern, Switzerland: Hans Huber.

Sprinthal, R. C. (2003). *Basic statistical analysis* (7th ed.). Boston: Allyn & Bacon.

Sternberg, R. J., & Davidson, J. E. (Eds.). (1986). *Conceptions of giftedness.* Cambridge, England: Cambridge University Press.

Treffinger, D. J. (1991). Future goals and directions. In N. Colangelo & G. A. Davis (Eds.), *Handbook of gifted education* (pp. 441–119). Boston: Allyn & Bacon.

Wakefield, J. F. (1992, February). *Creativity tests and artistic talent.* Paper presented at the Esther Katz Rosen Symposium on Psychological Development of Gifted Children, Lawrence, KS. (ERIC Document Reproduction Service No. ED355697)

Wiggins, G. (1989). A true test: Toward more authentic and equitable assessment. *Phi Delta Kappan, 70,* 703–713.

CHAPTER 27

DEVELOPING TALENTS IN CULTURALLY DIVERSE LEARNERS

E ducators need to learn about the culturally diverse students in their classes and understand the various cultural perspectives and practices that affect students' and families' approach to learning, school, and giftedness. Talents among culturally diverse learners are best located by alternatives to traditional identification. In addition to the identification of culturally diverse high-ability learners, school practices that enhance academic persistence are emerging.

WHAT WE KNOW

As the numbers of culturally and linguistically diverse learners increase, the need for identifying and developing their talents in culturally diverse students also increases (Baldwin, 2002; Bernal, 2002; Frasier & Passow, 1994). The more schools understand and include cultural and linguistic diversity in the educational experience, the more successful and interested students will be. With an expanding culturally and linguistically diverse population, educators need to acknowledge the special attributes talented, diverse students bring in terms of their own histories, languages, and cultural values and how these values may contribute to their giftedness (Strom, Johnson, Strom, & Strom, 1992).

Variability Among Culturally Diverse Learners

Culturally diverse groups are not homogeneous and should not be culturally stereotyped. For example, it would be a disservice to assume all Asian and Pacific Americans bring to the classroom the same background and values. Asian and Pacific cultures vary in country of origin, language, religion, attitudes, and social practices (Kitano & DiJiosia, 2002; Tomine, 1991). The Chinese culture promotes advanced education for gifted students, while the Japanese culture encourages a belief in equality (Stevenson, Lee, & Chen, 1994). Yet, similarities do exist across several Asian and Pacific cultural groups. For example, most Asian learners believe personal issues should not be discussed and emotions not expressed outside the family (Plucker, 1996; Sue & Sue, 1991; Tomine). In terms of Native American Indian peoples, Tonemah (1987) pointed out that there are 177 different tribes, each having its own culture with varying degrees of acculturation. Other researchers have suggested even greater numbers of distinctive tribal groups, thus diversity *within* this population is assured (Callahan & McIntire, 1994). Within-group diversity characterizes Latino and Hispanic groups who are immigrant and nonimmigrant, who differ in their bilingual orientation, and who present a complex variety of cultural perspectives (Osterling, 2001). African American high-ability learners come from urban, suburban, and rural homes with varying income levels and from geographically diverse regions of the country. A theme of the descriptive research on culturally diverse high-ability learners is that differences exist within, as well as across, cultural groups.

Cultural Views of Giftedness

It is important for educators of culturally and linguistically diverse students to understand the ways parents approach the education of their children and the cultural distinctions they may bring to the educational process. Not every culture defines giftedness according to stated and federal definitions. Although all cultural groups have a lens, the case of Native American Indians is a clear example. Native American Indians see giftedness in relationship to development within the tribe. Kirschenbaum (1988) stated that problem-solving abilities are extremely important in determining giftedness in the Indian culture. The earlier a child demonstrates certain abilities, especially being an active listener, the more likely the child is thought to be gifted. There is a strong sense of what the gifted child brings to the tribe as an effective leader and creative problem solver (Tonemah, 1987).

Identification of Culturally Diverse Gifted Learners

According to many researchers, culturally diverse gifted learners are underrepresented due to the identification procedures most commonly used (Alamprese & Erlanger, 1989; Baldwin, 2002; Frasier & Passow, 1994; Kirschenbaum, 1988; Robinson, Bradley, & Stanley, 1990), deficit thinking by educators (Ford, Harris, Tyson, & Trotman, 2002) or a combination of both (Ford & Grantham, 2003). Teacher perceptions have been found to be a factor in identification of diverse gifted learners. For example, Fernandez, Gay, Lucky, and Gavilan (1998) found teachers of Hispanic students were more likely to indicate that the ability to express oneself through a large vocabulary was more important than the ability to speak more than one language when identifying linguistically diverse students for giftedness.

Alternative methods of identifying culturally diverse gifted learners suggested by Frasier and Passow (1994) include teacher recommendations, parent and peer recommendations, student portfolios, and student performance tasks. Sarouphim (2001) investigated and reported some successes with the DISCOVER method, which includes tasks selected or developed from a multiple intelligences (MI) framework, administered in a classroom setting, and scored by trained observers. Tonemah (1987) suggested tests that are culturally based, and Sheets (1994) recommended language-specific tests for monolingual and bilingual students. Sheets investigated Hispanic students who were considered at risk and who were speakers of Spanish as their primary language but who did not read or write in Spanish. They were placed in an Advanced Placement (AP) Spanish Language and Literature honors course along with other AP students. The study involved 29 Spanish-speaking students over a period of 3 years. The course emphasized language, culture, and value of the culture, as well as pride in one's culture. These same at-risk students achieved success in AP Spanish tests. Twenty of the 29 passed the AP Spanish language test, the AP Spanish literature test, or both, and received college credit. Thus, this identification strategy can be conceptualized as an extended "try-out."

The use of nonverbal assessment instruments to identify culturally diverse gifted learners has been recommended repeatedly and has generated considerable attention and debate (Lohman, 2005; Naglieri & Ford, 2003). The most frequently recommended nonverbal group assessments are the Raven Standard Progressive Matrices and the Naglieri Nonverbal Abilities Test. Shaunessy, Karnes, and Cobb (2004) compared the relative effectiveness of three nonverbal measures with 169 students in grades 2–6 and found that Cattell's Culture-Fair Intelligence Test and the Raven Standard Progressive Matrices identified more students than the Naglieri Nonverbal Abilities Test. Robinson et al. (1990) found the Raven to be effective in identifying African American students for an enriched and accelerated mathematics program. Mills and Tissot (1995) also investigated the use of the Raven Matrices for identification. Lidz and Macrine (2001) used a dynamic assessment procedure with the Naglieri Nonverbal Ability Test and increased the number of culturally diverse students identified as gifted in an elementary school. At present, the research indicates that nonverbal assessments are promising, although the studies differ on which tests are used and on their relative effectiveness.

Schools, Parents, and the Culturally Diverse Gifted Student

To understand cultural diversity in the school context, Clark (1984) suggested four major considerations. First, family ethnic and racial background does determine how other groups respond to culturally diverse learners. Second, different ethnic and racial groups have particular social histories that lead to different personal histories and opportunities for economic and educational resources. Third, residential segregation over a period of time has led to different family approaches to survival. And, fourth, regardless of ethnic, occupational, income, or instructional differences, the same communication dynamics and processes account for academic success or failure.

How to serve high-ability youth effectively has been a preoccupation of the field (Robinson & Clinkenbeard, 1998). Programs successful in educating culturally diverse students share common elements in terms of the teacher and the mode of instruction (Garcia, 1993). The teachers were experienced educators, they were flexible, they participated in professional development regarding cultural diversity, and they incorporated the history, language, and traditions of the culturally diverse learner into the curriculum. The curriculum was generally theme-oriented. The instruction most often involved small-group activities, learning centers, and less whole-class instruction. In other words, instruction was student-centered rather than teacher-centered.

Montgomery (2001) collected data through interviews with staff and written reports from high school students concerning a Jacob K. Javits project focused on 120 rural, Native American Indian learners and reported that the linkages formed between students, schools, and the community were recognized by the participants as an important aspect of the program, Project LEAP. She reported that as a result of participating in a differentiated curriculum, students increased their performance on ACT and SAT scores, actively pursued postsecondary education, and applied for financial aid during the college application process.

Worrell (Worrell, Szarko, & Gabelko, 2001) investigated the return rate of culturally diverse high-ability learners to a summer program on a university campus. In a sample of 316 students, he found a return rate of 44% for nontraditional gifted learners who received a financial aid package to attend the program and were supported by counseling and mentor/tutor labs. The return rate for the nontraditional gifted learners exceeded the return rate of regular program attendees (40%).

Counseling, not only for the talented student, but for parents as well, is important. They need help in exploring career possibilities, applying for college, and applying for scholarships and grants. Case studies by Nieto (1992) of several culturally diverse high school students' experiences verified the need for career and academic guidance targeting the family. Chavkin and Williams (1993) also stressed the importance of educating parents, sometimes through an interpreter if necessary, of the resources available and the value of higher education.

Culturally diverse parents approach the role of school and their relationship to their children's education in different ways. Chavkin and Williams (1993) pointed out the belief that culturally diverse parents are not as knowledgeable, interested, or concerned about their children's education as Anglo American parents. Their studies, along with Clark (1984), Frasier and Passow (1994), and VanTassel-Baska (1989) did not support those beliefs. Cultural differences may limit the degree of parent involvement, but does not limit parent interest in the child's education. For example, Nieto (1992) indicated that Hispanics and Asian Americans tend to be less comfortable with teachers and defer to schools more than African Americans and non-Hispanic White parents. They tend to be more differential in their attitude toward schools, and therefore, have less contact. However, a survey conducted by Ritter, Mont-Reynaud, and Dornbusch (1993) suggested that these parents are very caring in terms of their child's education. For example, a survey of Hispanic parents found that 97% wanted teachers to provide them with ways to help their children with homework. In a report on Project Mandala, a Jacob K. Javits project, Damiani (1996) noted that among the 87 families served by the project, confusion about what the school provided for their gifted child was frequently reported. She concluded that school programs needed to review their methods of communication with the home and increase family involvement in educational planning. In case studies of young, culturally diverse gifted children, Tomlinson, Callahan, and Lelli (1997) observed that parental involvement encouraged family interest, harmony, and an understanding of the gifted child. Further, Clark (1984) reported that a major factor in successful, culturally diverse students was parent involvement in the child's academic experience. Specifically, fostering the homework habit, reviewing assignments, and conversations regarding the assignments contribute to academic achievement. These conversations, according to Clark, provide a line of communication between parent, child, and the school. Whether parents are physically present in the schools or supportive and encouraging at home, research suggests that student achievement can, in part, be due to parental encouragement and support. Culturally and linguistically diverse parents do care, and it is the role of the schools to initiate and encourage their participation in the schools.

WHAT WE CAN DO

At School

❧ Offer teachers, counselors, and administrators the opportunity to learn about the perspectives of each of the cultures their students represent.

❧ Encourage the inclusion of multicultural curriculum and culturally responsive teaching in the educational program of the classroom and the school as a whole.

❧ Seek alternative ways of identifying giftedness among diverse high-ability learners that consider the language and cultural expectations of students.

❧ Communicate with parents to build a bridge between home and school. Inform parents about what gifted programs can offer their children, what schools mean by giftedness, and what parents can do to assist their children.

❧ Address the social and emotional needs of culturally diverse high-ability learners through proactive interventions and the development of warm, personal relationships between students and teachers.

❧ Counsel with parents and students about postsecondary planning and the career opportunities available.

REFERENCES

Alamprese, J., & Erlanger, W. (1989). *No gift wasted: Effective strategies for educating highly able, disadvantaged students in mathematics and science.* Washington, DC: COSMOS Corporation.

Baldwin, A. Y. (2002). Culturally diverse students who are gifted. *Exceptionality, 10,* 139–147.

Bernal, E. M. (2002). Three ways to achieve a more equitable representation of culturally and linguistically different students in GT programs. *Roeper Review, 24,* 82–89.

Callahan, C. M., & McIntire, J. A. (1994). *Identifying outstanding talent in American Indian and Alaska Native students.* Washington, DC: U.S. Government Printing Office.

Chavkin, N., & Williams, D. L. (1993). Minority parents and the elementary school: Attitudes and practices. In N. Chavkin (Ed.), *Families and schools in a pluralistic society* (pp. 107–119). Albany, NY: State University of New York Press.

Clark, R. (1984). *Family life and school achievement.* Chicago: University of Chicago Press.

Damiani, V. B. (1996). The individual family support plan: A tool to assist special populations of gifted learners. *Roeper Review, 18,* 293–298.

Fernandez, A., Gay, L., Lucky, L., & Gavilan, M. (1998). Teacher perceptions of gifted Hispanic limited English proficient students. *Journal for the Education of the Gifted, 21,* 335–351.

Ford, D. Y., & Grantham, T. C. (2003). Providing access for culturally diverse gifted students: From deficit to dynamic thinking. *Theory Into Practice, 42,* 217–225.

Ford, D. Y., Harris, J. J., Tyson, C. A., & Trotman, M. F. (2002). Beyond deficit thinking. *Roeper Review, 24,* 52–59.

Frasier, M. M., & Passow, A. H. (1994). *Toward a new paradigm for identifying talent potential* (Research Monograph No. 9412). Storrs: National Research Center on the Gifted and Talented, University of Connecticut.

Garcia, E. (1993). Language, culture, and education. In L. Darling-Hammond (Ed.), *Review of research in education* (Vol. 19, pp. 51–98). Washington, DC: American Educational Research Association.

Kirschenbaum, R. (1988). Methods for identifying the gifted and talented American Indian student. *Journal for the Education of the Gifted, 11*(3), 53–63.

Kitano, M. K., & DiJiosia, M. (2002). Are Asian and Pacific Americans overrepresented in programs for the gifted? *Roeper Review, 24,* 76–80.

Lidz, C. S., & Macrine, S. L. (2001). An alternative approach to the identification of gifted culturally and linguistically diverse learners. *School Psychology International, 22,* 74–96.

Lohman, D. F. (2005). Review of Naglieri and Ford (2003): Does the Naglieri Nonverbal Ability Test identify equal proportions of high-scoring White, Black, and Hispanic students? *Gifted Child Quarterly, 49,* 19–28.

Mills, C., & Tissot, S. (1995). Identifying academic potential in students from underrepresented populations: Is using the Raven's Progressive Matrices a good idea? *Gifted Child Quarterly, 39,* 209–217.

Montgomery, D. (2001). Increasing Native American Indian involvement in gifted programs in rural schools. *Psychology in the Schools, 38,* 467–475.

Naglieri, J. A., & Ford, D. Y. (2003). Addressing underrepresentation of gifted minority children using the Naglieri Nonverbal Ability Test (NNAT). *Gifted Child Quarterly, 47,* 155–160.

Nieto, S. (1992). *Affirming diversity: The sociopolitical context of multicultural education.* White Plains, NY: Longman.

Osterling, J. P. (2001). Waking the sleeping giant: Engaging and capitalizing on the sociocultural strengths of the Latino community. *Bilingual Research Journal, 25*(1 & 2), 1–28.

Plucker, J. (1996). Gifted Asian-American students: Identification, curricular, and counseling concerns. *Journal for the Education of the Gifted, 19,* 315–343.

Ritter, P., Mont-Reynaud, R., & Dornbusch, S. (1993). Minority families and their youth: Concern, encouragement, and support for school achievement. In N. Chavkin (Ed.), *Families and schools in a pluralistic society* (pp. 107–119). Albany, NY: State University of New York Press.

Robinson, A., & Clinkenbeard, P. R. (1998). Giftedness: An exceptionality examined. In J. T. Spence (Ed.), *Annual review of psychology* (Vol. 49, pp. 117–139). Palo Alto, CA: Annual Reviews.

Robinson, A., Bradley, R., & Stanley, T. D. (1990). Opportunity to achieve: Identifying mathematically gifted Black students. *Contemporary Educational Psychology, 15,* 1–12.

Sarouphim, K. M. (2001). DISCOVER: Concurrent validity, gender differences, and identification of minority students. *Gifted Child Quarterly, 45*, 130–138.

Shaunessy, E., Karnes, F. A., & Cobb, Y. (2004). Assessing potentially gifted students from lower socioeconomic status with nonverbal measures of intelligence. *Perceptual and Motor Skills, 98*, 1129–1138.

Sheets, R. (1994, April). *College Board Advanced Placement Spanish Literature for at-risk native speakers: A model with multicultural, bilingual, and gifted dimensions.* Paper presented at the annual meeting of the American Educational Research Association, New Orleans, LA.

Stevenson, H., Lee, S., & Chen, C. (1994). Education of gifted and talented students in mainland China, Taiwan, and Japan. *Journal for the Education of the Gifted, 17*, 104–130.

Strom, R., Johnson, A., Strom, S., & Strom, P. (1992). Educating gifted Hispanic children and their parents. *Hispanic Journal of Behavioral Sciences, 14*, 383–393.

Sue, D., & Sue, D. W. (1991). Counseling strategies for Chinese Americans. In C. C. Lee & B. L. Richardson (Eds.), *Multicultural issues in counseling: New approaches to diversity* (pp. 79–90). Alexandria, VA: American Association for Counseling and Development.

Tomine, S. I. (1991). Counseling Japanese Americans: From internment to reparation. In C. C. Lee & B. Richardson (Eds.), *Multicultural issues in counseling: New approaches to diversity* (pp. 91–105). Alexandria, VA: American Association for Counseling and Development.

Tomlinson, C. A., Callahan, C. M., & Lelli, K. M. (1997). Challenging expectations: Case studies of high potential, culturally diverse young children. *Gifted Child Quarterly, 41*, 5–18.

Tonemah, S. (1987). Assessing American Indian gifted and talented students' abilities. *Journal for the Education of the Gifted, 10*, 181–194.

VanTassel-Baska, J. (1989). The role of the family in the success of disadvantaged gifted learners. *Journal for the Education of the Gifted, 13*, 222–226.

Worrell, F. C., Szarko, J. E., & Gabelko, N. H. (2001). Multi-year persistence of nontraditional students in an academic talent development program. *Journal of Secondary Gifted Education, 12*, 80–90.

CHAPTER 28

PROMISING LEARNERS FROM LOW-INCOME BACKGROUNDS

T he United States has a greater percentage of children born into poverty than any other developed country in the world—one out of every five children (U.S. Bureau of the Census, 2004). Many schools serve children enveloped by pockets of poverty. For example, in one southeastern state, two out of three children enrolled in school are eligible for the Free and Reduced Price School Lunch Program. Among the children born into high-poverty homes and attending schools in low-income communities are academically promising learners. Facing the barriers of poverty, they are often overlooked and underserved in programs and services for high-ability learners. Identification practices may not work in their favor, and assumptions are made by educators, parents, and policymakers about their potential for academic success. Although they confront grave challenges, evidence suggests that low-income promising learners have resiliency and the ability to succeed under the stressful conditions of poverty and low expectations. Furthermore, programs and services that are of sufficient intensity and duration and that take into account family circumstances can increase achievement and ultimately leverage these learners into a successful learning trajectory.

WHAT WE KNOW

Significant numbers of children and adolescents are born into poverty worldwide. Even among developed countries, poverty affects families and translates into negative outcomes for children. Among the poor, children are more likely to suffer health risks, cognitive difficulties, and compromised educational achievement (Parrish, 2004). Against the canvas of childhood poverty, however, there are promising learners who demonstrate high achievement or the potential to do so. They are underrepresented in programs and services for talented learners in comparison to their more affluent peers (Alamprese & Erlanger, 1989; Konstantopoulos, Modi, & Hedges, 2001). Robinson (2003) suggested that equity efforts in gifted education be directed toward high-ability learners living in poverty.

In reviewing and synthesizing the literature on low-income talented learners and their underrepresentation in gifted programs, three themes occur in terms of evidence-based practices. The first theme involves the practices used in the identification of giftedness. A second theme lies in the crucial role of family support systems. The third theme focuses on school expectations and practices and the family's understanding of those practices. Although these three themes are not independent of one another, each will be discussed separately.

Identification of Low-Income Promising Learners

Despite an increased use of multiple criteria, the identification of gifted and talented students continues to be dominated by the use of standardized test scores. These are generally paper-and-pencil aptitude and achievement tests. High-scoring students are considered gifted and recommended for programs and services. Giftedness, therefore, is associated with a test score in practice, if not philosophically. Low-income promising learners can be identified through traditional test scores, but many of them are overlooked. To address the problem, numerous researchers have advocated alternative or extended ways of identifying them (Callahan, Tomlinson, Moon, Tomchin, & Plucker, 1995; Frasier et al., 1995; Passow & Frasier, 1996; Sarouphim, 1999). In a national survey of identification practices, Hunsaker (1994) found alternative strategies included teacher checklists and rating scales, social interaction in the classroom, indicators of creativity, problem-solving activities, student portfolios, and provisional placement in gifted programs as a tryout period.

Supported by a Jacob K. Javits project, intensive screening procedures, assessment, and observation of kindergarten students were successful strategies for locating promising young learners through a case study approach

(Borland & Wright, 1994). On a statewide scale, increased numbers of low-income talented learners have been identified through the use of performance tasks introduced with preteaching examples (VanTassel-Baska, Johnson, & Avery, 2002). After 2 years of placement and performance in programs, teachers and program coordinators in two thirds of the schools surveyed perceived that students identified through these tasks were motivated and making progress (VanTassel-Baska, Feng, Quek, & Struck, 2004). Another approach to the identification of low-income promising learners is the classroom tryout procedure, in which every student in the class is given the same opportunities to solve problems and to participate in "gifted-like" activities in order to show his or her readiness to participate in gifted programs (Jatko, 1995).

The advantage of the use of extended and alternative systems is that they provide the opportunity for more students to be served. Such approaches are, however, not without disadvantages. The validity and reliability of alternative approaches or multiple measures, especially if locally developed, may be suspect (Plucker, Callahan, & Tomchin, 1996). Applying extensive identification procedures may be time consuming and therefore expensive. Cost is an important concern in schools that have large numbers of low-income students, and labor-intensive identification procedures can absorb scarce resources so that few dollars remain to serve the students.

Serving Low-Income Promising Learners

Although the issue of identification has garnered most of the attention, successful programs and services have been developed and documented. For example, Project Synergy identified low-income promising kindergarten students, moved them into a gifted program in a laboratory school at grade 2, and followed them longitudinally until they were in grade 8 (Borland, Schnur, & Wright, 2000). Key features identified by the researchers included transitional services classes, tutoring, parental support, and a message communicated to the students and their families that they were special.

Similar key features characterize another program serving low-income promising learners through school and university collaboration. Project EXCITE was developed to leverage more culturally diverse learners into science and mathematics opportunities in high school; however, the program also serves a high proportion of students reportedly eligible for the Free and Reduced Lunch Program (Olszewski-Kubilius, Lee, Ngoi, & Ngoi, 2004). Specifically, school officials report that 48.7% are eligible, and 51.3% are not; thus, one of every two students is from a low-income home. The program services begin at grade 3 with afterschool academic enrichment at local high schools and summer enrichment classes. These opportunities are followed with Saturday enrichment classes for students in grades 4, 5, and 6, with mandatory mathematics and science course selections beginning in grade 5. By grade 6, students are required to attend the summer program on the campus of

Northwestern University. Again, they choose a mathematics or science course. Project EXCITE also provides individualized support through preparation for the prealgebra placement test and collaborative study groups scheduled during school time. An array of professionals are available, including Project EXCITE instructors, school psychologists, high school student mentors, and a translator for Hispanic families. The program has followed three student cohorts and reports a 79.2% retention rate for Cohort 1, a rate of 78.9% for Cohort 2, and a rate of 77.8% for Cohort 3. Olszewski-Kubilius et al. (2004) also found that students "earned high grades in school, and performed well on state criterion-referenced tests in math and science." (p. 127). As in the case of Project Synergy, Project EXCITE is a multiyear program.

Case studies of promising learners living in poverty also echo the necessary intensity and duration of school services required for low-income children and youth (Hébert, 2002). High expectations from their teachers, real-world problem-solving opportunities, extracurricular activities, and the sustained involvement of caring adults were repeating themes in programs and services that made a difference. In terms of the effective education of low-income promising learners, the evidence currently exists to guide schools, but resources and the collective will of society are needed to initiate and maintain the practices that work.

The Role of Parents: Making the Connection Between Home and School

Parents can and do play an important role in the development of opportunities for talented children regardless of family income (Gelbrich & Hare, 1989). Studies by Clark (1983); Reis, Colbert, and Hébert (2005); and Werner (1995) have investigated students' resiliency to stressful, high-poverty environments; they suggest that the connection between parents, other family members, and mentors is an extremely important factor in student success. Low-income families need to know what they can contribute to the educational development of their talented child. Programs and services effective with low-income promising learners have involved parents as key participants. For example, a case study by Barone and Schneider (2003) found that a high-ability, low-income child in an at-risk urban school followed this pattern. The mother provided a rich literacy environment for her son and two younger siblings, engaged in learning discussions at home, and readily involved herself at school. A follow-up study of Head Start children at grade 3 confirmed that the highest achieving low-income children were characterized by parents with positive attitudes toward parenting and toward school (Robinson, Lanzi, Weinberg, Ramey, & Ramey, 2002). Among older low-income promising youth, the mother's role in supporting achievement retained its salience as adolescents moved into grade 9 (Newman, Myers, Newman, Lohman, & Smith, 2000). Across the age span, many low-income promising learners were protected and assisted in reaching their academic goals by supportive family members. Thus, gifted programs that ignore the importance of the family and do not include them explicitly in program services risk being ineffective.

WHAT WE CAN DO

At Home

&⃗ Parents who believe their child is gifted should insist upon alternative or extended assessment strategies if traditional methods don't work. Parents should ask teachers and administrators about guidelines used to identify gifted students and share with teachers their perceptions of their child's abilities.

At School

&⃗ Share information with parents of low-income promising learners. Don't exclude them in the preparation of their child's academic program. Many parents feel they have little input and understanding of what they can do to assist the development of talents in their child or adolescent. Awareness of academic goals in school can help parents and other family members provide supportive learning experiences at home. Building the "homework habit" becomes another line of communication between the school, the child, and the parent. Parental education and partnership between home and school are important factors with regard to parental understanding of what giftedness means and what actions should be taken to foster its development.

&⃗ Focus on family strengths. Do not assume a lack of parental or extended family support in a low-income home. High expectations and aspirations are not limited by income or family structure. Do assess the support system for each student and build a program that augments the social support systems of each individual student, be it through school clubs to develop leadership, academic support as needed, cultural enrichment activities, summer programs, or a mentorship program (Olszewski-Kubilius, Grant, & Seibert, 1994).

&⃗ Address parental distrust of schools. Many low-income parents had negative experiences in school themselves or felt alienated from them; they are suspicious about what schools might offer their children. In contrast, low-income parents who visit the schools when they haven't been summoned because of a disciplinary situation can assist the school with information that contributes to student development and achievement (Clark, 1983).

&⃗ Make time available for school personnel to provide social and emotional support to low-income promising learners and their families. Such activities include guidance in setting tangible goals, developing motivation toward learning, visiting student homes to talk with parents, and counseling middle school and high school students about career opportunities and applying for scholarships.

৯৶ Develop individualized programs that focus on the student strengths, not weaknesses or deficiencies. Too often school programs for low-income learners tend to be remedial in nature rather than exploratory and enriching. Low-income promising learners require exploratory, enriching, and accelerative services.

৯৶ Extend the time students spend learning. Afterschool, weekend, and summer programs; independent study; and collaborative study groups are strategies for increasing the intensity of services.

৯৶ Administrators should provide appropriate professional development to sensitize teachers and counselors to any biases they may hold about low-income promising learners.

৯৶ Teachers need to learn more about the family context and the community culture in the lives of their low-income promising students.

৯৶ Finally, create a cadre of people who will help to develop the financial resources for programs. In many districts, serving low-income highly able students is not the highest priority. In such cases, financial commitment to serving low-income, high-ability students should be cultivated. Sometimes that financial support comes from sources outside the district funds, but it also requires advocacy to make budgetary resources part of the district goals for talented learners.

REFERENCES

Alamprese, J., & Erlanger, W. (1989). *No gift wasted: Effective strategies for educating highly able, disadvantaged students in mathematics and science.* Washington, DC: COSMOS Corporation.

Barone, D., & Schneider, R. (2003). Turning the looking glass inside out: A gifted student in an at-risk setting. *Gifted Child Quarterly, 47,* 259–271.

Borland, J. H., & Wright, L. (1994). Identifying young, potentially gifted economically disadvantaged students. *Gifted Child Quarterly, 38,* 164–171.

Borland, J. H., Schnur, R., & Wright, L. (2000). Economically disadvantaged students in a school for the academically gifted: A post-positivist inquiry into individual and family adjustment. *Gifted Child Quarterly, 44,* 13–32.

Callahan, C. A., Tomlinson, C. A., Moon, T. R., Tomchin, E. M., & Plucker, J. A. (1995). *Project START: Using a multiple intelligences model in identifying and promoting talent in high risk students* (Research Monograph No. 95136). Storrs: National Research Center on the Gifted and Talented, University of Connecticut.

Clark, R. (1983). *Family life and school achievement: Why poor Black children succeed or fail.* Chicago: University of Chicago Press.

Frasier, M. M., Hunsaker, S. L., Lee, J., Finley, V. S., Frank, E., Garcia, J. H., et al. (1995). *Educator's perceptions of barriers to* the *identification of gifted children from economically disadvantaged and limited English proficient backgrounds* (Research Monograph No. 95216). Storrs: National Research Center on the Gifted and Talented, University of Connecticut.

Gelbrich, J. A., & Hare, E. K. (1989). The effects of single parenthood on school achievement in a gifted population. *Gifted Child Quarterly, 33*, 115–117.

Hébert, T. P. (2002). Educating gifted children from low socioeconomic backgrounds: Creating visions of a hopeful future. *Exceptionality, 10*, 127–138.

Hunsaker, S. L. (1994). Adjustments to traditional procedures for identifying under-served students: Successes and failures. *Exceptional Children, 61*, 72–76.

Jatko, B. (1995). Using a whole class tryout procedure for identifying economically disadvantaged students in three socioeconomically diverse schools. *Journal for the Education of the Gifted, 19*, 83–105.

Konstantopoulos, S., Modi, M., & Hedges, L. V. (2001). Who are America's gifted? *American Journal of Education, 109*, 344–382.

Newman, B. M., Myers, M. C., Newman, P. R., Lohman, B. J., & Smith, V. L. (2000). The transition to high school for academically promising, urban, low-income African American youth. *Adolescence, 35*, 45–66.

Olszewski-Kubilius, P., Grant, B., & Seibert, C. (1994). Social support systems and the disadvantaged gifted: A framework for developing programs and services. *Roeper Review, 17*, 20–25.

Olszewski-Kubilius, P., Lee, S-Y., Ngoi, M., & Ngoi, D. (2004). Addressing the achievement gap between minority and nonminority children by increasing access to gifted programs. *Journal for the Education of the Gifted, 28*, 127–158.

Parrish, M. (2004). Urban poverty and homelessness as hidden demographic variables relevant to academic achievement. In D. Boothe & J. C. Stanley (Eds.), *In the eyes of the beholder: Critical issues for diversity in gifted education* (pp. 203–211). Waco, TX: Prufrock Press.

Passow, A. H., & Frasier, M. M. (1996). Toward improving identification of talent potential among minority and disadvantaged students. *Roeper Review, 18*, 198–202.

Plucker, J. A., Callahan, C. A., & Tomchin, E. M. (1996). Wherefore art thou, multiple intelligences? Alternative assessments for identifying talent in ethnically diverse and low-income students. *Gifted Child Quarterly, 40*, 81–92.

Reis, S. M., Colbert, R. D., & Hébert, T. P. (2005). Understanding resilience in diverse, talented students in an urban high school. *Roeper Review, 27*, 110–120.

Robinson, N. M. (2003). Two wrongs do not make a right: Sacrificing the needs of gifted students does not solve society's unsolved problems. *Journal for the Education of the Gifted, 26*, 251–273.

Robinson, N. M., Lanzi, R. G., Weinberg, R. A., Ramey, S. L., & Ramey, C. T. (2002). Factors associated with high academic competence in former Head Start children at third grade. *Gifted Child Quarterly, 46*, 281–294.

Sarouphim, K. M. (1999). DISCOVER: A promising alternative assessment for the identification of gifted minorities. *Gifted Child Quarterly, 43*, 244–251.

U. S. Bureau of the Census. (2004). *Income, poverty, and health insurance coverage in the United States* (Table B-2). Retrieved May 3, 2006, from http://www.npc.umich.edu.poverty/#5

Van Tassel-Baska, J., Feng, A. X., Quek, C., & Struck, J. (2004). A study of educators' and students' perceptions of academic success for underrepresented populations identified for gifted programs. *Psychology Science, 46*, 363–378.

VanTassel-Baska, J., Johnson, D., & Avery, L. D. (2002). Using performance tasks in the identification of economically disadvantaged and minority gifted learners: Findings from Project STAR. *Gifted Child Quarterly, 46*, 110–123.

Werner, E. E. (1995). Resilience in development. *Current Directions in Psychological Science, 4*(3), 81–85.

CHAPTER 29

PROFESSIONAL DEVELOPMENT FOR TEACHERS

Perhaps there is no intervention more completely researched and confirmed in the field of education than the efficacy of teacher preparation and professional development. The last decade brought verification of earlier studies showing that in every area of instruction, teachers who develop their craft lead their students to greater success than those who do not. Teachers of gifted students experience the same distinction; when they have professional preparation, they are more sensitive to the needs of gifted children, have more strategies to use to meet these needs, and provide more avenues to success for the students (Hansen & Feldhusen, 1994). New attention has been given in recent research to understanding how teachers' beliefs and personal history impact their success in making changes in their teaching to benefit gifted students (Brighton, 2003). Standards for knowledge and skills of teachers of gifted students have been articulated.

WHAT WE KNOW

Times, children, families, and society have all changed. Teachers are charged with keeping up with the changes so that the children in their classrooms—whoever they may be and whatever talents and difficulties they may have—are given every opportunity to grow, learn, and become self-assured, self-actualized contributing members of society. That means teachers must constantly continue to grow, too. School districts use staff development, in-service training, workshops, and other deliveries of information to keep teachers growing in the craft of teaching. Professional development efforts to prepare all school personnel who provide for gifted students' needs are vital to the goal of educating this population of students (Dettmer, Landrum, & Miller, 2006).

For years, there have been efforts to draw a clear picture of the personal characteristics and beliefs and the professional competencies of successful teachers of gifted students (e.g., Bishop, 1968; Feldhusen & Hansen, 1987). The intent has been to identify what works and teach that to all instructors. In the past 10 or so years, gifted education's professional organizations designated a set of Standards for Graduate Programs in Gifted Education (National Association for Gifted Children, 1995), a section of the Pre-K–12 Gifted Education Program Standards dealing with professional development (Landrum & Shaklee, 1998), and a set of joint standards for initial teacher licensure in gifted education (Council for Exceptional Children, The Association for the Gifted [CEC-TAG], & National Association for Gifted Children [NAGC], 2004). The importance of preparing all school personnel to meet these standards is reflected in the recommendation of professional-growth activities utilizing best-practice, absolutely doable adaptations within the structure and pressures of daily classroom life (Dettmer et al., 2006).

Professional development has three important aspects, each necessary to the maturation of a teacher: (a) preservice training, (b) in-service or staff development, and (c) personal professional growth. Because each addresses a different perspective, it is critical to understand how all are to be integrated for maximum benefit to students and personal satisfaction for the teachers. Together, these growth areas improve teaching and keep good teachers in the job.

Preservice Teachers

Preservice teachers are anxious to get to the business of teaching, and most feel they are ready to meet the challenges of the classroom. They have certain beliefs about children and how schools work that they gleaned from their own education. In today's heterogeneous classrooms, the traditional views prove inadequate for meeting the needs of so many students; however, research over the years points out that these university students change their belief systems very little during their courses of instruction (Kagan, 1992; Lasley, 1980;

Tabachnick & Zeichner, 1984). Pajares (1992) makes the point that individuals who choose teaching as a career are most likely to be those who were successful in school and have no reason to change their beliefs about teaching. Unless preservice programs address gifted education and unless preservice teachers have positive experiences in practica and student teaching, they will not be prepared to deliver appropriate curricula and environments for their gifted students (Fullan & Hargreaves, 1992). Tomlinson et al. (1994) found that student teachers believe in student differences, although they are not clear about assessing and meeting those differences. They are focused on classroom management and covering the material, and they are not rewarded by university supervisors and cooperating teachers for attending to the needs of gifted students. On the other hand, Goodnough (2000) investigated a university course that had as one main goal to challenge undergraduate students' beliefs about gifted children. The results showed that all of the students who participated in the study reported changes in their beliefs and attitudes about giftedness. Those who held narrow beliefs took on broader conceptions of the range of abilities and talents, and those who believed able learners needed little support to succeed began to understand the importance of differentiating the curricula in the classroom for all—including gifted children. In fact, more universities are offering at least one course with a practicum component for undergraduates, and the early research holds similar findings (e.g., Bangel, Enersen, Capobianco, & Moon, 2006); however, the courses are not usually required and so they only affect a small group of preservice teachers.

It has long been thought that new teachers may leave university with fresh, contemporary ideas, but the truth is that they are unprepared for the stresses of their first positions, and they tend to revert to the teacher-centered approach with which they are familiar (Calderhead & Robson, 1991; Veenman, 1984). They find they do not have the management skills or the teaching strategies to meet the needs of the many learning levels of students in their classrooms (George & Rubin, 1992; Hallahan & Kaufman, 1994). They may actually lack basic teaching skills, not know where to find help in their new setting, and feel isolated among more experienced peers (Moon, Callahan, & Tomlinson, 1999).

Tomlinson et al. (1994) found that preservice teachers report the following: (a) although they assert a belief in student differences, they are (b) unclear about the identification of those differences and what they mean for students; (c) they have an inadequate view of how to differentiate instruction; (d) they feel it is logical to rely on high-ability children to lead cooperative groups or to tutor; and (e) they are clearly overwhelmed with all of the responsibilities of teaching. They feel that they have little or no exposure in their university background from which to draw strategies for change (pp. 109–112). As Robinson (1994) put it, ". . . regular education novices have acquired the compassionate rhetoric of accommodating all learners; they have not acquired the understanding or skills to put compassion to work" (p. 100).

Robinson and Kolloff (2006) examined the challenges of preparing teachers to work with gifted students in secondary school settings. While most of the literature does not address this level for preservice teachers, Robinson and Kolloff extrapolated from studies of elementary teachers and their own experience with secondary teachers' needs and responsibilities. In addition to the necessary background on the nature of giftedness, they discussed the unique talent development, social, and emotional needs of gifted adolescents. They pointed out the crucial role differentiation of curricula in the various content areas plays in meeting the needs of students with high levels of ability in math, science, language, art, or any area of secondary study.

In-Service Teachers

The last three decades are replete with research showing that classroom teachers who receive training in the nature and needs of gifted children, as well as instruction and coaching in appropriate strategies to use with able learners, are better qualified to identify and meet their students' needs (Borland, 1978; Feldhusen, 1985; Hansen & Feldhusen, 1994; Hultgren & Seeley, 1982; Maker, 1975; Reis & Westberg, 1994; Robinson, 1985; Sisk, 1975; Whitlock & DuCette, 1989). Cashion & Sullenger (2000) tempered that sweeping statement in their "one-year-later" study of teachers who had taken part in a summer institute about teaching gifted children. Although the teachers described increases over the intervening year in changing their practices for individual students and for whole-group strategies, as well as in advocacy and leadership, they also related obstacles that lessened their commitment and their success. Lack of time, discouragement, restrictions like class size, and feelings of isolation made the teachers' progress inconsistent.

Gentry and Keilty (2004) described in-service staff development experiences that put into place cluster-grouping innovations in both rural and suburban schools. The long-term success of these schools is testimony to years of careful, step-by-step planning and the understanding that it would take substantial time for teachers to buy into the changes. They advise that innovations of this kind begin with promoting conversations, both formal and informal, among teachers; providing site visits and relevant research to build an information base; asking teachers' input on choosing a course of action to solve problems (such as what can we do for gifted children when we do not have financial resources for a resource room or a gifted education specialist); carefully implementing the innovation; supporting the plan in ways such as providing time for staff development for all school personnel; and including maintenance and growth objectives.

New teachers often report their first years of teaching to be extremely difficult. The findings of Tomlinson et al. (1994) listed for preservice teachers (above) are not just concerns; they are reality for novices. However, there are success stories of teachers who seem to have the right beliefs, attitudes, knowledge, intuition, and other characteristics that help them make good decisions and learn quickly how to manage a classroom. Joffe (2001) described one such new teacher as able to handle the complexity and challenges of a classroom of diverse-ability learners. She used strategies such as beginning the year with a series of short units of different styles to see what would work with her students. She rewrote textbook lessons to make them more open and differentiated. She used other teachers and parents as resources. She was an astute observer of her students, and her intuition led her to solve problems in creative and appropriate ways. She worked hard, but she also possessed many characteristics of a talented teacher. With the joint standards fashioned by CEC-TAG and NAGC (2004), administrators now have guidance in their hiring decisions for teachers who will have gifted children in their classrooms and who are vibrant, knowledgeable, reflective, creative, and committed to continuing to grow (Callahan, Cooper, & Glascock, 2003). Included in the standards are guidelines for understanding laws pertaining to educating all students; historical and theoretical foundations; characteristics of gifted children and their families; instructional strategies and environments; assessment; cultural, ethnic, language, and economic diversity issues; gender issues; and needs of gifted students who also have a disability (Dettmer et al., 2006; Robinson & Kolloff, 2006).

A recent focus of professional development is on the personal history and belief system of teachers. Brighton's (2003) study of middle school teachers began with a discussion of how teachers' successes and failures as learners impact their view of new ideas. Cohen (as cited in Brighton) stated eloquently:

> Teachers . . . who try to carry out such change are historical beings. They cannot simply shed their old ideas and practices like a shabby coat and slip on something new. . . . They reach out with their old professional selves, including all the ideas and practices comprised therein. (p. 179)

Brighton found that attitudes and beliefs about the nature of teaching and learning had a great deal to do with how teachers accepted the challenge to change their practices with gifted students. They took part in intensive professional development experiences over 3 years, coaching sessions, demonstration lessons, and direct instruction to build their knowledge and skill. Those teachers whose preexisting beliefs aligned with the philosophy of addressing the diverse academic needs of their students had greater success in making the changes espoused in the instructional experiences they received. A study about beliefs that involved a workshop approach by Megay-Nespoli (2001) asked novice teachers about their attitudes toward gifted children, their confidence in teaching them, and the strategies they used for appropriate instruction for gifted students. The results showed that after the workshops, the teachers were more aware of the needs of able learners; however, they still struggled to put their newfound skills into practice.

A promising idea that embraces the tenets of reflective teaching, self-directed goal-setting, and personalized growth is the Individual Professional Development Plan (Collins, 1997; Sparks & Hirsh, 1997). Karnes and Shaunessy (2004) applied this plan to teachers of gifted children to make continuing education more meaningful and useful. It includes a reflection guide to help teachers learn more about themselves, their teaching styles and needs, and their students' styles and needs. They created questions that are of vital interest to them personally—as opposed to taking part in activities planned by school administrators. The plan they design includes how they will study and how they will document their accomplishments, as well as an evaluation of the effectiveness of the plan. It is not a one-time event, but a continuing process that increases the possibility of success. The plans may develop around non-traditional in-service formats and may be made in conjunction with someone else, as in the case of peer coaching, joint work (Collins), and collaboration and consultation (Landrum, 2001).

Personal Professional Growth

Implicit in the Individual Plan described above are particular characteristics of a teacher who is willing and even enthusiastic about doing personal-development work. This area of a teacher's development must begin in the individual him- or herself. It comes from the desire to remain vital and knowledgeable about one's profession and to keep the experience of learning fresh in one's mind.

Teachers who are serious about improving their ability to meet the needs of all of their students may take on the personal challenge of rigorously studying their own teaching. Hughes (1999) reported her qualitative study of her own classroom. After reading the pertinent literature, she arranged for several weekly observations of her class by administrators, specialists, and peers. She found that the study opened new possibilities to her for meeting the needs of her most talented learners. She studied the tools of flexible grouping, acceleration strategies, enrichment, and differentiated instruction (Tomlinson, 1995), and discovered how they could work to her gifted students' advantage within the regular classroom. A side effect of modeling for those who observed her added influence to her efforts.

Those teachers who hold the goal of helping to create the desire to be lifelong learners in their students are also those who have the same goal for themselves. They continue to develop and fine tune their craft, they become reflective teachers and readers, they study their students and the options they have for them, they find others who are more mature in their understandings and learn from them, they look for help from experts—not fads, and they are enthusiastic about learning. Are there some people who are "born to teach?" If so, they are surely those who have these qualities undergirding their professional preparation and knowledge.

School districts that offer pay increases and fee remissions for university courses, bring courses to the building, connect with local universities to create opportunities through involvement with preservice teachers, make time in busy schedules for professional development, and recognize teachers who attain higher levels of education give the message that continuing education is desired, important, and an integral part of professional life.

WHAT WE CAN DO

At School

ₔ Work with universities to infuse gifted education principles and experience into all preservice education classes. Provide information on the nature and needs of gifted children and strategies for differentiating instruction in all disciplines to those who teach methods classes.

ₔ Create substantive licensing or certification for recognizing those preservice and in-service teachers who prepare to teach gifted children. Work with the national and state associations to include best practices in the requirements. Advocate for hiring those who hold beliefs, attitudes, and characteristics that make them successful in addressing academically diverse learners' needs, and protect their teaching positions in times of budget cuts.

ₔ Use technology to create information sources for teachers. Translate empirical research findings into a format that will assist teachers.

ₔ Support teachers who are interested in improving skills by taking courses and studying their own teaching practices. Bring coursework to a local area and make it personally relevant to the teachers' classes.

ₔ Try the Individual Professional Development Plan.

ₔ Educate school board members and other administrators about the need for hiring and protecting the positions of teachers who are prepared to teach gifted students. Help parents speak to the issues that are impacted at budget meetings.

REFERENCES

Bangel, N. J., Enersen, D. L., Capobianco, B., & Moon, S. M. (2006). Professional development of preservice teachers: Teaching in the Super Saturday program. *Journal for the Education of the Gifted, 29*, 339–361.

Bishop, W. E. (1968). Successful teachers of the gifted. *Exceptional Children, 34*, 317–325.

Borland, J. (1978). Teachers' identification of the gifted. *Journal for the Education of the Gifted, 2,* 22–32.

Brighton, C. M. (2003). The effects of middle school teachers' beliefs on classroom practices. *Journal for the Education of the Gifted, 27,* 177–206.

Calderhead, J., & Robson, M. (1991). Images of teaching: Student teachers' early conceptions of classroom practice. *Teacher and Teacher Education, 7,* 1–8.

Callahan, C., Cooper, C., & Glascock, R. (2003). *Preparing teachers to develop and enhance talent: The position of national education organizations.* Reston, VA: ERIC Clearinghouse on Disabilities and Gifted Education. (ERIC Document Reproduction Service No. ED477882)

Cashion, M., & Sullenger, K. (2000). "Contact us next year": Tracing teachers' use of gifted practices. *Roeper Review, 23,* 18–21.

Collins, D. (1997). *Achieving your vision of professional development.* Greensboro: SERVE, University of North Carolina at Greensboro.

Council for Exceptional Children, The Association for the Gifted, & National Association for Gifted Children. (2004). *Draft joint standards for initial teacher preparation in gifted education.* Washington, DC: Author.

Dettmer, P. A., Landrum, M. S., & Miller, T. N. (2006). Professional development for the education of secondary gifted students. In F. A. Dixon & S. M. Moon (Eds.), *The handbook of secondary gifted education* (pp. 611–648). Waco, TX: Prufrock Press.

Feldhusen, J. F. (1985). The teacher of gifted students. *Gifted Educational International, 3,* 87–93.

Feldhusen, J. F., & Hansen, J. (1987). Selecting and training teachers to work with the gifted in a Saturday program. *Gifted Education International, 4,* 82–94.

Fullan, M., & Hargreaves, A. (1992). *Teacher development and educational change.* London: Falmer.

Gentry, M., & Keilty, B. (2004). Rural and suburban cluster grouping: Reflections on staff development as a component of program success. *Roeper Review, 26,* 147–155.

George, P. S., & Rubin, K. (1992). Tracking and ability grouping in Florida: Educator's perceptions. *Florida Educational Research Bulletin, 23,* 3–4. (ERIC Document Reproduction Service No. ED353683)

Goodnough, K. (2000). Fostering liberal views of giftedness: A study of the beliefs of six undergraduate education students. *Roeper Review, 23,* 89–90.

Hallahan, D. P., & Kaufman, J. M. (1994). *Exceptional children.* Boston: Allyn & Bacon.

Hansen, J. B., & Feldhusen, J. F. (1994). Comparison of trained and untrained teachers of gifted students. *Gifted Child Quarterly, 38,* 115–121.

Hughes, L. (1999). Action research and practical inquiry: How can I meet the needs of the high-ability students within my regular education classroom? *Journal for the Education of the Gifted, 22,* 282–297.

Hultgren, H. M., & Seeley, K. R. (1982). *Training teachers of the gifted: A research monograph on teacher competencies.* Denver, CO: University of Denver, School of Education.

Joffe, W. S. (2001). Investigating the acquisition of pedagogical knowledge: Interviews with a beginning teacher of the gifted. *Roeper Review, 23,* 219–226.

Kagan, D. (1992). Professional growth among preservice and beginning teachers. *Review of Educational Research, 62,* 129–169.

Karnes, F. A., & Shaunessy, E. (2004). The application of an individual professional development plan to gifted education. *Gifted Child Today, 27*(3), 60–64.

Landrum, M. S. (2001). Resource consultation and collaboration in gifted education. *Psychology in the Schools, 38*, 457–466.

Landrum, M., & Shaklee, B. (Eds.). (1998). *Pre K–grade 12 gifted program standards.* Washington, DC: National Association for Gifted Students.

Lasley, T. (1980). Preservice teacher beliefs about teaching. *Journal of Teacher Education 31*(4), 34–41.

Maker, C. J. (1975). *Training teachers for the gifted and talented.* Reston, VA: Council for Exceptional Children.

Megay-Nespoli, K. (2001). Beliefs and attitudes of novice teachers regarding instruction of academically talented learners. *Roeper Review, 23*, 178–182.

Moon, T. R., Callahan, C. M., & Tomlinson, C. A. (1999). The effects of mentoring relationships on preservice teachers' attitudes toward academically diverse students. *Gifted Child Quarterly, 43*, 56–62.

National Association for Gifted Children. (1995). *Standards for graduate programs in gifted education.* Washington, DC: Author.

Pajares, M. (1992). Teachers' beliefs and educational research: Cleaning up a messy construct. *Review of Educational Research, 62*, 307–322.

Reis, S. M., & Westberg, K. L. (1994). The impact of staff development on teachers' ability to modify curriculum for gifted and talented students. *Gifted Child Quarterly, 38*, 127–135.

Robinson, A. (1985). Summer institute on the gifted: Meeting the needs of the regular classroom teacher. *Gifted Child Quarterly, 29*, 20–23.

Robinson, A. (1994). Teachers, talent development, and talented students. *Gifted Child Quarterly, 38*, 99–102.

Robinson, A., & Kolloff, P. B. (2006). Preparing teachers to work with high-ability youth at the secondary level: Issues and implications for licensure. In F. A. Dixon & S. M. Moon (Eds.), *The handbook of secondary gifted education* (pp. 581–610). Waco, TX: Prufrock Press.

Sisk, D. (1975). Teaching the gifted and talented teachers: A training model. *Gifted Child Quarterly, 19*, 81–88.

Sparks, D., & Hirsh, S. (1997). *A new vision for staff development.* Alexandria, VA: Association for Supervision and Curriculum Development.

Tabachnick, B., & Zeichner, K. (1984). The impact of the student teaching experience on the development of teacher perspectives. *Journal of Teacher Education, 35*(6), 28–36.

Tomlinson, C. (1995). *Report from National Association for Gifted Children Task Force in the interface between gifted education and general education.* Washington, DC: National Association for Gifted Children.

Tomlinson, C. A., Tomchin, E. M., Callahan, C. M., Adams, C. M., Pizzat-Tinnin, P., Cunningham, C. M., et al. (1994). Practices of preservice teachers related to gifted and other academically diverse learners. *Gifted Child Quarterly, 38*, 106–114.

Veenman, S. (1984). Perceived problems of beginning teachers. *Review of Educational research, 54*, 143–178.

Whitlock, M., & DuCette, J. (1989). Outstanding and average teachers of the gifted: A comparative study. *Gifted Child Quarterly, 33*, 15–21.

CONCLUSION

The principal conclusions of this text are contained in the reviews of the 29 evidence-based practices that anchor our bulleted guidance for action. Our purpose here is to offer some general thoughts about the project, its relationship to our previous work on recommended practices in gifted education, patterns in the practices, and our hopes for the future of evidence-based practices in the field.

OVERVIEW OF THE EVIDENCE-BASED PRACTICES PROCESS

We identified and examined the research supporting 29 practices for the development of talents at home and school. In our search for evidence-based practices, we were aided by the conceptualization and recommendations of the steering group for the project—a cross section of researchers, state department personnel, and school-district leaders in the field. We also capitalized on the knowledge of three current journal editors who were in constant touch with emerging research through their review of new manuscripts. We were guided by three major questions: "What questions do we need to be able to answer about educational and home practices effective with high-ability youth?" "How do we frame these questions to be maximally useful to practitioners?" and "What existing research informs these practical questions?" In a face-to-face 2-day working meeting, the steering group generated 150 questions, identified the most important questions that might be directly translated into practice, and suggested specific research to inform them.

Following the conceptualization, we met as authors and pounded out the key features we wished these practical reviews to include: a capsule overview of the practice, a brief review of the research literature, and a set of bulleted actions that might be taken by parents or educators. We also derived searchable terms from the questions generated by the steering group, searched them, and began to read and think about the story the research had to tell. In fact, we even constructed what we called "story spines" to capture the flow from research to the specific actions found in the *What We Can Do* section of each review.

EVIDENCE-BASED PRACTICES AND RECOMMENDED PRACTICES

The work in this text differs from, but was informed by, our previous work on practitioners' needs for practical, evidence-based information about what to do for talented youth. Previously, two of us (Shore and Robinson) coauthored with Dewey Cornell and Virgil Ward the book *Recommended Practices in Gifted Education: A Critical Analysis* (1991). Our conceptualization of a recommended practice in the *Recommended Practices* book differs from the evidence-based practices the reader will find here. First, a *recommended* practice means that someone, in some book somewhere suggested that we should do something in gifted education. Many of these recommended practices were useful suggestions, but they were not necessarily based on research. In contrast, the 29 evidence-based practices reviewed through this project do have research support, and that research support can be translated into specific actions parents and educators can take at home and school.

Patterns in Practices

Empirical research in the form of meta-analyses, large-scale studies, small-scale studies, cross-case analyses, and single case studies exists in the field, and information on parenting and school practices for high-ability youth is extractable from the knowledge base on gifted education. Although more scholarly investigations are always needed, a core set of practices for high-ability learners with research support does exist. Here are some selected observations about them.

First, several of the practices focus on curricular content areas. Mathematics, science, reading, language arts, and an instructional practice in history are all represented in the practices. They also illustrate an interesting point about the nature of the research that informs evidence-based practices. Contrast two areas—mathematics curricula and primary sources in history. These both focus on different levels of practice. Using primary sources in history is an instructional practice. The practice itself is rich, and incorporates the way adult historians engage in their discipline; however, it is a focused practice and results in a set of specific actions for instruction to meet the needs of high-ability learners. In contrast, evidence-based practice for mathematics curricula is broader, includes both instructional and curricular research, and has a relationship to the literature on gender differences. To extend our use of the story metaphor, using primary sources in history is an elegant short story, whereas mathematics curricula is a large and episodic novel.

Second, the pattern of the evidence-based practices also reveals a cluster focused on special populations of high-ability youth—culturally diverse, low-income, and twice-exceptional learners—and what to do for them at home. In some cases, there are specific practices, and therefore, chapters are titled to reflect that focus, but information about what works with special populations of gifted learners also appears integrated throughout the practices. Some practices address special populations of high-ability learners in specific ways. Extremely precocious young children appear in the chapter on "Early Literacy for Precocious Readers" and in the work on prodigies in "Developing Specific Talents." Second language learners appear in both "Learning Multiple Languages" and in "Developing Talents in Culturally Diverse Students."

Third, some practices changed shape before our very eyes. For example, the evidence-based practice in the chapter titled "Learning Multiple Languages" began with a literature on the study of French, Spanish, or German in the secondary schools and grew into the inclusion of classical language study, early exposure to languages in the elementary school, and the linguistic talents of bilingual learners.

Finally, the patterns of evidence-based practices reveal some important gaps. For example, as a field we are heavily occupied with the topic of underachievement of high-ability youth. No individual practice on underachievement appears among the 29 in this text, although echoes of underachievement appear in other topics such as gender, for example. Its story remains to be told. We know about the behaviors associated with underachievement; the research literature includes studies of the ways underachievers differ from achievers. We have hints of specific actions that look promising—reversing underachievement with interest-based projects or attribution retraining for young women. But, this is a complex story. The reasons that high-ability youth underachieve are extremely varied. The learner who underachieves because of a disability differs from the learner who underachieves because of low expectations, who differs from the learner who underachieves because of a lack of motivation, who differs from the learner who underachieves because of family trauma. To return to our literary metaphor for evidence-based practices, we have healthy set of stage directions, but not a completed drama. We have yet to write the third act that will help us clearly articulate what works for gifted underachievers in a replicable way.

What's Next?

The future of evidence-based practices is a bright one. In an age of accountability and scarce resources for schools, educators, advocates, and decision-makers increasingly turn to evidence to inform their decisions. In many cases, the evidence is empirical research. We were guided in this project by the importance of connecting empirical evidence with parent, practitioner, and policymaker concerns. The connection between research and practice is often loosely coupled to the marked frustration of researchers, practitioners, and policymakers alike. This project sought to bridge the gap.

ABOUT THE
AUTHORS

Donna Enersen is a long-time educator of children, parents, and teachers. She spent 25 years as a classroom teacher and elementary school reading and curriculum specialist in Pennsylvania and Florida, and the last 17 years as a teacher educator at Purdue University in Indiana. She was one of the first gifted education specialists in Pinellas County, FL, where she also created parent classes and led professional development for teachers. She directed the summer residential programs and the Super Saturday program for children and taught gifted education certification courses for teachers at Purdue University's Gifted Education Resource Institute (GERI). She initiated parent-education courses at GERI and throughout the central-Indiana area. She has consulted with school districts as they evaluated and developed their services to gifted children. Through her work at the schools, Enersen became acquainted with individual children and their families who needed guidance, and she became an advocate in the schools for them, designing appropriate educational plans. Through the volunteer organization Partners for the Americas, Enersen has worked in southern Brazil, South America, teaching and consulting in the schools and universities.

Ann Robinson is professor of education and founding director of the Center for Gifted Education at the University of Arkansas at Little Rock. She is a former editor of *Gifted Child Quarterly*, serves on the board of directors for the National Association for Gifted Children as the finance secretary, and has received the Early Leader and the Early Scholar Awards from the association. In 2004, she and coauthor Sidney Moon received the *Gifted Child Quarterly* Paper of the Year Award for "The National Study of State and Local Advocacy in Gifted Education." With Shore, Cornell, and Ward, Robinson coauthored *Recommended Practices in Gifted Education: A Critical Analysis*, identified as one of the 50 most influential works in gifted education by a division of the National Association for Gifted Children. She was a charter board member of the Special Interest Group on Giftedness and Talent of the American Educational Research Association. In 2000, Robinson was recognized as the Purdue University Alumna of Distinction for the College of Education. Her own institution honored her with the University Award of Faculty Excellence in Research in 1999 and the University of Award for Public Service in 2001. Robinson is the president of the Arkansans for Gifted and Talented Education, the immediate past president of the Arkansas Association of Gifted Education Administrators, and is active in advocacy at the state and national levels. In 2006 she received the NAGC Distinguished Service Award.

Bruce M. Shore received his bachelor's degree, teaching diploma, and master's degree from McGill University; taught secondary mathematics; and then obtained his Ph.D. in educational psychology from the University of Calgary. Dr. Shore is a licensed psychologist in Quebec and was president of the McGill Association of University Teachers. He began in McGill's Department of Educational and Counselling Psychology in 1970, where he was chair for 9 years. In 2006, he completed a 5-year term as dean of students at McGill University. As dean, he was the senior academic administrator of student services, overseeing academic integrity policy and processes, and an active participant in general dialogue among students and student and university leadership. Shore has returned to his position as professor of educational psychology in McGill's Department of Educational and Counselling Psychology. He is author or coauthor of 9 published or forthcoming books, 23 chapters, and 73 journal articles on giftedness as evolving cognitive expertise, inquiry-driven teaching and learning, inquiry-education outcomes (his current primary research focus), and related topics. He received the 1995 Distinguished Scholar Award from the National Association for Gifted Children.

ABOUT THE STEERING COMMITTEE MEMBERS

Phyllis Aldrich is an adjunct professor at Skidmore College. She served as coordinator for gifted education for a five-county Board of Cooperative Educational Services (BOCES) in New York State, where she established a resource center and clearinghouse of information on gifted education. She served as president of a statewide advocacy organization of educators and parents. On a national level, she serves on the Advisory Committee on Exceptional Children for the U.S. Department of State Office of Overseas Schools, as well as the National Assessment of Educational Progress (NAEP) Governing Board.

Joan Becker is the Associate Vice Provost for Academic Support Services at the University of Massachusetts, Boston. She serves as the chief daily operations officer for Academic Support Services, which includes Academic Support Programs, the University Advising Center, the Honors Program, and Pre-Collegiate and Educational Support Services. Initially hired by the university to develop the Urban Scholars Program for talented and gifted urban youth, Becker served as the director of that program from 1984–1998.

Laurence J. Coleman is the Judith Daso Herb Chair in Gifted Studies at the University of Toledo. He is the former editor of the *Journal for the Education of the Gifted*. Among his many publications is *Nurturing Talent in High School: Life in the Fast Lane*, reviewed as "destined to be a seminal work in the field of gifted education." In 1995, he received a Fulbright study grant to India. He has been honored with the 2000 Distinguished Scholar Award from the National Association for Gifted Children, the 2001 *Gifted Child Quarterly* Paper of the Year award, and the 2004 Outstanding Leadership and Service Award from The Association for the Gifted of the Council for Exceptional Children.

Peggy A. Dettmer is professor emerita at Kansas State University. Dettmer authored several books and numerous journal articles in the field of gifted education. Her text, *Consultation, Collaboration, and Teamwork for Students with Special Needs*, coauthored with Norma Dyck and Linda Thurston, is in its fifth edition. She served as the chair of the Professional Development Division of the National Association of Gifted Children and was a founding member of the Professional Training Institute that preceded the work of this division.

Bessie Duncan is a former supervisor of gifted and talented education for the Detroit Public Schools. She serves on the Gifted Education Resource Institute Advisory Board at Purdue University. She was a member of the steering group for *National Excellence: A Case for Developing America's Talent*, published by the U.S. Department of Education.

Evelyn Hiatt was the senior director for advanced academic services in the Texas Education Agency prior to her retirement in 2004. She was president of the International Baccalaureate North America & Caribbean Board of Directors. She has served on many boards and committees and held leadership positions for several state and national associations.

Scott Hunsaker is an associate professor of educational foundations and gifted and talented education in the Department of Elementary Education at Utah State University in Logan, UT. His work at Utah State has been honored by its College of Education and Human Services with the Teacher of the Year Award (2000) and the Undergraduate Research Mentor of the Year Award (2005). He is a former member of the National Association for Gifted Children board of directors and former president of the Utah Association for Gifted Children. His leadership in gifted education was recognized by NAGC with the Early Leader Award in 1991 and by UAGC with the Jewel Bindrup Award in 2006. His research interests focus on advanced readers, professional decision making, and creativity.

James A. Kulik is director and research scientist at the University of Michigan's Office of Evaluations and Examinations. Since 1976, he has used meta-analytic methods to summarize research findings in various areas of social science research. His meta-analytic projects have resulted in approximately 75 publications, including journal articles and a comprehensive monograph on meta-analytic findings and results in educational research.

Rosa Perez is a program specialist and teacher of highly gifted students in the San Diego City Schools gifted program. She is an author and consultant in early intervention and giftedness and the culturally and linguistically diverse learner.

Joyce VanTassel-Baska is the Jody and Layton Smith Professor in Education and executive director of the Center for Gifted Education at the College of William and Mary and current president of the National Association for Gifted Children. She has worked as a consultant in gifted education in all 50 states and for key national groups, including the U.S. Department of Education, the National Association of Secondary School Principals, and the American Association of School Administrators. She has published widely, including 20 books and more than 345 articles, chapters, and scholarly reports. She is the past president of The Association for the Gifted of the Council for Exceptional Children and the former editor of *Gifted and Talented International*.

Herbert J. Walberg is research professor of education and psychology at the University of Illinois at Chicago. He has written and edited more than 55 books and 350 articles on such topics as educational effectiveness and exceptional human accomplishments. He served on the National Assessment Governing Board, and as a fellow of the American Association for the Advancement of Science, the American Psychological Association, and the Royal Statistical Society. For the U.S. Department of Education and the National Science Foundation, he carried out comparative research in Japanese and American schools. He also employs research synthesis to summarize effects of various educational conditions and methods on learning and other outcomes, the results of which have informed the policies of educators and legislatures.

INDEX